The economics of unemployment in Britain

The economics of unemployment in Britain

Edited by John Creedy

Butterworths
London Boston Sydney Wellington Toronto Durban

First published 1981

© Butterworth & Co (Publishers) Ltd 1981

British Library Cataloguing in Publication Data

The Economics of unemployment in Britain.
  1. Unemployment – Great Britain
  I. *Creedy*, John
  331.13´7941   HD5765.A6   80-41940
  ISBN 0-408-10703-0

Typeset by CCC in Great Britain
by William Clowes (Beccles) Limited, Beccles and London
Printed in England by Redwood Burn Ltd, Trowbridge & Esher

Acknowledgments

I should like to thank the staff of Butterworths for their interest in this book and for advice throughout its preparation. This project would not have been possible without the friendly cooperation of the authors who have contributed to the book, and who have worked to a very tight timetable. I have gained much from reading their work, and am grateful for the privilege. Finally, I am very grateful to Patricia Wears, who has coped quickly, efficiently and cheerfully with an extremely heavy burden of typing.

John Creedy

The economics of unemployment in Britain

Contributors

J. Creedy is Professor of Economics and Head of the Department of Economics at the University of Durham. He has previously lectured at Reading University, and has worked at the National Institute of Economic and Social Research. His main research interests are concerned with the distribution of income, public policy, and the history of economic thought.

R. B. Thomas is Senior Lecturer in Economics at Durham University. He was previously lecturer at Salford University and was a Research Fellow at the SSRC Industrial Relations Research Unit at the University of Warwick. His main research interests are in the operation of labour markets. He is co-author, with David Deaton, of *Labour Shortage and Economic Analysis* (1978).

M. C. Casson is Reader in Economics at Reading University. He is the author of *Youth Unemployment* (1979) and *Unemployment: A Disequilibrium Approach* (1981). His research interests include the economic theory of the entrepreneur and the theory of the multinational enterprise.

H. Armstrong is Lecturer in Economics at the University of Lancaster. He has previously been a Lecturer at Loughborough University of Technology, and Visiting Lecturer at the University of British Columbia, Canada. His main research interests are regional policy and problems in the United Kingdom and the EEC.

J. Taylor is Reader in Economics at the University of Lancaster. He joined the staff at Lancaster in 1964 and has since taught at the University of Pennsylvania and at the University of British Columbia in Canada. His main research interests are concerned with regional economic policy and with the economics of unemployment. He is the author of *Unemployment and Wage Inflation* (1974).

A. B. Atkinson is Professor of Economics at the London School of Economics. He has previously been Professor of Economics at the University of Essex and Professor of Political Economy at University College London. He is Editor of the Journal of Public Economics and was a member of the Royal Commission on the Distribution of Income and Wealth 1978–1979. His most recent books include *Lectures on Public Economics* (with J. E. Stiglitz), and *The Distribution of Personal Wealth in Britain* (with A. J. Harrison).

R. Disney is Lecturer in Economics at the University of Kent at Canterbury. He has previously lectured at the University of Reading and the University of Addis Ababa. His research interests include the economics of underdeveloped countries and labour economics.

J. Ashworth is Lecturer in Economics at Durham University. He was previously a Research Fellow at the University of Stirling, working on the Taxation and Labour Supply project. His main research interests are in the econometric analysis of individuals' labour supply, and in the macroeconomic analysis of the determinants of wage and price inflation.

S. Lord is in the Department of Health and Social Security as a member of the Government Statistical Service. His current responsibilities involve the collection, analysis and application of statistics relating to incapacity and disablement benefits. Until recently he had similar responsibilities in relation to benefits for the unemployed and for child benefits. He has been involved in the provision of statistical advice to the Lane Committee on the Working of the Abortion Act, analysis of data from social and nutritional surveys, and work on social indicators.

List of tables

List of figures

Contents

Introduction

After the relatively low levels of unemployment experienced in Great Britain from the end of the Second World War to the late 1960s, when the aggregate unemployment rate hardly rose above 1½%, the 1970s were years of significant increases. At certain times during the late 1970s there were over 1½ million people on the unemployment register, and they formed about 6% of the labour force. It was also rather disturbing that the high and rising unemployment was also accompanied by high and rising rates of inflation. There have consequently been considerable changes, both in the scale of the problem and in the constraints on government policy, over a fairly short period[1]; and there is unfortunately little to suggest that the problem of unemployment will be significantly reduced in the 1980s*.

While it is undoubtedly true that the analysis of, and policy towards, unemployment in the 1980s must take into consideration many factors which were not present during either the extremely high unemployment of the inter-war years or the low unemployment of the 1950s and 1960s, it is useful to place the 'problem of unemployment' in historical context. Many of the issues which are raised are not in fact as new as they may initially appear to be. Section 1.1 of this Introduction thus very briefly considers some aspects of past unemployment experience in Britain.

The purpose of the remaining sections of this Introduction is then to raise a number of the general issues relating to unemployment which are examined in detail in subsequent chapters of this book. First, it is necessary to clarify what is, or what may not be, meant by the term 'unemployment'. This is the subject of Section 1.2, where unemployment is examined in the context of a brief discussion of different types of economic systems. This section does not pretend to provide an analysis of the many problems which are raised, but hopes to place some of the analyses of later chapters in 'analytical' context.

---

* Indeed, by late 1980 the number of unemployed had risen to over 2 million.

Section 1.3 then emphasizes the fact that unemployment should be examined in dynamic, rather than static, terms. Unemployment represents a transition period, although for some people it may be rather long, and for others it may be experienced repeatedly over their working lives. This section stresses some simple, but important, points about unemployment 'stocks' and 'flows'.

Section 1.4 then describes the plan of the book, and relates the chapters to the issues raised in Sections 1.2 and 1.3.

1.1 Unemployment past and present

Despite the fact that the *Oxford English Dictionary* dates the word 'unemployment' from 1888 and 'unemployed' from 1882[2], and that neither the first *Dictionary of Statistics*, compiled by Mulhall in 1884, nor the first edition of Palgrave's *Dictionary of Political Economy* (1894) has entries for either of these words, the problem of unemployment is certainly much older than 100 years. Indeed, after a detailed account of the economic history of England, taking three large volumes, Lipson concluded

> Thus the problem of finding work for the unemployed, without producing adverse reactions upon the economic system as a whole, is one which has been the subject of repeated experiments and incessant discussions: and it is one of the cardinal problems that confront our own generation[3].

The manorial system of the Middle Ages did of course ensure the absence of large scale unemployment of the 'able bodied', but a number of factors combined in the sixteenth century to produce a drastic need for an organized system of poor relief. Very briefly, these factors include the break-up of the manor and the depopulation of villages resulting from the growth of sheep farming at the expense of corn growing, the consolidation of farms and displacement of peasants from their holdings, the growth of industry and the growth of foreign trade. The latter introduced a further element of instability into a system which was already sensitive to the disruptive effects of wars[4].

The maintenance of employment has indeed been an important argument in most instances where pressure for tariffs has been strong. This may be traced from the mercantilists exemplified by Mun's *England's Treasures by Forraign Trade* (1664), to the beginning of this century and the Tariff Reform League of Chamberlain, and in fact to the present policy recommendations of the Cambridge Economic Policy Group.

The effects of these changes were also strongly exacerbated by the dissolution of the monasteries, which had previously played an important role in the relief of poverty. In considering past causes of unemployment it is also most important not to neglect the considerable influence of wars, and other 'disruptions' produced by rapid technological change and the discovery of new sources of raw materials or exhaustion of regular supplies.

While the problem of unemployment has been of importance since the sixteenth century, three main stages may be distinguished in government attitudes. First, the age of mercantilism, what has been called the 'first planned economy', involved a considerable amount of government authority over such things as establishing long contracts, and forcing employers to keep men in work during recessions[5]. Then after the English Civil War and Restoration, the movement towards *laissez faire* acquired increasing momentum, and the principles adopted during this period are of course reflected in the Poor Law Amendment Act 1834 and in much of the writings of the classical economists. An extreme view is reflected, towards the end of this period, in the statement of Gladstone in 1893 that action to prevent or relieve unemployment was, 'outside the legitimate sphere not merely of legislation but of parliamentary discussion'[6].

Finally the significant structural changes of the late 1880s and early 1900s imposed excessive pressure on local, trade union, and voluntary schemes, and eventually unemployment again became recognized as a 'problem of industry', rather than being regarded as a problem of individual character[7]. This resulted in the establishment in 1911 of the National Insurance scheme which was the starting point of many subsequent policy experiments which have continued to the present.

It is worth stressing that over the long history of the relief of the unemployed, and also of the working poor, the policy experiments have followed *in response* to observed difficulties which had been created by exceptional transition problems or dislocation of the economy, caused often by war and subsequent adjustment to peace conditions. For example, in the early 1900s it was found to be impossible to implement fully the provisions of the 1834 Poor Law, and in the 1930s the 'dole' was introduced for the many who had exhausted unemployment benefits under the Insurance scheme. Furthermore, the need to maintain incentives has always been given very high priority by those planning administrative mechanisms for the relief of unemployment; what Lipson (quoted above)[3] refers to as, 'adverse reactions upon the economic system'.

1.2 Economic systems and unemployment

Having very briefly discussed British experience, it is perhaps useful to consider several kinds of economic systems in a rather more abstract way. This should help to isolate some of the issues which are considered in other chapters of this book.

First, it is obvious that in a system in which each individual is entirely self-sufficient, there would be no such thing as unemployment. Such a system would of course require a clear set of property rights, however established, but these are not directly relevant here. Population control and other economic 'sanctions' would be rather severe, and the average 'standard of living' would not be expected to be very high. Each person would probably have some difficulty in surviving unforeseen exigencies, depending on his ability to save, and safely store, out of current production.

A cooperative society

Consider next a small society which recognizes the potential gains from the division of labour, and is fully cooperative in the sense that decisions about the allocation of labour, the composition of final output and the distribution of the gains are made following a consistent plan. The process by which decisions are made may be ignored here; that is, whether by a leader (however 'chosen'), or by some kind of voting system. If potential output exceeds current requirements, then a decision must be made about the appropriate division between 'leisure' and investment for the future, but this decision will be made explicitly, and clearly there can be no 'unemployment'. There would obviously have to be rules relating to the indolent and to those incapable of work, but again they are not of direct relevance here. Such a cooperative society would also have schemes for labour training. But it would not be faced by problems caused by fluctuations in, and uncertainty about, the demand for various goods—other than those arising from 'crop failure' or other hazards, and dislocation caused by the need to defend itself from aggressors[8]. But particular individuals who were unable to provide their appropriate share of output, because of sickness or accident, would be temporarily supported by the rest of society which 'pools' such risks and is fully acquainted with the individual circumstances.

An individualistic society

The decision-making and organizational problems of such a cooperative society are obviously very complex, and these will increase significantly as the size of the society increases. However, for present purposes the most interesting development occurs if the society becomes much more individualistic. In this case each individual chooses his own specialization and must make his production decisions on the basis of expectations of demand, however these are formed. In such an exchange economy the gains from specialization and exchange are obtained, although the distribution of the gains does not result from conscious overall planning. Here the achievement of a consistent set of individual plans becomes more difficult, since each transactor has much less information about the likely demand for his specialization or the production decisions of other individuals. (In the preceding system most individuals do not actually need much information, of course.)

If an individual finds that there is little or no demand for his output, it is very difficult for him to estimate the extent to which the reduction is permanent. It may also be the case that if the individual were to reduce the price of his output, he could not expect to obtain a level of income which he regards as 'reasonable' (given his previous standard), or which would maintain a conventional level of subsistence. Since the same difficulty also applies to the rest of the society, it will be willing to subsidize a period of 'unemployment', provided that the members of the society are satisfied that the 'privilege' is not being abused. Furthermore, the society would expect that if the person is still unemployed after a certain length of time, it is reasonable to assume that the demand reduction is permanent, so that the individual must then be expected to change his specialization and perhaps his place of residence, if necessary. The details of any administrative arrangements for supporting the unemployed will depend on a large number of complex factors, but it is clear that unemployment would exist in such a society and that it would increase during periods of adjustment which are imposed by exogenous changes. Such changes include the discovery of new techniques or materials, or the exhaustion of certain supplies.

Individualistic society with labour contracts

The final type of society which is of interest here is the individualistic community which recognizes the advantages of specialization and exchange, but in which the majority of individuals are employees, and are hired for a specified period by employers who must also purchase (or hire) a significant amount of capital equipment to be used by employees (either individually or in teams). The information requirements of this kind of system are clearly considerably greater than any of those previously discussed. To the extent that there is competition between producers, and conflict between employees and employers, attempts will also be made to conceal certain types of information. Each person must make decisions not only about his training (his occupational choice), but also about the industry in which he would prefer to work. There is of course also a decision to be made about whether to be 'self-employed' or to be an employee, and in the latter case about the particular firm in the industry for which he would prefer to work. In attempting to obtain employment he faces the task of communicating the nature of his aptitudes and abilities to a potential employer. In turn, each firm must attempt to attract suitable labour, and must of course offer contracts to, and pay, its employees well in advance of the date at which its final products are sold. The behaviour of both workers and firms depends crucially on their expectations and guesses about other people's plans, and these expectations are based on access to different kinds of information. Furthermore, firms and employees face different costs of acquiring information and of making incorrect decisions.

This society, while predominantly individualistic, recognizes the benefits from exchange, interdependence and cooperation in production—along with the difficulties just mentioned of achieving a consistent set of plans—to such an extent that individuals are prepared to give up some of their current income to support those who are temporarily out of work. As before, this is conditional on the system not being abused. The society would also recognize the advantages of supporting institutions, such as a network of labour exchanges, which may help to increase the flow of information about job opportunities and thereby reduce the time during which people are unemployed[9].

The problem of adjusting to any exogenous change, in terms of required changes in the structure of industry and the allocation of labour, will be considerable in this kind of system. An implication of the absence of complete information is that employees will find it very difficult to estimate how their real wage is changing, or is likely to change in the future. One response is to base behaviour explicitly on a more limited, but more accessible, set of data such as relative money wages. Employees may also find it useful to support a small number of individuals who can collect information and carry out negotiations on their behalf. In this case they may obtain sufficient information on which to negotiate in terms of real wages as well as differentials. But of course there may be groups of workers in certain industries or types of firms who are unable to become so organized.

What is clear is that individuals and firms will often base their behaviour on 'rules of thumb' which, on average, produce 'reasonably workable' results. But it is by no means clear that the individual and institutional responses to change will ensure that the stock of individuals unemployed at any time, or the average time between jobs, will not increase or remain for long periods above an 'acceptable' minimum. Indeed, this kind of question has occupied many economists for many years.

Definition of unemployment

It is necessary to examine the meaning which may be attached to the word 'unemployment' since, like most definitions in economics, it is by no means straightforward[10]. For example, unemployment obviously does *not* refer to the difference between 'potential aggregate labour input' and the actual input recorded through market transactions[11]. It must be recognized that there is a large 'conventional' element in the definition of unemployment, and this may not always correspond with the measure of unemployment which is available from official data. Individuals who are below school-leaving age or over retirement age, who are ill or otherwise prevented from accepting employment, are not usually regarded as being unemployed. Furthermore, individuals who decide to share income within a household, and recognize that the value of their household services exceeds the net amount which they could obtain at work, would not be regarded as being unemployed. However, circumstances may change (for example, the household earner may become unemployed) making it necessary for individuals who were not in the labour market to begin actively seeking employment. Whether such individuals are then recorded as being unemployed depends on the particular method of data collection used by the authorities, and the extent to which those individuals make use of all the official facilities available to them.

Consider next the case of an individual who decides, on the basis of information available at the time of the decision, to enter a particular occupation and to devote much energy to the acquisition of special skills (which may also involve foregoing earnings for some time). After a period of employment with a firm the individual finds that, because of circumstances beyond his/her control, he/she is made redundant. It may be possible for that person to obtain employment fairly quickly in a very different job offering lower wages than he/she expected (given his/her skills), but because of the existence of unemployment benefits he/she is able to wait for an opportunity to apply for a job which is regarded as suitable. In the meantime, vacancies for unskilled jobs will be filled by other individuals (some of whom have few skills while others, after a long spell of unemployment, perceive that their skills are obsolete). It is clear that the willingness of society to finance benefits to this type of person may affect the rate of flows of individuals from unemployment to employment, and in particular will affect the composition of the stock of unemployed. But it is by no means clear that such a person can be usefully described as 'voluntarily' unemployed. Different methods of placing the unemployed in vacancies will obviously affect the rate of flow of individuals between jobs, and reduce the stock of unemployment at any time, but few people would describe this as a change in 'voluntary' unemployment[12].

1.3 Stocks and flows

A very important point to stress is that the number of individuals who are observed to be unemployed at a particular time (the 'stock' of unemployed) is a very poor indicator of the number of individuals who have experienced unemployment over a specified period of time, such as a year. It is also a poor indicator of the private and social costs of unemployment. Quite simply, the stock of unemployment results from two flows the first consisting of those becoming unemployed and the second consisting of those who leave unemployment. For example, when the stock of unemployed in the mid 1970s was approximately $1\frac{1}{4}$ million on any day (4–5% of the labour force), the monthly inflow to the unemployment register was about 350 000[13]. The inflow has been surprisingly stable over quite long periods, so that the stock of unemployed is much more sensitive to the rate at which unemployed individuals leave the register. The probability that an unemployed person will leave the register during any week, which crucially affects the average time spent on the register, has been the subject of much research in recent years, although knowledge of this process is still unfortunately limited[14].

A further important point about the interpretation of the unemployment rate was made early in this century by Bowley, who stated that

> If the [average monthly rate] is 4% it means that . . . one person in 25 is on the average unemployed throughout the year. This average may be made up by one man in each 25 having no work in the year, or each man losing one week in 25, or any distribution of unemployment between these extremes[15].

Bowley's point is that information about the concentration of unemployment experience would be useful. It is of course well known that the unemployment rate differs widely between certain occupations and regions. For example, during the inter-war period some areas in Britain experienced unemployment rates well over 50%, while in others unemployment was very low. But the concentration of unemployment need not be directly related to unemployment rates, as Bowley clearly argued. To obtain appropriate information it is of course necessary to trace the experience of individuals over long periods.

It is also easy to forget that there are more kinds of 'labour market flows' than that from employment to unemployment and vice versa. Some people leave the unemployment register because they become sick, retire or otherwise leave the labour force (sometimes only temporarily). Similarly, a number of flows into unemployment are by people who are just entering the labour market or who have been ill[16]. Changes in labour force participation, sometimes associated with demographic changes and household formation, therefore produce changes in the structure of the labour force and in the composition of the unemployed.

The labour force has in fact changed considerably during the last 60 or so years. For example, between 1921 and 1971 the labour force grew by 30% (to 25 million). The major change has been in the proportion of married women workers. Indeed, in 1921 only 30% of the labour force consisted of women, of whom just over 13% were married. The Department of Employment estimates that by 1991 women will compose 39% of the labour force, and it is expected that about three-quarters of these women will be married. Furthermore, in 1971 almost half of the employed married women were working 30 or fewer hours per week[17]. As a consequence of this change, women and especially part time women workers form a larger proportion of the stock of unemployed than formerly. These changes obviously have implications for the administrative procedures which are used to deal with the unemployed, and with government policy and attitudes towards the problem of unemployment.

1.4 Plan of the book

When considering some alternative economic systems in Section 1.2, it was stressed that a modern complex society such as Britain faces considerable problems of adjusting to exogenous changes. This is particularly important, since long periods of stability are very much the exception. Disturbances exacerbate the considerable difficulty faced by employers and employees in obtaining the information on which they must base their output, pricing, and labour supply and demand decisions.

An analysis of unemployment in such a complex system must

therefore investigate the kinds of adjustments which are in practice made in the labour market. For example, there are numerous ways in which a firm may respond to a sudden decrease in the demand for its output. It may increase stocks of finished goods in the expectation that the reduced demand is temporary; reduce the price of the good; reduce wages, or output, or it may reduce its labour input by reducing hours or workers. If it decides on the latter strategy, it may either make workers redundant or not replace those who retire or resign. Each kind of policy has a different effect on the number of people employed by the firm, and the probability of an unemployed person obtaining a job within the firm during a specified time period. In examining such adjustments, it is most important to recognize explicitly the special features of the labour market which distinguish it from other markets, those, for example, dealing in commodities or financial assets. In particular, it is necessary to distinguish those 'variables' about which firms and individuals may make decisions, and the technical, financial, institutional and other *constraints* which limit the extent of choice.

These problems, among others, are dealt with by R. B. Thomas in Chapter 2. This chapter examines not only the nature of labour market adjustments, but indicates how the composition of the unemployed and the concentration of unemployment have been crucially affected by the adjustment methods commonly used.

The extremely difficult problem of analysing how a complex system responds in aggregate to exogenous change, and the absence of complete information about other individual's plans, has also been raised in Section 1.2. Indeed, this problem is so difficult that for many years economists have concentrated explicitly on examining the characteristics of equilibrium positions. In some cases, notably Walras (1874) and Edgeworth (1881), stylized processes have been invoked as mechanisms for achieving equilibrium; by ensuring either that one person has sufficient information and authority to set the equilibrium prices which transactors take as given, or that the information is communicated at zero cost through the formation of provisional contracts which may subsequently be broken when more advantageous bargains have been negotiated. Edgeworth also showed that the two processes achieve the same results, so long as there is a large number of competitors, but he stated explicitly that

> We have no general dynamical theory determining the path of the economic system from any point assigned at random to a position of equilibrium. We know only the statical properties of the position[18].

The specification of models that allow for the fact that transactors base their plans on a limited set of information, that they use realized market outcomes as the basis for forming expectations, rather than attempting the virtually impossible task of discovering what other people would prefer to do if only their own plans were not frustrated, is considered in detail by M. C. Casson in Chapter 3.

This chapter concentrates on an analysis of the system in which considerable emphasis is given to the fact that most transactions take place out of equilibrium. Again the importance for the analysis of distinguishing between variables which are generally exogenous, and those which are endogenous, becomes very clear. In connection with this point, the extent to which transactors are constrained, and to which they correctly perceive those constraints, turns out to be crucial. The chapter also considers the extent to which producers will attempt to fulfill certain implicit commitments to individuals as both consumers and workers. It shows that such commitments are a rational response to uncertainty and variability, and investigates their implications for the incidence of unemployment among workers. Although the importance of uncertainty and expectations has been recognized in general terms, the author demonstrates the crucial role played by profit expectations, and the fact that the separation of ownership from the control of firms inhibits the flow of information to shareholders.

Chapter 3 not only provides valuable new insights into the workings of an economy, relating to, for example, the role of money; but also generates powerful results concerning the effects of government policies, in particular, attempts to reduce unemployment by reducing wages.

Chapter 4, by H. Armstrong and J. Taylor, then turns to the practical problem of the provision of information to policy-makers about the nature of unemployment. Clearly not all unemployment can be eliminated by policies which provide a general stimulus to consumer demand. There will be situations in which vacancies exist in particular industries and geographical areas for particular types of workers, while suitably qualified workers are unemployed but living in a different area. Furthermore, some occupations may be more liable than others to seasonal fluctuations in unemployment. Decisions about appropriate policies, such as providing labour training in special skills, or attempting to stimulate the transfer of either workers or firms between areas, require detailed information about the structure of unemployment in addition to information relating to the costs of those policies.

In the absence of the complete data which would ideally be required for such an exercise, the authors provide a method of categorizing the stock of unemployed at any time, which is based on information about unemployment and vacancies. Suggestions for developing the method are also made, in addition to providing a sensitivity analysis of some of the assumptions which were necessitated by the lack of more complete data. This aspect of the work is of course very important, since data collection is extremely expensive and it is useful to know precisely which additional data would be most useful. Notice that this chapter does *not* attempt to measure the chimerical 'voluntary unemployed'.

In Section 1.2 it was also suggested that a society would support the unemployed only if it were satisfied that individuals were in some sense 'genuinely' unemployed. Indeed, the fear that a system of unemployment benefits may encourage some people to become and/or to remain unemployed for longer than otherwise, has always been a dominant influence on the design of systems, as also indicated at the end of Section 1.1. The separate influence of unemployment benefits on unemployment flows, and thereby also on the stock of those in unemployment at any time, is extremely difficult to isolate. Indeed, it would be extravagant to claim that much more than a tentative beginning has been made. The problems are considered in detail by A. B. Atkinson in Chapter 5, in the context of a critique of a number of attempts to measure incentive effects in Britain. Suggestions are also made about possible directions for future work in this area.

The question is then raised about the most appropriate method of treating the unemployed. For example, it is not immediately obvious that a system of unemployment insurance would be preferred to a general scheme which aims to help all those who, for a variety of reasons, fall below a conventional poverty standard. Each alternative itself raises further questions. Thus, should individuals be left to make private arrangements for insurance? If a system is to be operated by the state, how should it be financed (from special contributions or from taxation?), and which individuals should be excluded from receiving benefits? If a general scheme of income support is preferred, should this be operated through a rigorous system of means-testing or through something like a negative income tax? (The latter obviously involves a kind of means test, but on a very different level.) These important issues are considered in Chapter 6, by R. Disney. This chapter examines the economic arguments for alternative systems, and critically examines the National Insurance system which operates in Great Britain. It also examines the extent to which the present system provides support to those whom it was originally designed to help.

Chapter 7, by J. Ashworth, then turns to a question which has occupied many economists over the past two decades; that of the relationship between changes in average wages (or earnings) and the rate of unemployment, and the extent to which such a relationship may be affected by various government policies. The issue relates to the consistency (or 'tradability') of policy objectives, in particular those of reducing unemployment and the rate of inflation. This has of course been considerably complicated by the coexistence of rising unemployment *and* inflation during the 1970s. The analysis of this problem provides a further example of the difficulty of testing economic theories which are formulated in terms of variables which are extremely difficult, if not impossible, to measure, and where problems of aggregation cannot be ignored.

Chapter 8 provides a detailed summary of the vast amount of data relating to unemployment in Britain, and which are available to researchers working in this area. The chapter, by J. S. Lord, shows how the collection of data and kind of data available are intimately connected with the administration of the National Insurance scheme. Any researcher must be thoroughly aware of the precise meaning and limitations of the data, and these are discussed in the chapter.

Finally, it is worth recalling the statement of Alfred Marshall concerning the study of industrial fluctuations, that

> . . . though economists have not yet succeeded in bringing that study to a successful issue, the cause of their failure lies in the profound obscurity and ever-changing form of the problem; it does not lie in any indifference on their part to its supreme importance[19].

Notes

1. Unemployment therefore provides an example of the important point made by Malthus, that

   The laws which regulate the movements of human society have an infinitely stronger claim to our attention, both because they relate to objects about which we are daily and hourly conversant, and because their effects are continually modified by human interference. (Malthus, 1820, p. 10).

2. For further details concerning the origins of these words see Harris (1972, p. 4).
3. Lipson (1943, III, p. 487).
4. For example, details of the disruptive effects of the wars with Spain are given by Lipson (1943, III, p. 303). Mulhall (1884,

p. 34) notes that the expenditure on poor relief in the period after Waterloo was four times as great as in the previous ten years.

5. For example, the Statute of Apprentices (1563) stipulated, among other things, that no person in certain trades should be taken into service for less than a year. This applied to agricultural workers, textile workers, shoemakers, cutlers, bakers, brewers, millers and others. See Lipson (1943, III, p. 301). The classic study is by Davies (1956).

6. Quoted by Harris (1972, p. 100).

7. The phrase is taken from the book by Beveridge (1909).

8. It may be of interest to consider trade between cooperating societies of this kind, but it is not crucial in the present context.

9. In fact early forms of labour exchanges may be traced to the work of craft guilds in, for example, London (1370), York (1495), Worcester (1497), Coventry (1553) and Norwich (1573). For further details see Lipson (1949, I, p. 348).

10. In a different context Edgeworth remarked that, 'International trade meaning in plain English trade between nations, it is not surprising that the term should mean something else in political economy' (1925, II, p. 5).

11. Similarly, unemployment does not include those who are in employment but not actively working, such as a shop assistant who is not serving or a worker who is waiting to be assigned to his next task. It is part of the 'contract' that the person should be available for work between specified hours.

12. For further discussion of the use of the term 'voluntary' unemployment, see Worswick (1976). It is obviously important to distinguish this from abuse of a system of relief. For a useful discussion of the latter see *Report of the Committee on Abuse of Social Security Benefits* (1973).

13. During the late 1960s and early 1970s the quarterly flows were between $1\frac{1}{4}$ and 2 times the stock at the beginning of each quarter. See Leicester (1976, p. 189).

14. Most research has concentrated on the process of leaving the unemployment register, but has had to use data relating to incomplete spells of unemployment. It is known that the aggregate probability of leaving the register declines as unemployment duration increases. But the data do not allow discrimination between the alternative assumptions that the probability declines for each individual, and that the probability is constant but differs between individuals. See Cripps and Tarling (1974), and Salant (1977).

15. Bowley (1910, p. 158). It is of interest that Bowley wrote before

unemployment statistics were collected in the process of operating the Unemployment Insurance scheme; yet it is still difficult to obtain appropriate information. For details of statistics before 1914 see also Harris (1972, pp. 371–382). For further discussion of the concentration of unemployment see Disney (1979).

16. For further discussion of labour market flows see Clark and Summers (1979) for the US, and Creedy and Disney (1981) for Great Britain.
17. See the Department of Employment *Gazette* (October, 1975).
18. Edgeworth (1925, II, p. 311).
19. Marshall (1961, p. 712, n. 1).

References

Bowley, A. L. (1910). *An Elementary Manual of Statistics*. London; Macdonald and Evans

Clark, K. B. and Summers, J. H. (1979). Labour market dynamics and unemployment: A reconsideration. *Brookings Papers* **1**, 13–72

Creedy, J. and Disney, R. (1981). Changes in labour market states in Great Britain. *Scottish Journal of Political Economy* **28**, (forthcoming)

Cripps, T. F. and Tarling, R. J. (1974). An analysis of the duration of male unemployment in Great Britain 1932–73. *Economic Journal* **84**, 289–316

Davies, M. G. (1956). *The Enforcement of English Apprenticeship: A Study in Applied Mercantilism 1563–1642*, Harvard University Press

Disney, R. (1979). Recurrent spells and the concentration of unemployment in Great Britain. *Economic Journal* **89**, 109–119

Edgeworth, F. Y. (1881). *Mathematical Psychics*. London; Kegan Paul

Edgeworth, F. Y. (1925). *Papers Relating to Political Economy*, vol. II. London; Macmillan

Harris, J. (1972). *Unemployment and Politics: A Study in English Social Policy 1886–1914*. Oxford; Clarendon Press

Leicester, C. (1976). The duration of unemployment and job search. In Worswick (ed.) (1976), pp. 185–202

Lipson, E. (1949). *The Economic History of England, Volume I, The Middle Ages*, 10th Edition. London; Adam and Charles Black

Lipson, E. (1943). *The Economic History of England, Volume III, The Age of Mercantilism*, 3rd Edition. London; Adam and Charles Black

Malthus, R. (1820). *Principles of Political Economy*. Reprinted by Augustus M. Kelley, New York (1951)

Marshall, A. (1961). *Principles of Economics*, 9th Edition (ed. by C. W. Guillebaud). London; Macmillan

Mulhall, M. G. (1884). *Dictionary of Statistics*. London; G. Routledge & Sons. Reprinted (1970). London; Gregg International Publishers

Report of the Committee on abuse of Social Security Benefits (1973). HMSO, Cmnd 5228

Salant, W. W. (1977). Search theory and duration data: A theory of sorts. *Quarterly Journal of Economics* **91,** 39–57

Walras, L. (1874). *Elements of Pure Economics*. English edition (ed. by W. Jaffé) (1954). London; George Allen & Unwin

Worswick, G. D. N. (ed.) (1976). *The Concept and Measurement of Involuntary Unemployment*. London; George Allen Unwin

Labour market adjustments

2.1 Introduction

Labour market flows

The marked rise in the level of unemployment over recent years has been a prominent feature of the UK economy. The stock of unemployed persons will change whenever the inflows to the stock are not equal to the outflows, and these flows are typically large in relation to the size of the stock. In 1978, for example, 4.48 million people joined the unemployment register (some of these would be counted several times if they experienced repeated spells of unemployment) and 4.57 million people left it. Relatively modest variations in the flows will have a pronounced effect on the stock and an understanding of the nature and determinants of the flows is therefore important for understanding the problem of unemployment.

Some of the outflow from the unemployment register consists of people withdrawing from the labour force, and a tiny fraction is people setting up in business on their own, but the largest part is people accepting employment with firms. Firms' hiring behaviour is thus of major significance. The inflow to the unemployment register comprises new entrants and re-entrants to the labour force and, most importantly, separations from firms, most of which are involuntary as *Table 2.1* shows. The table indicates that for males, who account for the majority of the stock of unemployed, if those who left their last job because of ill-health are excluded, then over two-thirds of separations are involuntary. (These figures relate to the stock and do not strictly tell us about the flows, but it is reasonable to suppose for present purposes that the composition of the inflows is similar to that of the stock.)

It is clear that the decisions of firms are important in determining the inflow to and outflow from the unemployment register. It is usually employers who assign workers to the employed or unemployed state and the analysis of firms' employment behaviour is essential for understanding unemployment. The supply side obviously cannot be

Table 2.1 Reasons for leaving last job (Great Britain 1978)

Unemployed persons aged 16 and over who have ever worked	Males (%)	Females (%)	Total (%)
Made redundant, sacked	53	28	48
Dissatisfied with last job	20	21	20
Ill health	15	13	14
Last job temporary	4	4	4
Retirement	2	1	1
Domestic reasons/other	8	36	20

Source: *General Household Survey 1978*. London; HMSO. (Percentages do not sum to 100 since some people gave more than one reason for leaving their last job).

neglected. Individuals must decide whether to enter or leave the labour force, whether to accept some job offer, whether to quit their job, and so on, and much theoretical literature in the last decade has focused on these decisions. Search theory, in particular, has been a notable if not entirely fruitful development. The examination of firms' behaviour has received much less attention.

In the absence of widely accepted theory of firms' behaviour, this chapter aims to identify the principal ways in which employers adjust their labour to changes in product demand[1] and to show how the impact on unemployment will differ with the particular response adopted. In addition to their influence on the stock of unemployed through the scale of hiring and firing, firms will affect the composition of the stock because of preferences for the particular sorts of worker that they hire and fire. Furthermore, the timing of changes in unemployment depends on the speed with which firms act, and the location of unemployment may be affected by decisions on, say, whether to shut down a complete plant or to run all plants at slightly below capacity. Finally, it is evident that firms' behaviour affects not only measured unemployment but also unrecorded 'unemployment' in the form of underutilized labour.

Price and quantity adjustments

When faced with a fall in the demand for their product, firms will normally reduce their demand for labour and are likely to make some adjustments in wages (the price of labour) or in the quantity of labour input. The more they adjust wages, the less will be the quantity adjustments and vice versa. If wages were reduced sufficiently, the same quantity of labour may be employed since the lowering of production costs would permit a reduction in product prices and output would be maintained. If on the other hand wages were not adjusted at all, the adjustment would have to fall on the employment level and this would directly affect unemployment. In practice most of the adjustments in the labour market are of quantities rather than wages. Wages are sticky and employment is reduced.

Much of the discussion in this chapter is concerned with these quantity adjustments and how firms' decisions to alter their stocks of employees, through changes in the inflows of workers to and outflows from the firm, affect unemployment. The possible reasons why there should be this emphasis on employment, rather than wage, changes are also considered.

Utilization

Apart from changing its stock of employees, a firm may choose to alter its input of labour services by altering the rate of utilization of the stock through variations in the number of hours worked per employee. Such changes will generally have no impact on unemployment though there may be a minor effect in some instances. For example, if the hours reduction were drastic and permanent it may be that different workers are used. If part-time workers are substituted for full-time workers some of them are likely to be drawn from outside the measured labour force (e.g. secondary workers not registered at employment offices), whereas redundant full-time workers are more likely to join the pool of unemployed than to withdraw from the labour force. Discussion of how firms determine the optimum mix of persons and hours per person is deferred until Section 2.4. It is apparent that if the relevant economic concept of 'unemployment' includes underutilization of labour then sometimes changes in the measured stock of unemployed persons may be offset by changes in the utilization rate.

Non-market adjustments

Some adjustments by firms bypass the labour market altogether and such responses mean that the impact on unemployment could be quite small[2]. In the short run, for instance, stocks of finished goods may be built up and labour not adjusted at all. This is likely where the downturn is expected to be temporary and where adjustment costs are significant. There may also be some scope for cutting product prices. This need not reduce profits if there is organizational slack, though there will be some loss on the part of whoever was benefiting from the X-inefficiency.

One particular product market response, which is probably most common in the public sector, is variations in product quality. The post-1979 Conservative government's evident difficulty in reducing the number of civil servants simply by reducing public expenditure indicates that some of the impact is via product quality. There are two circumstances where this type of adjustment may be expected. The first is where there is a low elasticity of demand with respect to quality. The government, or consumers faced with no alternative suppliers, accept reduced standards of service, at least in the short run, given the slowness of the institutional machinery for registering public preferences. The second is where there are, in effect, labour-managed firms. Large government departments or universities, for example, are likely to ensure that the interests of the staff are served at least as well as those of consumers[3].

Thus, if adjustments take place through variations in the utilization of the stock of employees, or through changes outside the labour market, the impact on unemployment may be negligible. Before turning to a detailed consideration of changes in the stock of employees, some special features of labour markets are described since some appreciation of these is helpful for the understanding of employer behaviour.

2.2 Labour markets

A simple economic view of the labour market assumes that wages, based on an individual's contribution to output, act as signals to which free decision-makers respond such that allocative efficiency is achieved. A realistic understanding of labour markets requires some modification of this model and some of the features of labour markets are considered in this section.

Uncertainty

One thing labour markets have in common with other markets is that buyers and sellers face uncertainty about the state of the world. For example, decisions frequently have to be taken before all the relevant prices are known. In the case of employers this is likely to lead to a lower level of factor demand. The effect of uncertainty in the product market is usually modelled by postulating a random price with a known probability density function and a mean equal to the price under certainty. If output decisions are made before the price is observed they will depend on the probability density function of the random price variable, the risk-averseness of the firm and the cost function. Risk-averse firms generally select lower outputs than in the certainty case and this will cause less labour to be demanded. Uncertainty in the labour market has been modelled in various ways, for example by assuming random input prices or an uncertain flow of labour services from a given stock of labour. As in the case of product market uncertainty, most models predict that labour demand will be less than under certainty.

There are two other effects of uncertainty. The first is that employers' responses are likely to be delayed because they will not be able to discern the precise nature of the uncertainty. For example, when shocks occur it may not be apparent immediately whether they are temporary or permanent, or whether a fall in demand is confined to the firm or industry. Employers may, for instance, try to recoup market shares and boost sales rather than lay off workers if they do not perceive the fall in demand to be general. The second effect is that labour is likely to be more variable than other inputs, and if the labour input is decomposed into persons and hours per person then (as will be argued in Section 2.4) hours are more likely to be used as an adjustment than persons. This stems from putty-clay technology where capital is chosen before the realized value of product market prices is known and where labour can be used as an *ex post* adjustment. It may be possible, for example, to compensate for poor design in the capital input by a suitable choice of labour input[4].

Uncertainty thus tends to reduce the level of employment, delay adjustments and perhaps make employment more variable. It is a characteristic of most markets but there are other features of labour markets which are less evident elsewhere.

Human capital

One peculiarity of labour market stems from Marshall's observation that 'the worker sells his work but retains capital in himself'. There is normally no opportunity for investing in others, and since the decision to invest in human capital has to be a once-for-all decision on the part of workers, some regularity in wages over time is essential if expectations are not to be continually disappointed[5]. Flex-wage systems give way to fix-wage systems and this in turn puts more emphasis on quality variations through employers' changes in hiring standards[6]. Volatile wages are incompatible with the efficient functioning of the market, particularly since coordination over time often requires the development of some sort of forward markets and these are typically absent in the case of labour. The attempts by transactors to secure some degree of regularity is greatly reinforced by the fact that sellers of labour have interdependent utility functions and are much concerned with fairness and status. Pay is therefore frequently set on the basis of equity, and allocation may often depend on rules and custom. The importance of comparability in pay-fixing is well recognized by all observers of the labour market, and in the short run it is quite possible for large increases in wages to emerge from collective bargaining even when demand is depressed. Instead of mobility (exit) being the only response to dissatisfaction with wages, protest (voice) is often a prominent reaction. These forms of behaviour may well lead to different management tactics in response to falls in demand.

The employment contract

An important implication of the desire for regularity is that particular forms of contract and institutions develop in the labour market. One of the most important characteristics of the employment relation is that it is a continuing one. A degree of mutually beneficial 'attachment'[7] between employers and employees develops, so simple spot contracts which do not allow adaptation in response to changing circumstances are unsuitable. An alternative possibility is to have contingent claims contracts where the delivery of a particular labour service at some future time is contingent on particular future events. It is however impossible to measure quickly and accurately all the variables describing the contingencies (except in the case of linking wages to some price index). There is also the problem of moral hazard if the contract is contingent on variables, such as reported sales or profits, which one of the parties can influence. This has led some writers to characterize the employment transaction as an authority relationship where payment is made for some exact use of labour after uncertain events have unfolded[8]. Within some zone of indifference (the 'acceptance set') the employee will accept the employer's authority, and this enables the employer to postpone selecting particular tasks until after the contract is made. Where the employer selects an item outside the acceptance set then specific payments will normally be required, such as compensation for redundancy.

These views on the special nature of labour contracts have formed the basis for two quite separate lines of thought. One is the development of a special view of labour contracts as a means of risk-sharing. The other view is that, because of the inherent difficulties of contingent claims contracts and authority relations, internal labour markets develop. Both are devices for handling uncertainty in the market and both affect employer behaviour and consequently unemployment. Discussion of the risk-sharing idea of contracts is deferred until Section 2.4 and the present remarks are confined to internal labour markets.

In internal labour markets pricing and allocation is largely by administered rules, often unwritten, which derive their rigidity and legitimacy simply from having been in existence for a long time[9]. The rules serve to promote, and are themselves a consequence of, the stability which is the central feature of such markets. The internal markets are thus a means of minimizing uncertainty. They are created and preserved wherever there are firm-specific skills, jobs or technology[10], because of the advantages not only to employers in the form of reduced labour turnover, but also to workers by ensuring greater standards of equity and stability. The greater the specificity the stronger the internal markets are likely to be and their occurrence is associated with the growth in the size of firms and the move to single-employer bargaining[11].

There are two consequences of internal labour markets which are relevant to the present discussion. First, when faced with a fall in demand firms will prefer hours reduction rather than making redundant the workers embodying firm-specific human capital. Secondly, the nature of the rules, such as seniority rules with 'last in, first out' (LIFO) redundancy arrangements, will influence the composition of any lay-offs. Seniority rules are often desired by profit-maximizing employers. Not only are the most recently hired workers cheapest to lay-off, since redundancy compensation is related to length of service, but they have also acquired least firm-specific training, including the degree of integration into stable work teams.

The labour market features which have been outlined in this section indicate that there is often a high degree of attachment between firms and workers and neither side is indifferent to the identity of the other. There are, therefore, constraints on the extent to which impersonal market forces govern transactions. Indeed, employers sometimes treat labour as fundamentally different from other inputs. Some employers, especially in the public sector, pay attention to 'social obligations', and this might influence the adjustments by delaying redundancies. Apparent concern for employees may often be part of a cost-minimizing strategy but in some cases the welfare of employees may be an argument in the employer's utility function. This special treatment of the labour input is also evident on the part of the Government which has constrained managerial behaviour directly by rules, and indirectly by the impact of legislation on firms' labour costs.

2.3 Changes in the stock of unemployment

The size of the flows into and out of the unemployment register is, as noted earlier, large in relation to the size of the stock of unemployed. A remarkable feature of these flows is their comparative stability from month to month over a decade when unemployment has risen massively. *Table 2.2* shows that the size of the inflow to the register

Table 2.2 Standardized and seasonally adjusted inflows into unemployment in GB and unemployment: males 1967–1973. October each year ('000s)

Year	Inflows	Unemployment	Year	Inflows	Unemployment
1967	249	429	1974	238	507
1968	241	450	1975	264	855
1969	250	456	1976	242	972
1970	250	483	1977	245	1029
1971	254	684	1978	236	946
1972	227	655	1979	236	883
1973	206	425			

Source: Department of Employment *Gazettes*. December 1976, March 1980.

has shown no tendency to increase even though the size of the stock of unemployed has varied. Unemployment over this period must therefore have been largely due to increased duration. Thus the hiring policies of firms, as well as their lay-off and redundancy policies, are important.

Adjustments to hiring policy

When product demand falls there is likely to be a slowing or cessation of recruitment from the external market. This may be accompanied by a rise in hiring standards, or reduced search and selection effort to achieve the same quality of labour intake. Firms face a queue of applicants who may be ranked according to their training costs (widely defined)[12], starting with the least cost applicant. When the rate of recruitment slows there is less necessity to hire more expensive trainees and the training costs of firms will fall, assuming no change in the size and composition of the queue. An alternative way of viewing the fall in firms' costs is in terms of the reduction in the expenditure of effort on the extensive and intensive margins of search. If hiring screens are expensive there will be a preference for assessing performance on the job and using an active dismissals policy. There may also be more emphasis on internal recruitment when recruitment is slowed to a trickle, with consequent effects on the types of adjustment. For example, in the school teachers' market with the present expenditure cuts and falling pupil numbers, there is much redeployment of existing staff between schools rather than external recruitment.

Where increased hiring standards occur with no change in pay rates there is a fall in pay per efficiency unit of labour so these are, in a sense, price adjustments. New recruits are more productive and thus cheaper labour is substituted for dearer labour with unfavourable consequences for the less-well-qualified. More explicit cost cutting may occur if job redesign permits the use of less-qualified labour. In practice job redesign is frequently taking place: it is a choice variable, and need not always involve capital investment.

How far reduced inflows to firms affect the stock of unemployed depends on how far the recruits are drawn from this stock and how far they are drawn from elsewhere. The reduced inflow to firms means an increased average duration of unemployment, though the burden will fall most heavily on certain individuals, particularly the less-skilled who have difficulty meeting the increased hiring standards. Dual labour market theorists argue that even when firms are not experiencing a fall in product demand they might be quite restrictive in their hiring practices and do not attempt to cut across market segmentation by hiring from the slack parts of the market. This is because the increasing hiring costs outweigh the lower wages[13]. Thus workers in the secondary part of the market rarely get an opportunity to participate in the stable jobs of the primary market, and this is a more pronounced tendency in times of reduced hiring. Such workers with their low skills and poor history of 'attachment' to firms suffer repeated spells of unemployment[14].

Outflows from employment

A major downward adjustment is to increase outflows of labour from the firm. Voluntary quits can be influenced by the firm to only a limited extent: they can be increased by offering less favourable pay and conditions or promotion opportunities, but this is an unlikely strategy where firms pay attention to their reputation as employers, in order to facilitate subsequent recruitment in an upturn. In any case, with such strategies it is likely to be the most able workers who respond to such incentives. Other outflows, early retirements, dismissals, temporary lay-offs and most importantly, redundancies (see *Table 2.1*) are more directly controllable. The scope for achieving substantial adjustment by tighter dismissals policies is fairly limited and although early retirement policies have some contribution to make, especially where the required adjustment is small or phased over a long period, they are less significant than redundancies.

How far the stock of unemployed rises when there are redundancies depends on the overall state of the labour market and on the composition of the redundant workers. Some workers, such as older persons and married women, may withdraw from the labour force. Furthermore, the skill composition of those joining the unemployed will influence the duration patterns.

The selection of particular workers for redundancy will depend on the personal and firm-specific investment in human capital and on the rules dictated by the operation of internal labour markets and by unions. These tend to lead, as argued in Section 2.2, to an emphasis on seniority and on consequent use of LIFO procedures[15].

Short service workers and the less-skilled will be the first to be made redundant and much of the burden therefore falls on groups such as youths and the unskilled. Once unemployment becomes concentrated on a few particular types of worker there is a reinforcing effect, given the nature of the screening process. An important signal which employers use, especially when they are raising hiring standards, is job history. Repeated or prolonged spells of unemployment will be an unfavourable signal for most employers since it implies high training costs[16]. Thus the last to be employed are the ones on whom unemployment is concentrated. They are the young, the sick, the long-term unemployed, and the unskilled. But these are the first to be made redundant so that LIFO rules thus discriminate against those who are already disadvantaged in the labour market and they perpetuate the existing pattern of unemployment[17].

Although there can be little doubt of the importance of seniority rules, their role in the UK is sometimes exaggerated. In the foremost study of local labour markets in the UK, MacKay et al. (1971, p. 211) found that the seniority principle was rarely applied in an undiluted form and '. . . plants quite commonly declared married women redundant before single women or men . . ., or men and women near retiring age before workers in younger age groups; or "inefficient" employees before "efficient" employees'. Thus they found that employees with long service often suffered a high proportion of redundancy. The finding of MacKay et al. is important to the extent that in the case of married women and elderly workers at least, they may leave the labour force rather than add to measured unemployment.

In the US seniority rules probably play a more important role because of differences between unions in the two countries, and the lesser significance of internal labour markets in the UK. In the UK there has been a greater emphasis on craft-based unions and, although this is changing, there is still the resulting horizontal mobility between firms, at the same occupational level, rather than the vertical mobility of internal labour markets. So workers do not build up long chains of seniority entitlements[18]. There is also a tendency for British trade unions to seek full employment and high real wages through their influence on national policies rather than plant level measures to control jobs, as is more the case with US unions[19]. There has been more plant-bargaining in the US than in the UK though the picture has changed dramatically in the UK over the last decade. The growth of single-employer bargaining may strengthen seniority rules.

Internal labour markets are also less prominent in the UK than in the US. In some public sector industries such as steel or police there are well-developed internal markets but they are less significant in manufacturing and the volume of internal mobility in firms is often rather restricted. MacKay *et al.* (1971, pp. 398–399) concluded that in British engineering '. . . we are some considerable distance from a situation where the wages of those some way up the occupational ladder are insulated from market forces, because hiring only takes place at the bottom rung and progress up the ladder is determined purely by seniority'. All this suggests that whereas seniority rules do play a considerable role they are not the only forces at work in the selection of workers for redundancy.

2.4 Particular factors affecting adjustment

The discussion in the previous section showed how firms' hiring behaviour affects the size and composition of the stock of unemployed. More generally, in deciding on the choice of adjustment, including non-market adjustments and changes in the utilization of the stock of employees, firms will select adjustment instruments on a cost-minimizing basis. The decision is, however, complex and subject to numerous influences, many of which are best seen as constraints on choice. Some of these influences are discussed in this section. They help to explain why adjustments which have a larger impact on unemployment, that is, quantity adjustments rather than price adjustments, tend to be chosen.

One source of the failure of wages to clear labour markets may be simply that firms are ignorant of developments in other parts of the market and information diffusion is so slow that market clearing processes do not emerge. This view has some superficial attraction given the pervasive ignorance on both sides of the market and the costs of information acquisition, but persistent and substantial unemployment requires further explanation.

Labour contracts

It was noted in Section 2.2 that workers often have expectations of stability and long-term attachments to firms, and that a spot-auction view of the market is inappropriate. Fluctuations in income may occur for several reasons and firms may therefore draw up contracts in terms of a quantity of labour services to be provided and a wage to be paid as a function of the state of nature (usually represented in formal models by output price, which is assumed to be a random variable with a known probability distribution)[20]. The contracts are often implicit and are offered before the state of nature is known. Firms thus compete *ex ante* for workers by offering contracts specifying not just wages and hours but also the proportion of the firm's pool of labour which is to be employed in every state.

There are in fact two transactions which a worker engages in jointly with a single firm. First, the firm buys labour services for use in the production process and secondly, the firm sells insurance to workers against undesirable income fluctuations. Workers are generally more risk-averse than firms so the firms absorb some of the risk that the worker would otherwise bear[21]. The real wage may therefore no longer equal the marginal product of labour, for as Grossman (1979, p. 67) observes, '... a worker's nominal wage income equals either the value of his marginal product minus an implicit insurance premium or the value of his marginal product plus an implicit insurance indemnity, depending on whether the perceived real value of his marginal product is high or low'. Insurance aspects are likely to play a greater role where workers are highly risk-averse and where output fluctuations are large.

The effect of these contracts is to stabilize workers' incomes so that adjustments must take place through quantity changes. Employment may therefore be more variable than under flexible wages but it does not follow that the average level of employment would differ significantly. The nature of the contract can explain why lay-offs occur as long as workers have a preference for income stability. The existence of such a preference was noted in Section 2.2. It may also be that if workers have a preference for the bunching of leisure then the marginal utility of leisure may rise very sharply in the neighbourhood of full leisure even though it is diminishing everywhere else[22]. For a given level of consumption, workers may then prefer the gamble of a little or full leisure (temporary lay-offs) to a certain quantity of leisure which falls between these extremes. When output price is sufficiently low they may prefer to combine random vacations with periods of work at longer hours, to continuous employment when hours per week required to maintain full employment are small.

Some support for the contract theory is claimed by Abowd and Ashenfelter (1979) whose empirical work in the US indicated that workers experiencing higher expected unemployment and hours variability receive higher pay than those with more secure employment. This suggests that there is an element of compensation in wages for uninsured differences in the incidence of unemployment.

Contract theory thus appears to provide some interesting insights on the question of why lay-offs occur rather than wage changes. However, it cannot be accepted unreservedly. First, there may be incomplete shifting of risk from workers to firms because of the possibility of default on contracts, and because the existence of state unemployment benefits provides some income insurance outside the firm. There will be incentives to default wherever wages diverge from marginal products. In 'good' states of nature when the marginal product turns out to be higher than the contracted wage, workers may threaten to quit or demand higher temporary wages. And in 'bad' states employers may wish to substitute cheaper labour. The use of legally-enforceable contracts is rare in labour markets and extra-legal incentives for compliance must therefore be relied upon. The firm's concern with its reputation for reliability is important in this regard.

Secondly, the contract theories typically do not pay much attention to the fact that unemployment is concentrated on a few workers[23]. Perhaps workers of different seniority can obtain different implicit contracts because of their different risks, and this will affect their order of lay-off.

Thirdly, the principal phenomenon explained is that of temporary lay-offs, so that in a long-term sense there is still an attachment between employer and worker. In the UK such temporary lay-offs are very much less significant than redundancies and even in the US where the contract literature has been prolific and lay-offs are said to predominate, there has recently been a serious questioning of their importance[24].

Fixed costs

An important influence both on the level and on the variability of employment is the mix of workers and hours per worker. For any given level of labour services the optimal mix depends on technological and cost factors. Cost-minimizing employers will consider the ratio of the marginal contribution to labour services of an additional employee to that of an additional hour for all employees, and equate this to the ratio of the respective marginal costs of the two methods of increasing labour services[25]. Technology is discussed later and the present remarks relate only to costs.

Labour costs comprise wage and non-wage costs; of these the latter have attracted considerable attention in recent years. Many of these non-wage costs are fixed, or quasi-fixed, in that they vary less-than-proportionately with the number of hours worked. Some of these fixed non-wage costs are of a non-recurrent kind such as recruitment and selection costs whereas others are recurrent such as welfare and holiday pay and national insurance contributions (though in part these are pay-related). Some are contingent liabilities such as maternity benefits or redundancy payments. The latter form part of the 'adjustment costs': that is, the costs of changing the labour stock or its rate of utilization. There will also be adjustment costs which are not separable from the production process, such as operating at less than the capacity for which the plant was designed, and morale effects. Where team production is important such morale effects may reduce productivity through such factors as greater absenteeism, poor time-keeping, increased material wastage, or more disputes. In some cases formal opposition to lay-offs may be an important consideration in any rundown decision.

There has been a marked growth in these non-wage costs in recent years. In manufacturing industries they increased from 8.1% of the total costs in 1964 to 13.7% in 1975, and in extractive industries they jumped from 9.4% to 24.6% over the same period[26]. Nickell (1979) has documented some of the increases to those costs which are largely attributable to government legislation, particularly the employment protection legislation. Provisions relating to procedures for dismissals and employee's rights of appeal against unfair dismissal, and the periods of notice which employers are required to give before terminating employment have generally become more favourable to employees and their provision has been extended to cover more employees. It is usually assumed that these developments have increased the costs of reducing the labour force and have also made employers more selective in hiring because of the greater problems of dismissing workers.

This growth in non-wage costs has several consequences. First, increases in fixed cost will raise the marginal cost of labour services from additional workers relative to the marginal cost of labour from extra hours per worker. This will lead to the substitution of hours for workers, with adverse effects on unemployment[27]. In dynamic terms there may be some slight offsetting of this tendency because of adjustment costs leading to labour hoarding thereby increasing employment in a slump[28].

Secondly, the speed and extent of adjustment will be moderated by adjustment costs and by employers' expectations of the duration of the downswing. The adjustment costs dictate that adjustments will be slow and almost all empirical work strongly supports the idea that there is a hierarchy of adjustment speeds for the different inputs with hours adjusting more rapidly than workers in response to demand shifts[29]. This reduces the flows between the unemployment register and firms. Employment variability is lessened, and this tendency may well be reinforced by internal labour markets which are likely to be stronger where fixed costs are important.

The speed of adjustment may well be affected by the state of the labour market. For example, Peel and Walker (1978) found some empirical evidence to support the view that in times of high unemployment there may be a significant increase in the speed of adjustments compared with times when the employer is rationed in the labour market[30].

The fall in the inflows to the unemployment register from firms, as a result of fixed costs, is accompanied by increased average duration of unemployment. This is because employers are more reluctant to take on workers when they are more difficult to dismiss. Workers will only be hired when employers are confident that they are going to require them for long periods and that their screenings are sufficiently discriminating to require few dismissals on the grounds of unsatisfactory performance. The fall in the inflows to the unemployment register and the increased duration of unemployment will have opposite effects on the stock of unemployed, and the direction of the net effect is an empirical question.

Evidence from econometric studies and from surveys is available on the relationship between fixed costs and unemployment. One of the difficulties of attempting to estimate relationships statistically is the lack of appropriate data on many aspects of fixed costs. This means that the conclusions of studies which purport to show that fixed costs are an important influence on employment levels cannot be accepted unreservedly. For example, Nickell (1979) estimated regression equations of monthly inflows to unemployment and of the proportion of vacancies filled each month, and used these as a basis for assessing their contribution to changes in unemployment. He estimated that for males in the UK in the period 1970–1975 unemployment increased by about 23% due to the reduction in job offer probabilities and decreased by about 3.5% due to the reduction in the inflow. He regards this as consistent with the view that increases in unemployment are attributable to increases in fixed costs, particularly those resulting from government legislation. There was, however, no specific measurement of adjustment costs but simply an acknowledgement that one unmeasured trend during the period was tighter restrictions on dismissals. Other econometric attempts to relate the effect of the Redundancy Payments and

Employment Protection Acts to employment have found no significant effect[31].

Alternative evidence, from surveys of firms, suggests that there is little foundation for the view that employment legislation inhibits recruitment. Daniel and Stilgoe (1978), whose 1977 survey covered manufacturing firms employing between 50 and 5000 people, found that although many firms were recruiting fewer workers than previously, only 6% cited any aspect of the employment legislation as a contributory factor. A survey of smaller firms, employing less than 50 people, by Clifton and Tatton-Brown (1979) found similar results. Only 4% mentioned employment legislation or difficulties in reducing their labour force as a reason for not recruiting. (In both surveys these percentages rose considerably when firms were prompted about the legislation.)

The conclusion then is that fixed costs of employment have risen and this seems to have resulted in some substitution of hours for employment. But attempts to link this specifically with the higher fixed costs which are attributable to legislation are not well supported. Indeed, there is no clear estimate of the quantitative impact on labour costs of the legislation. There are more grounds for confidence in asserting that employment variation has been lowered with the higher fixed costs, and hours variation has increased. However, even this proposition requires some qualification since firms may be able to select the level of fixed costs they incur, particularly in terms of recruitment and selection expenditures. If firms choose to incur higher fixed costs in times of stable prices, and hence stable demand for labour, then it may be that high fixed costs are an effect rather than a cause of low employment variability.

A good deal more needs to be known before a large part of the increase in unemployment can be attributed to the rise in fixed costs.

Technology

Technology may influence both the choice and the speed of adjustment. The substitutability of different inputs will affect the responses firms make, and this is partly though not wholly dependent on the technology.

The separate contributions to output of the number of employees and the number of hours per employee can usefully be distinguished[32]. Their substitutability and their productivity may influence the extent to which an employer attempts to reduce workers or hours in making quantity adjustments, and there will be different consequences for unemployment. It is frequently assumed that the elasticity of output with respect to hours per employee (η_H) is greater than the elasticity with respect to employees (η_E). Flemming (1975) has argued that in such a case, if a given reduction in total manhours by hours reductions, and by reductions in the number of workers, were to reduce the wage bill by an equal amount then the decision might well depend on the effect on output of the alternative sources of reduction. If $\eta_H > \eta_E$ then hours reductions would have a bigger impact on output and reducing the number of workers would be preferred. Lay-offs thus may arise because of the technical nature of the production function.

The assumption that $\eta_H > \eta_E$ is, at first sight, plausible. If there is some starting-up time, the early hours will be less productive than the later ones so that even if the marginal product of the post-starting-up hours were constant it would exceed the average product. Variations in hours will thus affect output more than variations in workers. In addition, Flemming (1975) has argued that the employer closes marginal machines when the number of workers is reduced so that output changes relatively little, whereas with changes in hours he simply runs his good machines for a shorter period each day, thus having a greater impact on output. One factor offsetting these tendencies is the greater possibility of fatigue which may lead to diminishing marginal productivity of hours[33].

Early empirical evidence seemed to confirm the high postulated values of η_H[34]. Estimates of 2 or more suggested strongly increasing returns to hours, but such estimates were derived from aggregate production functions and generally took no account of the bias in the coefficients resulting from inter-industry effects. A recent attempt by Leslie and Wise (1980) to take account of such effects has led to a substantial downward revision of the estimated η_H. They report a figure of 0.64, about the same as their estimate of η_E, which shows diminishing returns to hours.

Empirical support for Flemming's argument is therefore questionable, and other explanations of lay-offs have to be sought. It does seem important to recognize differences between industries in discussing adjustments, for within any particular sector the appropriate technology may be rigid over quite wide ranges of relative input prices.

The importance of adjustment costs as a determinant of the speed of response has already been noted. Technology will affect some of these costs. Hazeldine (1978), for example, has argued that there will be a maximum productivity level of production and employment. Average productivity will be an inverted U-shaped function of employment and the sharper the reduction in productivity either side of the maximum, the greater are the costs of deviating from the maximum level. This affects the speed of adjustment, which is slower the greater the costs of departing from the optimum.

Long-run productivity growth can be enjoyed as increases in real wages or reduced working hours or some combination of the two. Over the course of this century most of the gains have been taken in the form of increased consumption rather than of leisure, and more recently an even greater share has been taken as consumption[35]. With the slowing down of the rate of growth of productivity, attributable in part to the expansion of the low-productivity labour-intensive service sector, major increases in leisure time are likely to be difficult to achieve. Thus, the more immediate policy questions are not so much in terms of more income versus more leisure but in terms of employment versus shorter hours. There have been many proposals to alleviate unemployment by cutting the average length of the working week, based on the argument that employees would be substituted for the smaller input of hours per worker. How far this is feasible depends crucially on the technology, and the low estimates of η_H produced by Leslie and Wise (1980) indicate that substantial reductions in unemployment are possible.

Unions

Unions may affect employers' adjustment behaviour in several ways. In the first place they may have an effect on pay levels and on the wage structure. There is widespread agreement that unions have an impact effect on wages and raise their members' pay above that of non-members, or more accurately, above that of those who are not covered by the collective agreement[36]. They also have a conservative effect in the form of rigidifying the wage structure. The emphasis on comparability in pay bargaining inhibits movements in differentials in response to market forces. There will also be some constraint in wage movements over time since unions exercise more power in resisting cuts in a downswing than they do in an upswing, when wage claims are much more readily conceded by employers and the very process of collective bargaining may slow down the pace of wage increases.

Unions' ability to control the price of labour means that they cannot also control the quantity, and this forms part of the explanation of the predominance of quantity adjustments in labour markets[37]. Unions may, however, be able to influence the composition of the available employment by implementing controls on the order of lay-offs or on vetting the workers hired.

How far employment is adversely affected by higher wages

depends on the relevant elasticities of demand, and in particular on the elasticity of substitution between union labour and other inputs. Unions will therefore attempt to constrain such substitution via so-called restrictive practices and there is considerable anecdotal evidence and also some statistical evidence which indicates that the elasticity of substitution is in fact reduced in unionized firms[38]. To some extent, of course, unions prosper best in circumstances where there is a low elasticity of substitution. They are therefore most likely to form there, which means that unions may be an effect rather than a cause of low substitution elasticities. The closed shop and resistance to technical change limit the use of non-union labour or capital within any firm. The greatest effect of unions is likely to be on *ex ante* substitution; once capital is in use unions will have less chance of altering the input combinations.

The adjustment costs of firms are likely to be increased by constraints which unions impose on managerial behaviour. For example, where the bargaining unit does not coincide with the area of market pressure adjustments may be more costly. In a downturn which is confined to a particular sector or product group, employers may be reluctant to facilitate redundancies by giving especially generous compensation if such provisions are automatically applicable to a much wider group of workers. More directly, unions may increase adjustment costs by disruptive strikes and sit-ins. They may delay the timing though they cannot ultimately avoid quantity adjustments if prices are fixed. This is why much union activity is often concerned with the broader target of attempting to influence macroeconomic policy.

The activities of unions in securing pay above workers' transfer earnings and in building up seniority rules and pension rights that may not be transferable, will lead to a preference for temporary lay-offs to preserve the attachment to the firm. These will also be favoured by firms when they are confident that workers with firm-specific human capital will return when recalled. Feldstein's (1978) empirical work in the US has shown that lay-offs were much more common among union members.

Resistance to wage-cuts is not confined to unions. Non-union labour will also resist for as Rees (1973, p. 226) has noted, 'workers universally regard a wage cut as an affront because they view their money wages as a measure of their worth and the esteem in which they are held'. A non-union employer may then fear that the resentment caused by wage cuts will lower productivity and perhaps cause the formation of a union. One consequence of this general resistance to wage cuts is that in a depression the employed and unemployed are essentially non-competing groups, and the supply

price of the unemployed is not relevant to determining the wage
level of the employed.

Government policy

Government policies can affect the adjustment decisions of firms in
various ways. In a general sense all government economic policy will
exercise an influence on firms but the remarks here are confined to
those policies which affect input costs. In addition to the employment
protection legislation, which has already been considered, there has
been a battery of subsidies, job creation and training programmes
aimed at alleviating or preventing unemployment.

In practice the government's approach to active labour market
policies has been rather *ad hoc* and the multiplicity of measures is
indicative of their temporary and changing character. In recent
years the following policy measures have been operative at one time
or another:

> the Temporary Employment Subsidy, the Short-time Working
> Compensation Scheme, the Small Firms Employment Subsidy,
> the Recruitment Subsidy, the Adult Employment Programme,
> the Job Creation Programme, the Special Temporary Employ-
> ment Programme, the Work Experience Programme, the Youth
> Opportunities Programme, the Job Release Scheme, Community
> Industry, Training Services Agency Courses for Young People,
> Training places in industry and the Job Introduction Scheme for
> disabled.

In view of this variety and the fact that some of them have
operated for limited periods only, it is unlikely that firms will have
made long-term employment decisions on the basis of these policies.
The impact on the general level of unemployment appears to have
been small. A number of studies have attempted to estimate the
effect of particular measures, but it is difficult to say with confidence
what the results have been since the individual measures have been
small and difficult to separate from the background of industrial,
regional, industrial relations and prices and income policies. Where
the measures may have had an impact is on the timing of lay-offs and
the short-term recruitment flows, especially for certain target groups
such as youths. There is a growing theoretical literature on the use of
labour subsidies but they have made little contribution to any
substantial fall in unemployment in the UK[39].

Apart from influencing labour costs by subsidies, various
government incomes policies may change the relative prices of
different labour inputs. Equal pay legislation has, for example, had

a pronounced impact effect on sex differentials. Median earnings of full-time female workers were about 50% of those of males for the whole of this century to 1970, when the legislation announced for 1975 caused the figure to rise. It reached 58% by 1975 and now appears to have levelled off at around 60%. The efficacy of price signals in determining the mix of different types of labour in the production process is much overstated, but that is not to say that price signals are totally irrelevant. The legislation may have the effect of reducing the employment prospects for women, and might contribute to further segregation along dual labour market lines into primary and secondary markets. The Sex Discrimination Act is obviously an important attempt to limit this process. Detailed empirical studies of the employment impact of the Equal Pay Act have not yet been undertaken.

More generally, anti-inflation incomes policies have often been alleged to rigidify differentials, or narrow them in the 1970s when the terms of some of the policies allowed equal absolute increases to all groups, and sometimes permitted no increase at all for the very highest paid. If this were true, then if employers base input mix decisions on relative input prices, there would be changes in the employment mix. The recent narrowing of skill differentials began, however, before the egalitarian incomes policies and is more associated with periods of inflation than unemployment. Furthermore, Brown (1979) has produced evidence which suggests that workplace bargainers generally adhere to the spirit of incomes policies but are often able to manipulate the distribution of increases between grades. This observation of 'flexible conformity' suggests that even apparently rigid incomes policies may not act as a complete constraint on employers' ability to manipulate factor prices.

If incomes policies have had a restraining effect on the general level of wages then there may be favourable employment consequences through the substitution of labour for other inputs. This argument has sometimes been suggested to explain the observation that falls in real wages were accompanied by falls in labour productivity in the incomes policy period 1975–1977. However, it is most unlikely that this was due to capital substitution over so short a period. The general conclusion must be that in practice incomes policies do not act as a powerful constraint on employers' adjustment decisions in times of high unemployment.

One other policy measure which has attracted considerable attention is the level of unemployment benefit. This has been examined in many countries and a positive relationship between the average duration of unemployment and the level of benefits has been found. This is usually explained in terms of supply-side analysis of job seekers' behaviour, but employers' behaviour may also be influenced by benefits. Feldstein (1978), for example, noted that the existence of benefits may make firms more prone to lay off workers for short periods in response to demand fluctuations, since there is less fear of creating costly ill-will. He argues that so strong is the propensity of firms to lay off workers when there is unemployment insurance that efficiency losses may result from distorting the firm to adjust in this way rather than through other means[40].

It seems then that the effect of government policies on adjustment behaviour are potentially very strong, but in practice have been limited.

Size of firm

The size of firms is likely to affect employment decisions. First, the growth in average firm size has been associated with increasing industrial concentration and this has implications for product pricing and employment stability. Secondly, the size of the firm has implications for plant level decision-making.

There are several reasons for supposing that more concentrated industries have less flexible price responses to demand changes. Oligopolists, for example, may practice 'entry-limit' pricing and keep prices below the short-run maximizing level, and in order to coordinate prices, firms with market power may prefer to space price increases evenly rather than adjusting swiftly as may be the case under competition[41]. To the extent that price stability exists, then quantity variation will be a more important response to demand fluctuations. This will lead to greater instability in employment and will counteract any tendency for greater organizational slack under oligopoly to lead to more employment stability via increased hoarding. Feinberg (1979) attempted to measure the effect of market structure on employment stability and found that highly concentrated industries were characterized by instability, so that some of the risk faced by firms is shifted onto employees[42]. The growth in concentration may therefore lead to a more volatile labour force and possibly, as a result, to more variation in the stock of unemployed.

The size of organization may also influence the sorts of decisions that are made. In larger organizations the decision-making processes are often complex and the instruments of adjustment are under the control of different decision-makers, so that it is often inappropriate to view the enterprise 'as if' it were a single rational decision unit[43].

Where there are different levels of decision-making, the discretion of individuals at the lower levels is often severely limited and this might have implications for the size, or at least the timing, of changes in unemployment in particular localities. When decisions are made at a parent company, complete plants may be closed; whereas the shut-down of a plant is likely to be delayed with decision-making by independent plants interested in survival[44]. Where decisions are made at many dispersed points within an organization, there is often a process of limited and sometimes uncoordinated adjustments because in large organizations with regularized bureaucratic procedures, 'habit' and caution may lead to a predilection for small departures from established procedures. This may be rational behaviour for risk-averse firms in an uncertain world but it does mean that choice of adjustment depends to some extent on the history of the firm; it will favour what is found familiar. Different departments in a firm have different responsibilities and authority for different adjustment instruments and this may lead to inter-departmental conflicts, the resolution of which is a complex political matter. What is observed, therefore, is considerable diversity between firms in apparently similar circumstances because of the differences in organizational structure and internal constraints.

2.5 Conclusions

This chapter has shown that the way firms adjust to changes in demand can influence the level, composition, variability and speed of changes in the stock of unemployed. Several explanations for the predominance of quantity rather than price changes were discussed. Most of these stem from supply-side preferences for stability of income. Unions' resistance to wage cuts, and the consequent willingness to tolerate periods of unemployment for some of their members, is probably a major factor. But it was also noted that employers of non-union labour may have good reasons for preferring cuts in employment to wage reductions. This was in part due to the fact that the employment relationship is a continuing one and employers are often concerned about their reputation. Technological explanations of quantity adjustments, in terms of differing elasticities of output with respect to persons and with respect to hours per person have been used to form the basis of a rationale for lay-offs. The best empirical evidence on the size of these elasticities does not, however, offer much support for this view. Finally, contract theorists have argued that the particular nature of the risk-sharing arrangements leads to lay-offs rather than price changes.

Several developments over recent years have affected unemployment via firms' behaviour. The growth of fixed costs of employment has lead to some substitution of hours for workers, thereby putting a greater burden of adjustment on hours variation than on employment variation. Such costs also lead to slower adjustment in the labour force. The increase in the size of public sector employment, now accounting for about 30% of all employment, means that more of the labour force is in enterprises where greater weight might be given to maintaining employment than is the case in many parts of the private sector. The great increase in the level of unemployment in the last decade has not lessened its concentration on just a few groups. The features of the labour market that have been described in this chapter indicate that the more persistent the unemployment is, the less likely are the disadvantaged groups to improve their lot.

There may be pronounced differences between firms in their adjustments. These are perhaps of little consequence in aggregate but in terms of the incidence of unemployment between particular individuals or localities, they can cause a redistribution of the burden. In any one firm there may be marked discontinuities in the adjustment process, with significant changes (such as altering the size of the capital stock, or employing an extra shift) being the end point of a period of gradually increasing pressure during which no responses occurred. Again, these factors may be important locally though there is likely to be smoothing in the aggregate.

It has not been possible to consider the welfare implications of the different adjustments which firms make but it is clear that there may be differences in the social and private costs and benefits of different adjustments. Optimal strategies for the firm may lead to socially sub-optimal levels of unemployment and such possibilities lead some writers to conclude, for example, that employers should be compensated for the costs of employment protection legislation. Such analysis requires specification not only of socially optimal levels of unemployment but also explicit consideration of distributional weights since, as has been argued throughout this chapter, the composition of unemployment in terms of the particular individuals who experience it is likely to be much affected by firms' behaviour.

A rich variety of adjustments has been indicated in this chapter. There is much formal modelling of some aspects of firms' decisions but there is a need for more comprehensive analysis of the firm, which would help to provide a basis for policy.

Notes

1. Most of the discussion does not therefore deal explicitly with responses to technological advance, though this may be an important source of change in the demand for labour.

2. It is impossible to describe labour market adjustments satisfactorily without considering what is happening elsewhere. In Fisher's (1971, p. 92) words 'economic analysis, *per se*, does not prescribe through which avenues adjustments are to be secured and one cannot maintain *ab initio* that it should not proceed to some degree through interdependence with other labour, factor and commodity markets'.

3. Unions may actively resist staff-trimming measures. Some public service unions have recently refused to produce manpower figures which would facilitate the appraisal of employment needs.

4. In such cases, as Hartmann (1976) has shown, the models soon become very complex and unambiguous results hard to obtain even in the case of risk-neutral firms. Indeed, most models of the impact of uncertainty on the labour market very soon become intractable. See Hey (1979) for a review of some of these.

5. See Crossley (1973). The observations and rationale of regularity has always been well known, see Hicks (1932, p. 55) and see also his second edition (1962, p. 317).

6. See Pissaridies (1976) for a formal modelling of these different systems.

7. See Pen (1959) for a discussion of the nature of attachment. He argued (on p. 72) that the market effectively dissolves into a series of bilateral monopolies. The plant becomes of central importance, as has been borne out in all empirical studies of labour markets since Reynolds' (1957) early work. See, for example, MacKay *et al.* (1971) and Rees and Schultz (1970).

8. See Simon (1979).

9. See Brown (1972) for a detailed description and analysis of the significance of custom and practice rules.

10. Williamson (1975) provides an account of the differences between firms arising from task idiosyncracies, when apparently similar jobs differ, for instance in the equipment, the processes or the communications systems and informal team accommodation which are often firm-specific.

11. An extensive survey reported by Deaton and Beaumont (1979) found that 75% of their sample had single-employer bargaining arrangements.

12. Thurow (1976) has developed this analysis fully. The training costs include not only the costs of acquiring any necessary skills but also of learning to adapt to all the firm's idiosyncracies and becoming an integrated member of the production team.

13. See Holt (1979). For evidence of the trade-off between worker quality and wages, see Rees and Schultz (1970).

14. There is little firm evidence to support the view that there is strong segmentation in the UK. In particular the dual market idea of a sharp division between primary and secondary markets seems exaggerated. See Mayhew and Rosewell (1979).
15. There are some exceptions in particular industries. In some areas in coal mining, for example, the union has insisted that workers to be made redundant are selected randomly.
16. See Johnson and Van Doorn (1976) for a view on the loss of skills with unemployment. Training costs will also be higher because workers are less practised at team integration.
17. See Disney (1979) for evidence on the concentration of unemployment amongst certain groups. Disney makes an important distinction between the number of spells of unemployment and the spell duration, and found that younger workers experience a high number of spells and older workers a high spell duration.
18. See Kerr (1954) for the initial analysis of these different mobility patterns.
19. See Addison and Siebert (1979, p. 305).
20. Some models use a vector of stochastic variables to describe the state of nature but a frequent simplifying assumption is that firms are price-takers and the exogenous output price is the only relevant stochastic variable.
21. See Grossman (1978) for an account of how these differences in risk-aversion between firms and workers emerge.
22. It is a commonplace observation that hours of work per year have fallen more rapidly than hours of work per week which suggests that workers do have such a preference.
23. Early contract models such as Azariadis (1975) assumed that available employment was evenly distributed among workers. However, markets have been modelled, by for example Baily (1976), in which one group of workers have considerable security and another act as a sort of buffer stock and experienced much more unemployment.
24. Feldstein (1978) has suggested that lay-offs account for about 50% of all unemployment in the US and he estimated that about 75% of laid-off workers returned to their former employer, a figure broadly supported by Medoff (1979, p. 390). More recently, however, careful estimates by Clark and Summers (1979) indicate that only about 50–60% return to their previous jobs.
25. This is pure demand-side analysis and implicitly assumes there are no supply constraints.
26. These figures are taken from *Labour Costs in G.B. 1964* (1968), HMSO, London and *Structure of Labour Costs* (1977), Eurostat,

Luxembourg. The costs are very much lower than in many other European countries. Whiting (1978) gives other evidence on the increase in such costs.

27. Conversely, workers will be substituted for hours if there is an increase in the wage rate, the overtime premium, or the number of hours paid at basic rates.

28. Nickell (1978) produces these intuitively appealing results on the basis of a rather restrictive formal model in which, for example, there are no voluntary quits.

29. There is an extensive literature on short term employment functions, which relate employment to output. Most of these show hours adjust faster than employment. See Wilson (1980) for a comparison of the performance of various models. Nadiri and Rosen (1973) used a system of interrelated factor demand functions to demonstrate empirically that the order of adjustment speeds was: capital utilization, hours, workers, and very slowly, the capital stock.

30. This finding is not universal. Hazeldine (1979), for example, using Canadian data found that downward employment adjustment is more difficult when unemployment is high, partly because of qualms about laying off workers.

31. See Beenstock (1979), though he estimated the elasticity of employment with respect to employment surcharges (such as national insurance contributions) as −1.4. That is, the surcharge depresses employment.

32. This is now a commonplace procedure. See, for example, Hart and Sharot (1978).

33. This idea has been incorporated into a number of models following Brechling (1965).

34. See Feldstein (1967) and Craine (1973).

35. See Levitan and Belous (1977).

36. Estimates of the union/non-union differential vary greatly but figures in the order of 20–30% are not unusual, though as Creedy (1979) shows, the usual method of estimating such differentials is open to serious questioning.

37. The fact that some unions impose work-sharing practices such as overtime bans indicates that wages are a dominant but not exclusive concern of unions.

38. See Freeman and Medoff (1977).

39. For an examination of some of these measures see Layard (1979). He found, for example, that the Small Firms Employment Subsidy did have positive employment effects, but the overall size of the programme is tiny.

40. Over recent years there has been very little change in the ratio

of benefits to average earnings in the UK so it is unlikely to have been a strong contributory factor to increased lay-offs by firms in the UK.
41. See Feinberg (1979) for an elaboration of these and other arguments.
42. He used US cross-industry data and took several different measures of concentration and instability. He also attempted to allow for greater labour hoarding in more concentrated industries.
43. See Beynon and Wainwright (1979) for an account of the decision-making in a large organization and the impacts on particular plants.
44. Several economists have tried to model the separation of decisions within firms (quite apart from the fully behavioural models of the firm). See, for example, Siven (1979), Pissaridies (1976) and Ehrenberg (1971).

References

Abowd, J. M. and Ashenfelter, O. (1979). Do market wages (still) compensate expected unemployment and hours variability. *Industrial Relations Section*, Working Paper 120. Princeton University

Addison, J. and Siebert, W. S. (1979). *The Market for Labor: An Analytical Treatment*. Santa Monica; Goodyear Publishing Company

Azariadis, C. (1975). Implicit contracts and underemployment equilibria. *Journal of Political Economy* **83**, 1183–1202

Baily, M. N. (1976). Contract theory and the moderation of inflation by recession and by controls. *Brookings Papers on Economic Activity* **No. 3**, 585–622

Beenstock, M. (1979). Do labour markets work? *Economic Outlook* June/July, 21–31

Beynon, H. and Wainwright, H. (1979). *The Workers' Report on Vickers*. London; Pluto Press

Brechling, F. (1965). The relationship between output and employment in British manufacturing industries. *Review of Economic Studies* **32**, 187–216

Brechling, F. (1975). *Investment and Employment Decisions*. Manchester; University Press

Brown, W. A. (1972). A consideration of 'custom and practice'. *British Journal of Industrial Relations* **10**, 42–61

Brown, W. A. (1979). Engineering wages and the social contract 1975-7. *Oxford Bulletin of Economics and Statistics* **41**, 51–62

Clark, K. B. and Summers, J. H. (1979). Labor market dynamics and unemployment: A reconsideration. *Brookings Papers on Economic Activity* No. 1, 13–60

Clifton, R. and Tatton-Brown, C. (1979). *Impact of employment legislation on small firms*. Research Paper No. 6. London; Department of Employment

Craine, R. (1973). On the service flow from labor. *Review of Economic Studies* 40, 39–46

Creedy, J. (1979). A note on the analysis of trade unions and relative wages. *Oxford Bulletin of Economics and Statistics* 41, 235–238

Crossley, J. R. (1973). A mixed strategy for labour economists. *Scottish Journal of Political Economy* XX, 211–238

Daniel, W. W. and Stilgoe, E. (1978). *The Impact of Employment Protection Laws*. London; Policy Studies Institute, No. 577

Deaton, D. R. and Beaumont, P. B. (1979). *The determinants of bargaining structure: Some large scale survey evidence for Britain*. Discussion Paper No. 15. University of Warwick, S.S.R.C. Industrial Relations Research Unit

Disney, R. (1979). Recurrent spells and the concentration of unemployment in Great Britain. *Economic Journal* 89, 109–119

Ehrenberg, R. G. (1971). *Fringe Benefits and Overtime Behaviour*. Lexington, Massachusetts; D. C. Heath

Feinberg, R. M. (1979). Market structure and employment instability. *Review of Economics and Statistics* LXI, 497–505

Feldstein, M. (1967). Specification of the labour input in the aggregate production function. *Review of Economic Studies* 34, 375–386

Feldstein, M. (1978). The effect of unemployment insurance on temporary layoff unemployment. *American Economic Review* 68, 834–846

Fisher, M. R. (1971). *The Economic Analysis of Labour*. London; Weidenfeld and Nicolson

Flemming, J. S. (1975). Wage rigidity and employment adjustment. In *Contemporary Issues in Economics* (ed. by J. M. Parkin and A. R. Nobay). Manchester; University Press

Freeman, J. F. and Medoff, J. L. (1977). *Substitution between production labor and other inputs in unionised and non-unionised manufacturing*. Discussion Paper No. 581, Harvard University, Department of Economics

Grossman, H. I. (1978). Risk shifting, layoffs, and seniority. *Journal of Monetary Economics* 4, 661–686

Grossman, H. I. (1979). Why does aggregate employment fluctuate? *American Economic Review* 69 (Papers and Proc.), 64–69

Hall, R. E. and Lilien, D. M. (1979). Efficient wage bargains under uncertain supply and demand. *American Economic Review* **69**, 868–879

Hart, R. A. and Sharot, T. (1978). The short run demand for workers and hours. *Review of Economic Studies* **45**, 299–309

Hartmann, R. (1976). Factor demand with output price uncertainty. *American Economic Review* **66**, 675–681

Hazeldine, T. (1978). New specifications for employment and hours functions. *Economica* **45**, 179–194

Hazeldine, T. (1979). Explaining differences in cyclical employment behaviour in 13 Canadian food and beverage processing industries. *Journal of Industrial Economics* **XXVIII**, 161–175

Hey, J. (1979). *Uncertainty in Microeconomics*. Oxford; Martin Robertson

Hicks, J. R. (1932). *The Theory of Wages*. London; Macmillan

Holt, C. C. (1979). Comment on labor market dynamics and unemployment. *Brookings Papers on Economic Activity* **No. 1**, 13–60

Johnson, P. S. and Van Doorn, J. (1976). Skill loss and unemployment: a note. *British Journal of Industrial Relations* **XIV**, 202–205

Kerr, C. (1954). The Balkanisation of labor markets. In *Labor Mobility and Economic Opportunity* (ed. by C. Kerr and E. W. Bakke). New York; John Wiley and Technology Press of Massachusetts Institute of Technology

Layard, R. (1979). The costs and benefits of selective employment policies. *British Journal of Industrial Relations* **17**, 187–204

Leslie, D. and Wise, J. (1980). The productivity of hours in U.K. manufacturing and production industries. *Economic Journal* **90**, 74–84

Levitan, S. A. and Belous, R. S. (1977). *Shorter Hours and Shorter Weeks*. Baltimore; Johns Hopkins University Press

Mackay, D. I., Boddy, D., Brack, J., Diack, J. A. and Jones, N. (1971). *Labour Markets Under Different Employment Conditions*. London; George Allen & Unwin

Mayhew, K. and Rosewell, B. (1979). Labour market segmentation in Britain. *Oxford Bulletin of Economics and Statistics* **41**, 81–115

Medoff, J. L. (1979). Layoffs and alternatives under trade unions in U.S. manufacturing. *American Economic Review* **69**, 380–395

Nadiri, M. I. and Rosen, S. (1973). *A Disequilibrium Model of Demand for Factors of Production*. New York; National Bureau of Economic Research

Nickell, S. J. (1978). Fixed costs, employment and labour demand. *Economica* **45**, 329–345

Nickell, S. J. (1979). Unemployment and the structure of labour costs. In *Carnegie–Rochester Conference Series* (ed. by K. Brunner and A. H. Meltzer) **11**, 187–223. Amsterdam; North-Holland

Parsley, C. J. (1980). Labor unions and wages: A survey. *Journal of Economic Literature* **XVIII**, 1–31

Peel, D. A. and Walker, I. (1978). Short-run employment functions, excess supply and the speed of adjustment: A note. *Economica* **45**, 195–202

Pen, J. (1959). *The Wage Rate Under Collective Bargaining*. Harvard; University Press

Pissaridies, C. A. (1976). *Labour Market Adjustment*. Cambridge; University Press

Rees, A. (1973). *The Economics of Work and Pay*. New York; Harper and Row

Rees, A. and Schultz, G. P. (1970). *Workers and Wages in an Urban Labour Market*. Chicago; University of Chicago Press

Reynolds, L. G. (1951). *The Structure of Labor Markets*. New York; Harper and Brothers

Simon, H. A. (1979). Rational decision making in business organisations. *American Economic Review* **69**, 493–513

Siven, C. H. (1979). A Study in the Theory of Inflation and Unemployment. *Studies in Monetary Economics*, Vol. 4. Amsterdam; North Holland

Thurow, L. C. (1976). *Generating Inequality*. London; Macmillan

Whiting, E. (1978). The economics of modes of employment. *Personnel Review* **Winter**, 40–52

Williamson, O. E. (1975). *Markets and Hierarchies: Analysis and Antitrust Implications*. New York; The Free Press

Wilson, R. A. (1980). Comparative forecasting performance of disaggregated employment models. *Applied Economics* **12**, 85–101

3
Unemployment and the new macroeconomics

3.1 Introduction
'Neoclassical' and 'Keynesian' approaches

In the postwar period there have been two conflicting approaches to macroeconomics: a 'pure' approach based on the general equilibrium (GE) model and an 'applied' approach based on simplified Keynesian theory.

The GE approach is developed from a small number of postulates about individual behaviour[1]. Individuals are supposed to be rational egotists: they have consistent preferences, defined over their own consumption, which they optimize by transacting in perfectly competitive markets. Competitive forces maintain continual equilibrium in each market; the simultaneous equilibrium of interdependent markets then determines the price and aggregate volume of transactions in each market. The problem with the GE approach may be summarized quite simply: in a perfectly competitive economy with no taxes or subsidies and no monetary asset there can be no unemployment. Since the existence of unemployment cannot be denied, it is necessary to relax the assumptions of the GE model.

Neoclassical economists claim that notwithstanding this difficulty, the basic structure of the GE model is sound. While it is admitted that competition applies, in a literal sense, to few if any markets, the principle that 'every commodity has a substitute' suggests that competition is present to some extent in all markets. Money is not considered important for unemployment because, it is argued, in the long run where money illusion is absent, money prices tend to adjust proportionately to changes in the money supply. Thus the effect of monetary changes resembles a change in the unit of account which leaves relative prices, and hence output and employment, unchanged. The explanation of unemployment typically focuses on the labour market: the distortion of incentives created by the payment of benefits to the registered unemployed, and the frictions that workers encounter when they change jobs. Particular attention has been given to the cost to the worker of learning about the wages available outside his own segment of the labour market[2].

The neoclassical approach claims to be in the tradition of the 'classical' economists such as Pigou and Robbins. However, it is much more doctrinaire because of its refusal to consider social and institutional constraints on labour market adjustment[3]. Nevertheless it shares with the classical economists the view that unemployment can be analysed by what is essentially a partial approach. The perfectly competitive model of the labour market is modified, but it is assumed that the consequences of these modifications for the rest of the system are negligible.

The partial approach was rejected by Keynes (1936), who argued that the existence of a monetary asset has major implications for unemployment. His analysis has two logically distinct stages. The first is a critique of the naive quantity theory of money, which led him to reject the classical dichotomy between real and monetary variables. The second is his theory of effective demand, in which he argued that unemployment due to demand-deficiency can arise when purchasing power is diverted into the building up of money balances. Keynes showed that from a theoretical standpoint the classical dichotomy is false. The real and monetary sectors are linked because the money rate of interest has a role in equilibrating both the money market and the product market.

It follows that GE models which contain no monetary asset omit an important influence on real variables. However, this does not imply that monetary factors are a cause of unemployment. Patinkin (1965) has demonstrated that the asset-demand for money can be integrated into a GE framework under certain simplifying assumptions. The demand for money is analysed by making households' utility dependent on the real value of their money balances. When households pursue an integrated plan of consumption, money asset accumulation and labour supply, decisions on each of these will be responsive to changes in the real wage, the money rate of interest, and the level of money prices. Competitive forces adjust the three 'price' variables to achieve simultaneous equilibrium in goods, labour and money markets. The interaction of real and financial markets maintains the economy at full employment. An important element in the equilibrating mechanism is the real balance effect, whereby price adjustment influences the real value of money balances, which in turn affects aggregate product demand.

It appears therefore that the introduction of the asset-demand for money does not have the immediate implications for unemployment that Keynes believed it did. Furthermore the second stage of Keynes' analysis—the formulation of his theory of effective demand—poses its own set of problems.

First, some of his macroeconomic relationships appear *ad hoc*;

their specification lacks any sound foundation. This is particularly true of the consumption function. As indicated above, a rational consumer will pursue an ingegrated plan of consumption, saving and labour supply, and in a competitive environment each of these decisions becomes a function of prevailing market prices[4]. Consumption should therefore depend on prices and not on income, which is an endogenous variable determined by labour supply. Furthermore, with an integrated plan, all decisions are a function of the same set of variables. So if consumption *does* depend upon income then so should other decision variables, including labour supply. But Keynes postulates that consumption depends upon income whereas he retains the classical assumption that labour supply depends solely on the real wage.

The second problem is an apparent conflict with Walras' law. One implication of this law (see Section 3.3) is that an excess supply in one market must be accompanied by an excess demand in another. Unemployment represents an excess supply of labour and so in the Keynesian model this should imply an excess demand for either goods or money. Keynes suggests, instead, that unemployment can coexist with equilibrium in all other markets.

The disequilibrium approach

Given that the introduction of a monetary asset is not sufficient to explain unemployment, some further relaxation of the GE assumptions is called for. Clower (1965, 1967) has suggested relaxing the equilibrium assumption. It is this assumption, applied to the labour market, that most obviously rules out unemployment. Although neoclassical economics has traditionally assumed that markets adjust to equilibrium, the process by which this occurs has until recently received only scant attention. It is not, as is often suggested, an immediate consequence of competition.

Once it is recognized that markets may operate in disequilibrium, it is possible to rationalize the apparent anomalies of the Keynesian model noted above. In disequilibrium, traders on one side of a market will be unable to buy or sell the exact amount they wish at the prevailing price. Such traders face not only a price constraint in the market, but also a quantity constraint. In particular, when the money wage is too high, households face a constraint on their labour supply, and in an otherwise competitive labour market their income becomes parametric. In other words, it is outside their control because it is no longer responsive to labour supply. Thus consumption becomes a function not only of prices but also of income. Thus the Keynesian relation between consumption and income is correctly specified once it is reinterpreted as a description of disequilibrium behaviour.

The disequilibrium approach also sheds light on the relevance—or strictly speaking the irrelevance—of Walras' law to Keynesian theory. For given that labour supply is constrained, consumer demand is constrained and hence so is aggregate product demand. Thus two concepts of demand must be distinguished: a notional demand which applies when equilibrium prices prevail, and an effective demand which applies when transactors are subjected to quantity constraints. Walras' law applies to notional demands; if Keynes was talking about effective demands then there is no reason why Walras' law should apply.

This chapter critically examines the assumptions about market behaviour and expectation-formation which underlie the disequilibrium approach. In the light of this criticism, certain aspects of the theory are extended and developed. But first it is necessary to develop a basic model of a monetary economy.

3.2 A simple model of a monetary economy

Outline of the model

This section introduces the basic model which is used for examining the microeconomic foundations of Keynesian theory. The main weakness of the model is that all decisions are made using a one-period time horizon. However this restriction is relaxed in Section 3.7, which extends the model to allow for intertemporal allocation.

It is assumed that there are three markets: for labour, a single good and a monetary asset. Money consists of notes and coins issued by the government and held by the private sector. (Bonds will be introduced in Section 3.7, however.) Given just three markets, there are two independent relative prices, the money wage and the money price.

There are three types of transactor: households, firms and government. Each household contains a single member of the working population. For simplicity it is assumed that all households are identical, all firms are identical, and that there are the same number of firms and households. This avoids aggregation problems and makes it possible to conduct the entire analysis in terms of a representative household and a representative firm.

The assumption of identical households is highly restrictive. Because all households are identical, unemployment appears not as a proportion of the working population wholly unemployed, but as an excess supply of hours of work by the representative household.

It is unlikely that the behaviour of a representative household on short-time working, when scaled up by the number of households, will resemble the aggregated behaviour of two different groups of households, one wholly employed and another unemployed[5]. Furthermore, borrowing restrictions and liquidity constraints are likely to be crucial for the wholly unemployed, whereas they may not be binding for those on short-time working[6]. The assumption of identical households also has implications for the specification of production technology. There are numerous technical reasons why the production function relating output to hours of labour will differ from that relating output to the number of employees. This, together with the fixed costs of employment, and the costs of recruitment and redundancy, means that the pattern of adjustment in terms of men will differ from that in terms of hours[7].

It is assumed that the money wage, W, and money price, P, are uniform and parametric, and for any wage–price combination each transactor has a unique demand or supply for each commodity (indicated by the superscripts d and s respectively). The representative household supplies labour n^s and demands consumption c^d; it anticipates a profit income Π^h and pays a lump sum tax T. The excess of after-tax income over consumption expenditure goes into savings, which take the form of additional holdings of the monetary asset, $\dot{M}^d$. Then

$$\dot{M}^d = M^d - M \tag{1}$$

where M^d is the demand for the stock of the monetary asset and M is the household's initial holding of it. Thus the household faces a budget constraint

$$Pc^d + \dot{M}^d = Wn^s + \Pi^h - T \tag{2}$$

The representative firm uses a single variable factor of production, labour, of which it demands n^d to supply an output y^s, giving a planned profit

$$\Pi^f = Py^s - Wn^d \tag{3}$$

which accrues to the households, as owners of the fixed factors. There is no investment.

The government spends G^d *per capita*, which it finances out of taxation and the issue of money. Thus the government's budget constraint in *per capita* form is

$$G^d = T + \dot{M}^s \tag{4}$$

where

$$\dot{M}^s = M^s - M \tag{5}$$

Real variables are defined by normalizing the monetary variables with respect to money price; they are denoted by small letters, i.e. $w = W/P$, $\pi = \Pi/P$, $g = G/P$, $t = T/P$, $m = M/P$, $\dot{m} = \dot{M}/P$. The budget equations (2)–(4) become, in real terms,

$$c^d + m^d = wn^s + \pi^h - t \tag{6}$$

$$\pi^f = y^s - wn^d \tag{7}$$

$$g^d = t + \dot{m}^s \tag{8}$$

Summing (6)–(8), and substituting in the equation of aggregate demand

$$y^d = c^d + g^d \tag{9}$$

and rearranging terms gives

$$(y^d - y^s) + w(n^d - n^s) + (\dot{m}^d - \dot{m}^s) + (\pi^f - \pi^h) = 0 \tag{10}$$

The first three terms on the left hand side of equation (10) represent net excess demand in each of the markets, and of course a negative excess demand corresponds to an excess supply. They may be denoted

$$\left. \begin{array}{l} z_y = y^d - y^s \\ z_n = n^d - n^s \\ z_m = \dot{m}^d - \dot{m}^s \end{array} \right\} \tag{11}$$

Substituting (11) into (10) gives

$$z_y + wz_n + z_m + (\pi^f - \pi^h) = 0 \tag{12}$$

This is *Generalized Walras' law* (GWL) for the economy.

It is conventional to assume that the households' perception of profit π^h agrees with the profit implied by the firms' production plans π^f. In this case the final term on the left hand side of (12) is zero and *Simple Walras' law* (SWL) is obtained: the total value of all excess demands in the economy is zero:

$$z_y + wz_n + z_m = 0 \tag{13}$$

It follows from SWL that

(1) if there is excess demand in one market then there must be excess supply in another market, whence
(2) it is impossible for one market alone to be in disequilibrium, whence
(3) if all markets but one are in equilibrium, then the final market is in equilibrium too.

It should be noted that GWL depends on only three assumptions: the existence of uniform parametric prices, the uniqueness of demands and supplies and the internal consistency of transactors' plans, as represented by their budget constraints. It is partly because GWL depends on such weak behavioural assumptions that it provides a useful benchmark in macroeconomic theory.

Form of demand and supply schedules

The next step is to strengthen the assumptions by specifying the form of the demand and supply schedules. It is assumed that the representative household maximizes welfare, u, derived from real consumption, leisure and the real value of its stock of money. The utility of money derives solely from its use as a medium of exchange (its role as a store of value is considered in Section 3.7)[8].

Maximizing the well-behaved utility function

$$u = u(c^d, n^s, m^d) \tag{14}$$

subject to the budget equation (2) and the stock–flow equation (1), gives the household demand and supply functions

$$\left. \begin{array}{l} c^d = c^d(w, \quad \pi^h, \quad m, \quad t) \\ \qquad (+)(+)(+)(-) \\ n^s = n^s(w, \quad \pi^h, \quad m, \quad t) \\ \qquad (+)(-)(-)(+) \\ m^d = m^d(w, \quad \pi^h, \quad m, \quad t) \\ \qquad (+)(+)(-)(-) \end{array} \right\} \tag{15}$$

The signs in brackets refer to the partial derivatives. Convexity of household preferences is not sufficient to determine all these signs; some additional restrictions need to be made, the most significant of which is that the supply of labour is everywhere an increasing function of the real wage. Labour supply is also shown as an increasing function of taxation because the latter is administered on a lump sum basis, so that the substitution effect on labour supply is zero.

The representative firm maximizes profit (7) subject to a technology which exhibits diminishing marginal returns:

$$y = y(n), \qquad dy/dn > 0, \qquad d^2y/dn^2 < 0 \tag{16}$$

This determines the labour demand and product supply functions

$$n^d = n^d(w), \qquad y^s = y^s(w) \tag{17}$$
$$\quad (-) \qquad\qquad (-)$$

and also the profit function

$$\pi^f = \pi^f(w) \tag{18}$$
$$\quad (-)$$

All the partial derivatives of (17) and (18) are unambiguously signed.

Finally, government demand and taxation are set exogenously in money terms.

Equilibrium requires that the excess demands in each of the three markets are zero:

$$z_y = z_n = z_m = 0 \tag{19}$$

and also that household profit expectations coincide with firms' planned profits:

$$\pi^h = \pi^f(w) \tag{20}$$

Substituting (8), (9), (15), (17) and (20) into (11) expresses the excess demands as functions of the endogenous variables W, P, and the exogenous variables M, T, G. Equations (19) then become:

$$z_y(W, \ P; \ \ M, \ T, \ \ G) = 0 \tag{21a}$$
$$(+)(-)(+)(-)(+)$$

$$z_n(W, \ P; \ \ M, \ T) \ \ \ \ = 0 \tag{21b}$$
$$(-)(+)(+)(-)$$

$$z_m(W, \ P; \ \ M, \ T) \ \ \ \ = 0 \tag{21c}$$
$$(+)(+)(-)(-)$$

Not all of the partial derivatives can be unambiguously signed; the signs here are typical of those assumed in the literature.

SWL indicates that only two of the three equations are independent. Full employment equilibrium is determined by solving any two of the equations for W^e, P^e, and then substituting into (17) to determine employment and output, n^e, y^e. A superscript e on a variable denotes its equilibrium value.

Graphical illustration of the model

The equilibrium is illustrated graphically in *Figure 3.1*. To assist in the economic interpretation, the axes represent not the money wage and the money price but the real wage and the reciprocal of the money price. The significance of the real wage is that if monetary factors are held constant, it is the real wage which governs equilibrium on the real side of the economy. The lower the real wage, the greater is firms' demand for labour and supply of output, and the lower is household supply of labour and demand for output. Adjustments of the real wage are thus an important equilibrating influence in both product and labour markets.

The reciprocal of the money price measures the value of money in

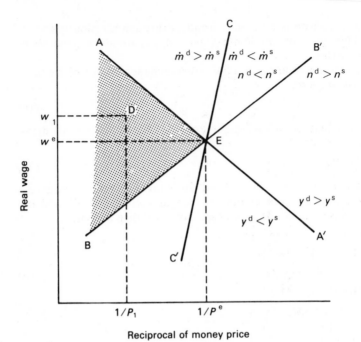

Figure 3.1 *Equilibrium conditions for a monetary economy*

terms of goods. When money price is low the real value of households' initial endowments of money is high and this encourages them to spend more on all 'normal' goods. This is the real balance effect— analogous to the income effect in consumer theory. There is no substitution effect because utility depends not on nominal money balances but on real money balances, the opportunity cost of real money balances in terms of real consumption is independent of money prices.

Equilibrium in the product market is represented by the locus AA′, derived from equation (21a). It has a negative (downward) slope because when the value of money is increased, the real balance effect stimulates consumption, and so to maintain product market equilibrium, supply must be increased by a reduction in the real wage. A lower real wage also helps to restore equilibrium by reducing household wage income, thereby reducing planned consumption.

Equilibrium in the labour market is represented by the locus BB′, derived from equation (21b). It has a positive (upward) slope because when the value of money is increased, the real balance effect encourages increased consumption of leisure, and hence a lower labour supply. To maintain equilibrium the demand for labour must be reduced by an increase in the real wage. The increase in the real wage may also encourage households to substitute work for leisure, and so help to counteract the reduction in labour supply.

Equilibrium in the money market is represented by the locus CC', derived from equation (21c). When the value of money increases, the real value of initial household money balances increases. At the same time the real balance effect increases household demand for real money balances. However, unless the demand for real money balances is highly income-elastic, the increase in real demand will be less than the increase in the real endowment. It follows that households will wish to decumulate nominal money balances. Given that the change in the supply of nominal money balances is exogenous, equilibrium must be maintained by further stimulation of nominal demand. This calls for an increase in the real money wage which will increase the nominal demand through an income effect. Thus to maintain equilibrium in the money market, an increase in the value of money must be associated with an increase in the real wage, and so the locus CC' has a positive slope, as shown in *Figure 3.1*.

Using *Figure 3.1* it is possible to distinguish various regimes according to the excess demand in each market. Suppose that the real wage is fixed at w_1 (say) and the money price level at P_1, as illustrated by the point D in the figure. Point D lies to the left of AA' which means that the value of money is too low for equilibrium in the product market. Because of the low real value of money balances, consumer demand is low and so there is excess supply in the product market. Point D also lies to the left of BB', which means that the value of money is too low for equilibrium in the labour market. The low real value of money balances encourages households to increase their labour supply, so that there is excess supply in the labour market. Point D also lies to the left of CC'. Thus the low real value of initial money balances encourages households to accumulate nominal balances, creating an excess demand for new nominal money balances.

Generalized excess supply

It can be seen that the point D represents a state of generalized excess supply on the real side of the economy; that is, excess supply in both product and labour markets. As predicted by SWL, this is associated with an excess demand for money balances.

A similar analysis can be applied to any wage–price combination. All points to the left of AA' and BB' are associated with excess supply in the product market and labour market respectively. All points to the left of CC′ are associated with an excess demand for new money balances and all points to the right of it with an excess supply. Thus the shaded area in *Figure 3.1*, containing all points to the left of both AA′ and BB′, represents the set of wage–price combinations which are associated with generalized excess supply on the real side of the economy. This case will be the focus of attention later.

In a perfectly competitive economy, money price will be bid up when there is an excess demand for the product and bid down when there is excess supply. Likewise, the money wage will be bid up when there is an excess demand for labour and bid down when there is an excess supply. Thus wage and price adjustments will tend to eliminate excess demands in labour and product markets.

General equilibrium is represented by the intersection E of the loci AA′, BB′, CC′. Because there are just two dimensions (real wage and reciprocal of money price), any two of the three loci can be used to determine full employment. SWL guarantees that if any two of the markets are in equilibrium then the third will be in equilibrium too.

3.3 The disequilibrium approach

The disequilibrium approach, as its name suggests, is based on the view that the typical market spends more time out of equilibrium than in equilibrium. It may be true that a world without exogenous change would, given sufficient time, adjust to an equilibrium in which it would remain indefinitely. But this has little relevance to the real world where markets are subject to continuous disturbance.

Orthodox equilibrium theory is essentially static. It postulates that prices are uniform and parametric, and that trading only takes place when excess demands have been eliminated. But it does not explain how these conditions are set up and maintained. It assumes the existence of a market adjustment mechanism, but does not explain what it is or how it works.

Price flexibility is a necessary but not sufficient condition for equilibrium. Adjustment to equilibrium requires a market *process*; that is, a sequential procedure which takes a market from an arbitrary initial state to an equilibrium[9]. This is essentially a question of information processing. It concerns the way in which individuals recognize excess demands, calculate the appropriate response to them, and announce their response to other transactors.

There have been two main attempts to model the dynamics of the competitive process. The first is a highly artificial model constructed by Walras[10]. The second, slightly more realistic model, is due to Edgeworth[11]. To simplify the discussion, these models are compared in the context of a partial analysis of a single market.

Walras and Edgeworth processes

Walras postulates that the market is organized by an auctioneer. The auctioneer begins by announcing a trial price, on the basis of which transactors determine their provisional bids for demand or supply. The auctioneer aggregates the bids to determine the excess demand. If it is zero he confirms the bids and transactions proceed. If it is non-zero then he announces a new trial price and a new set of bids is collected. If the excess demand is positive he raises the price, if it is negative he reduces the price. Provided that excess demand is a decreasing function of price, and that price adjustments do not overreact to excess demand, the process will eventually converge to equilibrium.

Edgeworth postulates that transactors bargain directly with each other over price. In the simplest variant of this model the buyers and sellers constitute two distinct groups: the buyers each wish to purchase one unit of the commodity while the sellers each wish to sell one unit[12]. A transaction is arranged as a two-party coalition between a buyer and a seller. To establish the coalition, it is necessary for the two parties to agree on a price. To bargain for the most favourable price each buyer explores possible coalitions with the other sellers, and vice versa. All coalitions remain provisional until everyone is satisfied that they cannot improve on their existing coalition. Anyone who is not satisfied can recontract—that is, can quit one coalition and form another. Price adjusts to equilibrium on the initiative of transactors whose plans are frustrated, and whose obvious strategy is to break up existing coalitions by offering sellers a higher price, or buyers a lower price, as appropriate. Higher prices attract new supplies and deter existing demand; lower prices have the opposite effect. Thus what begins as an attempt to bid away supplies or demands from other transactors, ends by altering the aggregate quantity traded.

Both the Walras and the Edgeworth mechanisms can be generalized to simultaneous transactions in many markets. The generalization is quite straightforward in principle, though in practice the amount of information required to implement the adjustment procedures increases considerably as additional markets are introduced.

In both the Walras and the Edgeworth mechanisms, prices are adjusted in response to notional excess demands. Equilibrium is guaranteed by the fact that the market does not open for actual trading until the set of planned transactions has been 'screened' for consistency. In the Walras mechanism the screening is done by the auctioneer. In the Edgeworth mechanism it is effected through recontracting among individual transactors.

Screening obviously involves processing considerable amounts of information. It is normally uneconomic for the processing of the same information to be replicated by different individuals. On these grounds the Walras mechanism, which centralizes information processing, is *prima facie* more efficient than the Edgeworth mechanism, which requires the transactors to process independently very similar information.

Problems with an auctioneer and recontracting

It may be rational, however, for transactors to refuse the services of a Walras' auctioneer. When transactions involve change of ownership, price acts not only as an allocator but as a distributor of rewards between the new owner and the old. Thus transactors face considerable risk in foregoing the right to negotiate over price. It could of course be argued that in a competitive situation they may as well accept the authority of the auctioneer as accept the discipline of impersonal market forces. But transactors may doubt the integrity of the auctioneer, who is required to be a non-profit maker. But it is difficult to see why a rational individual, who has a monopoly of intermediation, should accept such a constraint, and if he does so then he has little incentive to perform the job efficiently, since there is no longer a link between his performance and his reward.

Turning to the Edgeworth mechanism, it has already been noted that this may involve considerable negotiation and renegotiation of contracts before transactions can proceed. But protracted negotiations will delay completion and thereby incur costs for the impatient transactor. Also, the more protracted the negotiation the greater is the risk that market conditions will change and render obsolete the provisional contracts already established. But as negotiations are speeded up to avoid delays, so resource costs increase as faster communication and quicker decisions are called for.

The optimal strategy for the individual transactor is to trade off the resource cost of speeding up negotiations against the costs of delaying completion of the transaction. In the typical market unexpected changes are continually occurring, so the optimal strategy is likely to involve very fast negotiation and hence relatively high resource costs. Thus, even with the optimal strategy, the average cost per transaction is likely to be high. The Edgeworth process of costless recontracting must therefore also be rejected.

Use of realized excess demands

An obvious way for a transactor to economize on information costs is to respond to realized excess demand, thereby eliminating the calculation of notional excess demand prior to the transaction, and the renegotiation of contracts until notional excess demand is zero. The use of realized excess demands was explained in detail by Marshall (1961). Transactors proceed on the basis that they will trade today at yesterday's price, so long as none of yesterday's plans was frustrated. If yesterday's plans were frustrated they will trade at a new price which is estimated using a simple rule of thumb to eliminate yesterday's disequilibrium.

The advantage of this procedure is that in a changing environment it exposes the transactor to continual minor frustrations of his plans. The consequences of this are illustrated in *Figure 3.2*. Adjustment

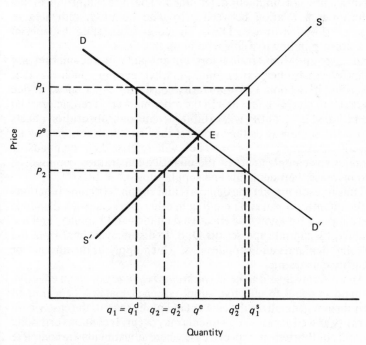

Figure 3.2 *Disequilibrium in a single market*

based on notional excess demands will determine price and quantity at E, the intersection of the supply and demand curves. If realized excess demand is used, then in the short run price will be set by rule of thumb, at say, P_1, in excess of the equilibrium price P^e. Demand is less than supply and, since trading is voluntary, sellers cannot insist on buyers taking all they have on offer. Consequently the quantity actually traded, q_1, is equal to the amount demanded, q_1^d. Similarly, if the price is set at $P_2 < P^e$, so that demand exceeds supply, then demanders cannot insist that suppliers meet all their needs. Consequently, quantity is set at $q_2 = q_2^s$.

In general, because transactions are voluntary, the quantity traded cannot exceed either the amount demanded or the amount supplied. And because traders will not forego opportunities for mutually beneficial transactions, the quantity traded will never be less than the minimum of the demand and the supply. It must therefore be equal to the minimum of demand and supply. This proposition is summarized by saying that *quantity is set at the short end of the market*[13].

It should be noted that, unlike the equilibrium model, price and quantity are not uniquely determined. The disequilibrium model determines a relation between price and quantity, indicated in *Figure 3.2* by the frontier DES'. The equilibrium state is a special case corresponding to a single point on this locus.

In disequilibrium, transactors on one side of the market are quantity-constrained. In a multi-market system—such as that described in Section 3.2—a quantity constraint experienced in one market will modify behaviour in the other markets. Transactors who are rationed by quantity will exhibit income and substitution effects in just the same way as they would if they had been rationed by an adverse movement of price. They will reduce their demands or supplies for complements of the quantity-constrained commodity, and increase their demands and supplies for substitutes[14].

Thus in each market the demands and supplies become functions of the quantity constraints binding in other markets. Such demands and supplies are known as effective demands and supplies, and are denoted by capital superscripts D, S, to distinguish them from the notional demands and supplies d, s, which apply in the absence of quantity constraints.

An economy is said to be in *constrained equilibrium* when effective demand is equal to effective supply in each market. Constrained equilibrium generalizes the concept of equilibrium to the case where quantity as well as price adjustments may occur. It contains orthodox general equilibrium as a special case where adjustments are complete and effective demands and supplies are equal to notional demands and supplies in each market.

A necessary condition for constrained equilibrium is that transactors perceive correctly the quantity constraints to which they are subject. In each market the effective demand and supply is based on expectations of the quantity constraints that will be binding in other markets. If these expectations were incorrect, then transactors would wish to alter their demand and supplies in other markets.

It is important to distinguish between transactors' expectations of a quantity constraint and the actual demand or supply that they signal to the market. From a strategic point of view, it pays a transactor who anticipates a constraint to signal a demand or supply which is larger than he expects to be able to achieve. It will pay him to signal the demand or supply that he would have were there no constraint prevailing in the market concerned[15]. Then if by any chance his expectation of trading opportunities is too pessimistic, he will be able to trade as much as he would like. If on the other hand he signals his willingness to trade only the amount he expects to be able to, and then if his expectations are too pessimistic, other transactors will not be aware of his willingness to trade more, and the opportunity will be lost. For example, in the labour market, workers who are unemployed, and who do not expect to be able to find employment, still register as unemployed (even though they may no longer be eligible for benefit) in the hope that their expectations are wrong. If all workers were discouraged from registering as unemployed because they did not expect to find jobs, then the unemployment problem would, from a statistical point of view, appear insignificant[16].

Thus a constrained equilibrium can exist even though quantity signals indicate excess demands and supplies in the various markets. Transactors signal the quantities they hope to trade, rather than the quantities they expect to trade. The fact that transactors are disappointed in their trading opportunities is quite consistent with their expectations being fulfilled.

3.4 Disequilibrium in a non-monetary economy

Suppose now that money is simply a unit of account, so that the demand and supply for money balances is zero. In this case disequilibrium can lead to unemployment only because the real wage is too high. To simplify the discussion government expenditure and taxation are ignored. The model of Section 3.2 then reduces to

$$\left.\begin{array}{ll} u = u(c^d, n^s) & \text{(household utility function)} \\ c^d = wn^s + \pi^h & \text{(household budget constraint)} \\ \pi^f = y^s - wn^d & \text{(firm's planned profit)} \\ y^s = y(n^d) & \text{(firm's production function)} \\ \pi^h = \pi^f & \text{(consistency of profit expectations)} \\ y^d = c^d & \text{(equation of aggregate demand)} \end{array}\right\} \quad (22)$$

Using this simplified model, unemployment equilibrium can be exhibited very easily in diagrammatic terms, as in *Figure 3.3*. Since all output is consumed and employment is measured by the hours of work of the representative household, the consumption/work preferences of the representative household can be shown in the

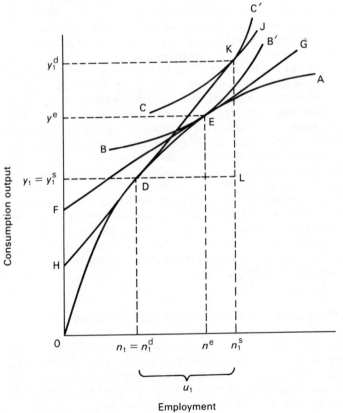

Figure 3.3 *Unemployment due to an excessive real wage*

figure. Because consumption is a 'good', and work a 'bad', and the marginal rate of substitution between consumption and leisure diminishes continuously, the indifference map is backward-sloping and concave to the vertical axis; this is illustrated by the shapes of the two indifference curves BB' and CC'. Technology, exhibiting diminishing returns to the variable factor labour, is represented by the production frontier OA.

Full employment is at E, where the indifference map is tangential to the production frontier. The equilibrium real wage w^e is determined by the slope of the tangent FG at E, and real profit π^e by its intercept OF on the vertical axis. The tangent FG has a dual role, as budget constraint for the household and as isoprofit line for the firm. The household is in equilibrium because, given its budget constraint, it is on the highest attainable indifference curve, and the firm is in equilibrium, because given its production technology, it is on the highest attainable isoprofit line.

Suppose now that the real wage is set above its full employment level at w_1, as indicated by the slope of the line HJ. Profit-maximizing firms plan to produce at D, demanding n_1^d units of labour and supplying y_1^s units of product. The profit implied by this production plan is OH. Households face the budget constraint HJ and they optimize at K by supplying n_1^s units of labour and demanding y_1^d units of product. The supply of labour exceeds the demand, and so with employment set at the short end of the labour market, there is unemployment of $u_1 = n_1^s - n_1^d$.

The excess supply of labour is associated with an excess demand for the product, which from SWL are equal. This is confirmed by the geometry of the right-angled triangle DKL: the base measures the excess supply of labour and the slope of the hypotenuse measures the real wage, so that its height measures the value of the excess supply in product units. But projecting the upright side of the triangle onto the vertical axis shows that it also measures the excess demand for the product.

With employment set at the short end of the labour market and output set at the short end of the product market, firms are in equilibrium producing at D. Households however are doubly-constrained: employment is restricted to $n_1^d < n_1^s$ and consumption is rationed to $y_1^s < y_1^d$. As a result, households who planned to be at K find themselves constrained to D. However these two constraints are mutually consistent in the sense that households who cannot supply more than n_1^d units of labour cannot afford to spend more than y_1^s on consumption. Consequently although households' notional demand for the product is y_1^d, their effective demand is only y_1^s. This is a very simple example of a quantity-constrained equilibrium.

3.5 Disequilibrium in a monetary economy

In a monetary economy disequilibrium can lead to unemployment even though the real wage is at or below its full employment level. If money price is fixed too high—so that the real value of households' initial stock of money balances is unacceptably low—then there may be an excess demand for new money balances. This generates excess supply in both labour and product markets, a downward spiral of output and employment adjustments, which ends only when the immiserizing effect of lower incomes has reduced the demand for money balances into equality with the exogenous supply.

This case of 'generalized excess supply' on the real side of the market was first systematically discussed by Barro and Grossman. Both households and firms experience quantity constraints (unlike the previous case in which only the households were constrained). Households cannot supply as much labour as they would wish at the prevailing money wage, while firms cannot sell as much output as they would wish at the prevailing money price. These two constraints had been considered separately, by Clower and Patinkin respectively, but the analysis of their interaction is due to Barro and Grossman[17].

Quantity-constrained equilibrium

When transactors are quantity-constrained their behaviour is governed by effective demands and supplies. The objective functions and budget constraints, which were specified in terms of notional demands and supplies, apply also to effective demands and supplies. In what follows, an equation which was first specified in terms of notional quantities and rewritten in terms of effective quantitites is indicated by a prime following the equation number. A capital superscript on a variable indicates that it is associated with a quantity-constrained plan.

Households maximize (14′) subject to (1′), (2′) and the inequality constraint $n^s \leqslant n$. When the constraint is binding the solution determines the effective demands and supplies.

$$c^D = c^D(y^H, P, M, T) \tag{23a}$$
$$n^S = n \tag{23b}$$
$$m^D = m^D(y^H, P, M, T) \tag{23c}$$

where

$$y^H = wn + \pi^H \tag{24}$$

is the income anticipated by households when they perceive an employment constraint n on wage income, and when their expectation of profit, π^H, allows for the fact that firms may be subjected to a sales constraint. The wage rate does not appear separately in equations (23) because at the margin it is employment-rationing and not wage-rationing that governs consumption/leisure choice. Equation (23a) is analogous to the consumption function of Keynesian theory.

Firms maximize (3′) subject to (16′) and the sales constraint $y^S \leqslant y$. When the constraint is binding, firms' optimal strategy is to employ just sufficient labour to meet demand for the product, so that

$$n^D = n^D(y)$$
$$y^S = y \tag{25}$$

and profit becomes

$$\pi^F = y - wn^D \tag{26}$$

Constrained equilibrium (indicated by the superscript E) implies that

$$y^D = y^S = y^H \tag{27}$$

all three variables being identically equal to y^E. Substituting the equation of aggregate demand (9) and the consumption function (23a) into (27) yields

$$c^D(y^E, P, M, T) + g^D = y^E \tag{28}$$

Given P, M, T and G, this determines equilibrium income y^E. Equilibrium employment n^E and profit π^E may then be determined from equations (25) and (26).

A diagrammatic illustration

A simple illustration of constrained equilibrium is given in *Figure 3.4*. Suppose that the economy is initially in full employment equilibrium and that W and P then increase in the same proportion. It may be imagined, for example, that a union-negotiated money wage increase is being passed on to consumers in higher administered product prices. Government expenditure and taxation are ignored, and the money supply is assumed to remain constant.

Since the real wage remains unchanged, and G, T and M are constants, the only variables are P, which is exogenous, and the endogenously determined equilibrium output and employment, y^E, n^E. For small variations in P it is possible to examine the induced variations in y^E and n^E using the differential of equation (28)

$$(\partial c^D/\partial y^E)\,\mathrm{d}y^E + (\partial c^D/\partial P)\,\mathrm{d}P = \mathrm{d}y^E \tag{29}$$

Grouping terms in $\mathrm{d}y^E$ gives the multiplier formula

$$\mathrm{d}y^E = [1 - (\partial c^D/\partial y^E)]^{-1}(\partial c^D/\partial P)\,\mathrm{d}P \qquad (30)$$

This formula determines the quantity adjustment $\mathrm{d}y^E$ implied by an exogenous price change $\mathrm{d}P$. The adjustment is equal to the change in consumption induced initially by the change in price, multiplied by the reciprocal of the household marginal propensity to save.

In *Figure 3.4* price- and quantity-adjustments are separated into the left-hand and right-hand sides of the diagram. The schedule BB',

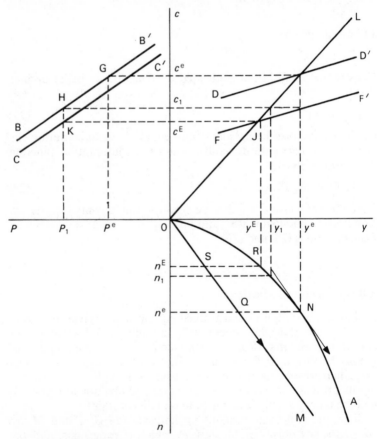

Figure 3.4 *Demand-deficiency due to too high a money wage and money price level.*

Note *Strictly speaking, the schedules BB', CC', DD', FF' apply only over the range of prices and output associated with notional excess supplies in the labour and product markets. Furthermore the schedules must be regarded only as first-order linear approximations valid in the region of the initial levels of price and output* in the top left-hand quadrant, shows how consumption responds to price when employment is fixed at the full employment level n^E, and the schedule DD', in the top right-hand quadrant, shows how consumption depends upon income when price is fixed at its full employment level P^e. An increase in the price to P_1 initially reduces consumption from c^e to c_1, as indicated by the movement along BB' from G to H. This is associated with an excess demand for real money balances of the same amount. This shifts down the schedule DD' in parallel fashion by $c^e - c_1$ to FF', creating an excess supply of output $y^e - y_1 = c^e - c_1$. The same effect would be produced in a Keynesian model by a fall in autonomous consumption. Firms are now sales-constrained and reduce output to y_1 to eliminate excess supply. They adjust along the production frontier OA, in the bottom right-hand quadrant, reducing employment to n_1. The reduction in household income to y_1 now feeds back into the top left-hand quadrant, shifting the price-consumption locus BB' downward and inducing a further fall in consumption. Equilibrium is achieved at J, the intersection of the consumption function FF' and the 45° line OL. Given the new price P_1, income-constrained consumption is just equal to the income which constrains it: $c^E = y^E$. Associated with the new lower level of income is the new price-consumption locus CC', with households consuming at K.

The distribution of income at the unemployment equilibrium may be determined from the bottom right-hand quadrant. Given the prevailing real wage, the wage bill is directly proportional to employment, as indicated by the line OM. At any given level of employment, real profit is measured by the horizontal discrepancy between the production function OA and the wage bill line OM. Consequently when employment is n^E, profit is SR. Profit is less than at full employment n^e, where firms achieved an unconstrained maximum profit QN. On the other hand, the geometry of the figure shows quite clearly that, although total profit has fallen, the share of profits in national income has increased.

3.6 Perception of quantity constraints on money

There is one aspect of the preceding model which has received surprisingly little emphasis in the literature. This is concerned with the question of why households apparently fail to respond to quantity constraints on the demand for money balances. Given the assumptions of the model, it is a consequence of generalized excess supply on the real side that there should be an excess demand for money. If households perceived this they would modify their consumption and labour supply strategy accordingly. Consumer demand would increase as money income originally intended to build up money balances is diverted into consumption, and labour supply would contract since one of the major uses of labour income would have been restricted. Thus household response would tend to diminish—and eventually eliminate—the excess supplies in product and labour markets. If this were indeed to occur then labour and product markets would adjust without any multiplier effect on income and employment.

The crucial point is that households do not perceive that they are rationed. Although rationed in the aggregate, no household perceives this rationing itself. The reason is that the rationed asset, being a medium of exchange, is in continual circulation. Each household believes that it can accumulate as large a money balance as desired simply by maintaining money expenditure below money income for a sufficient period. What it fails to perceive is that this strategy will reduce the money incomes of other households, who are recipients of its own expenditure, and that they in turn, by reducing their own expenditures, will ultimately reduce its own income. Consequently in the aggregate the individual efforts of households to accumulate money balances are self-defeating. Thus underpinning the entire analysis is the fact that money balances circulate, and that for this reason households do not perceive that money balances are rationed.

3.7 IS/LM analysis and the Keynesian model

The model presented in Section 3.5 differs from the usual Keynesian model in two main respects. First, it is based on a one-period analysis of household and firm behaviour. The role of money as a store of value is not considered, and no comparison is made between money and alternative stores of value, such as bonds and real assets. Secondly, the money price level is assumed to be fixed, whereas in the Keynesian model it is flexible[18].

These two defects are, however, easily remedied. Suppose that money prices continue to be fixed, but that households and firms now plan over a two-period time horizon. Households have a choice of two financial assets: money and bonds. Because of intertemporal planning, households now have a savings decision to make, and because there are two financial assets they have a choice of the form in which their savings are held. They must therefore decide both on the aggregate value of their savings, and on the composition of their savings portfolio.

When planning over two periods, firms endeavour to maximize the discounted sum of present and future profit. They have not only production and employment decisions to make, but an investment decision too. It is evident that the decisions of both households and firms will be strongly influenced by their expectations of the future period. But given these expectations, their demands and supplies in each of the markets for the present period will be determined by the prices currently prevailing, together with quantity constraints to which they are subjected.

Suppose that the bond market is maintained in equilibrium by adjustments in the money rate of interest, r, and that generalized excess supply prevails on the real side of the economy. It follows that, given prevailing wages and prices, all household demands and supplies are functions of the money rate of interest and anticipated real income y^H, while all firms' demands and supplies are functions of the money rate of interest and the anticipated sales constraint y^F. All other influences on demands and supplies are exogenous.

Let aggregate real savings be denoted s, and aggregate real investment i. The equilibrium condition

$$y^H = y^F \tag{31}$$

implies[19]

$$s^D(r, y) - i^D(r, y) = g - t \tag{32}$$

Equation (32) is the familiar condition for macroeconomic equilibrium: that the excess of saving over investment is equal to the government budget deficit. This condition determines an implicit relation between r and y, which is represented graphically by the curve IS in *Figure 3.5*. The equilibrium condition for the money market is

$$\dot{M}^D(r, y) - \dot{M}^S = 0 \tag{33}$$

Equation (33) is illustrated by the curve LM in *Figure 3.5*. The two equations may be solved to determine simultaneously the equilibrium rate of interest, r^E, and equilibrium income, y^E; the equilibrium is illustrated by the intersection E of the IS and LM curves.

Suppose now that the money price, P, is flexible, so that price adjustments maintain the product market in equilibrium. The money wage, however, is fixed too high, so that there is an excess supply of labour associated with an excess demand for money. Because price is flexible firms are no longer sales constrained; they produce on their product supply curve and employ on their labour demand curve. But households remain constrained because they cannot supply as much labour as they would wish at the prevailing money wage.

Since price is variable, it must now be exhibited as an argument

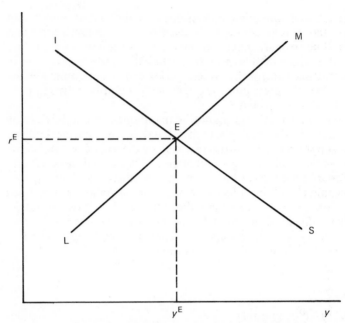

Figure 3.5 *Constrained equilibrium with fixed prices and two financial assets*

in households' and firms' demand and supply functions. Since firms
are unconstrained, real income is no longer an argument in firms'
demand and supply function, though it remains an argument in the
household functions. The appearance of an additional variable, P,
is matched by the appearance of an additional equilibrium condition,
namely that firms produce on their product supply curve. Consequently the conditions for constrained equilibrium now become

$$s^D(r, P, y) - i^D(r, P) = g(P) - t(p) \tag{34a}$$

$$\dot{M}^D(r, P, y) - \dot{M}^S(P) = 0 \tag{34b}$$

$$y(P) - y = 0 \tag{34c}$$

Substituting the supply curve (34c) into the modified IS and LM
curves (34a) and (34b) determines two implicit relations between r
and y, shown respectively by the lines HT and KN in the upper
quadrant of *Figure 3.6*. Both curves are sloped more steeply than
their counterparts in *Figure 3.5*. This means, for example, that if
there were an exogenous change in government budgetary policy,
which caused a shift in both IS and HT, then the impact on real
income would be less when price adjustment occurred. This accords
well with intuition, which suggests that, to some extent at least, price

adjustments and quantity adjustments are substitutes. The lower quadrant of the figure shows the graph BC of the supply curve. The steepness of this curve determines the relative magnitude of price and quantity adjustments. The form of the curve reflects the parameters of production technology, and in particular the speed with which diminishing marginal returns to labour set in. The faster diminishing returns set in the greater will be the price adjustments, and hence the greater the stability of output in the Keynesian model.

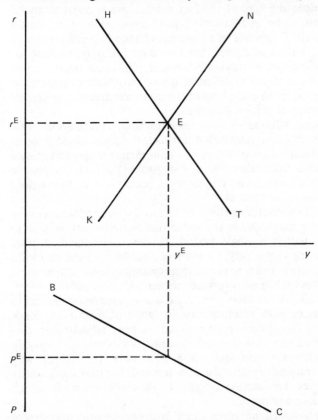

Figure 3.6 *Constrained equilibrium with flexible prices and two financial assets*

3.8 Quantity adjustment versus price adjustment

There is no doubt that the rejection of recontracting, by weakening the assumptions of competitive theory, has made economic analysis much more flexible. Emphasis on the informational aspects of market trading makes possible a more realistic account of transactors' behaviour.

However, the rejection of recontracting is by itself inadequate as the basis for a new macroeconomics. This inadequacy stems from the generality of the theory: the fact that, in principle, it applies to nearly all markets. However, the evidence suggests that some markets are much more prone to disequilibrium than others. For example, the labour market appears to suffer more from disequilibrium than does the typical product market, while most financial markets seem to be maintained close to equilibrium. One reason may be that the frequency of exogenous change is much greater in some markets than in others, but this does not fully account for observed differences in market behaviour. The main reason seems to be that prices adjust at different speeds in different markets, so that it is necessary to complement the non-recontracting approach with an analysis of price adjustment.

In Sections 3.3–3.6 an extreme assumption was made about price adjustments. It was assumed that transactors do not adjust price in response to realized excess demands. Thus money wages and money prices remain fixed throughout the time in which successive contractions of output and employment occur; that is, throughout the entire multiplier process.

One way of rationalizing this is to regard the multiplier process as a purely imaginary one, in the sense that the economy adjusts to equilibrium within a single period. However, for the multiplier process to work in this way, transactors must be involved in a kind of recontracting in order to revise their quantity plans, so that these quantity plans are mutually compatible when they are put into effect. In this case all that the theory has done is to replace recontracting in terms of prices with recontracting in terms of quantities. Since recontracting has already been rejected for price adjustments, it is most unsatisfactory to revive it for quantity adjustments. To justify the disequilibrium approach, it is necessary to explain why transactors respond to realized excess demands by adjusting quantity instead of price. This section investigates the conditions under which such behaviour will occur.

It is often assumed that transactors always prefer price adjustment to quantity adjustment. Failure to adjust price is attributed to externally imposed constraints such as statutory minimum wages and regulated prices[20]. But quantity adjustment may in fact be a well-informed transactor's rational response to other people's information costs. A transactor may well evaluate price and quantity adjustment and decide, quite correctly, that it is in his long-term interest to adjust quantity rather than price[21].

The role of goodwill

In most market economies it is firms that quote prices to households, rather than the other way round. It is hypothesized that firms maintain these price quotations stable in order to secure goodwill. There are two main variants of the theory. In the first, the firm which stabilizes its prices can charge on average a higher price (for the same quantity sold) than a firm which does not. In the second variant the firm can increase the proportion of 'regulars' among its customers, and reduce its labour turnover, by stabilizing prices and wages. In the first case the firm increases its long run average revenue, whereas in the second case it reduces its long run average cost; in either case the firms' long run profitability is increased by administering price stability. The two variants are considered in turn below.

The first is based on the idea that price stability is an information-efficient substitute for future markets and insurance markets. In an uncertain and changing world a household would like to be able to plan an intertemporal programme of consumption and work, with built-in insurance against contingencies. The household would enter into contracts for labour services to be supplied, and its consumer goods delivered, in specific amounts at particular dates according to conditions which prevail on or before these dates. But the information required to undertake such planning is far too much for a household with limited search-time and limited mental capabilities. For under such arrangements, planning for all possible future contingencies would be telescoped into a single period, involving the household in simultaneous transactions in an enormous number of different markets[22].

One way round the difficulty is for firms to assume a specialized role as market intermediaries, offering the household regular work at stable wages and regular consumption supplies at relatively stable spot prices. This provides the household with the insurance it requires, while committing the household only to a regular sequence of spot transactions in a limited number of markets. Risk-averse individuals become the customers and employees of firms, while those with less aversion to risk become the owners of firms, and receive profit as a reward for their specialized risk-bearing function. The more risk-averse individuals prefer to trade with firms offering such services, even though the cost of the service is included in the price. Consequently price and wage stability become particular aspects of the 'quality of service' offered by the representative firm to its customers and employees.

The second version of the goodwill model is concerned with price stability as a policy for reducing a firm's turnover costs. It is much cheaper for a firm to supply established customers—whose specific requirements and credit-worthiness it knows—than it is to take on new ones; and it is much more profitable to employ established workers, who have acquired firm-specific skills, than it is to take on new workers who have to be trained. In general, the firm cannot recover from the customers or workers it loses the costs it incurs in attracting and then integrating a replacement: these costs are internal to the firm, but external to the customers and workers who make the decisions. A rational strategy for the firm is to attempt to minimize these costs by influencing quit behaviour.

Suppose that customers and workers have very imperfect market knowledge. They know only the price and quality of service offered by the firm with which they regularly trade, although they are aware that the firm has competitors. They are presumably satisfied that when they first chose the firm it was competitive, and so they will continue with their trading habits until either the firm's quality of service deteriorates or the price moves adversely. An adverse price or wage movement encourages them to sample the competition, and once their trading habit is broken they are unlikely to return to the original firm. Even if the competition is no better, they may find it convenient to stay with the firm to which they have switched. A firm wishing to minimize turnover costs must therefore avoid adverse price or wage movements. It does this by not increasing its prices or reducing its wages when competitive circumstances are favourable to it, and it recovers its losses by not reducing prices or increasing wages when competitive circumstances are unfavourable to it.

Implications of goodwill

The goodwill theory suggests certain qualifications to the maxim that quantity is set at the short end of the market. It can be argued that firms that maintain prices fixed to generate goodwill may in certain cases set quantity at the long end of the market.

Consider first the product market. Both variants of the goodwill theory suggest that a firm which maintains its prices stable will also be committed to supplying all the product demanded at the quoted price. It is pointless for the firm to insure its customers against price movements unless supplies are actually forthcoming at the regular price. Unless supply is guaranteed, the typical customer is likely to find that just when the price is most favourable relative to the short-run equilibrium price, the increased demands of other customers result in quantity-rationing. Similarly, it is impossible to retain established customers by avoiding price increases if they have to find alternative supplies elsewhere because some of their demand cannot be met. Failure to meet demand will simply mean that in the long run regular customers quit even though the price is kept stable.

The role of open-ended quantity commitments in the product market is illustrated in *Figure 3.7*. If price exceeds the equilibrium level (at say $P_1 > P^e$) then quantity is set at the short end of the market, as before: $y_1 = y_1^d$. But if price is too low (at say $P_2 < P^e$) then firms still supply what is demanded, even though this exceeds the

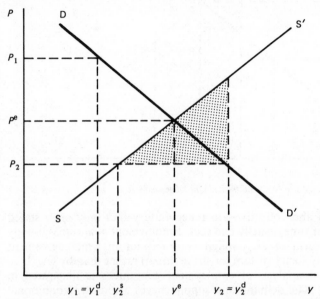

Figure 3.7 *Quantity commitments in the product market*

competitive supply, and output is set at $y_2 = y_2^d$. This is because firms are maximizing long-run profit rather than short-run profit. Instead of producing an output which equates marginal production cost to price (i.e. producing on the supply curve) they invest in goodwill by foregoing some of their short-run profits. The profits foregone by producing at the long end rather than the short end are measured by the shaded area in the figure. Thus, when the price is too low, the firms themselves bear the entire cost of the disequilibrium price. It follows that the locus of price–quantity combinations actually observed in the product market is given by the demand curve (the heavy line in the figure); the supply curve exerts no influence on the outcome unless, or until, price adjustment is initiated.

A similar argument can be applied to the labour market. Here the commitment to wage stability is apparent in agreements—both

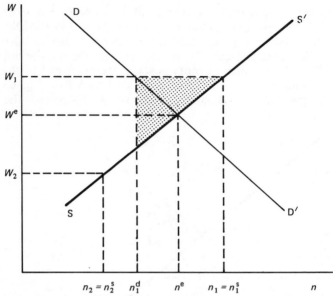

Figure 3.8 *Employment commitments in the labour market*

individual and collective—to renegotiate wages only after stated intervals of time, usually one year. Employment guarantees usually take the form of an implicit contract—an informal agreement enforced by social custom (or strike threat) rather than by law[23].

A partial analysis of employment guarantees is illustrated in *Figure 3.8*. The demand and supply curves are drawn conditional upon a given money price level. At the money wage W_1 above the equilibrium level W^e, firms offer all the employment workers demand, and so actual employment is $n_1 = n_1^s$. Employment exceeds firms' competitive demand for labour n_1^d because the firms are following long-run profit-maximization and so the marginal conditions underlying the competitive demand curve do not apply to them. Given that the money wage is fixed, the short-term profit foregone in maintaining workers' goodwill is measured by the shaded area in the figure. At the money wage $W_2 < W^e$ firms are constrained by the labour supply. Since households have no reciprocal commitment to supply all the labour firms require, employment is now set at the short end of the market: $n_2 = n_2^s$. It follows that the locus of wage–employment combinations actually observed is given by the supply curve (the heavy line in the figure). The demand curve is relevant only in determining the direction in which competitive pressure will tend to adjust the wage over time.

It is evident that a firm which endeavours to maintain the goodwill of both customers and employees by making price- and quantity-commitments in both the product and labour markets is exposed to a considerable degree of risk. It has to ensure that when labour is in short supply it is still able to meet product demand, otherwise customer goodwill expensively built up in the past may be lost. On the other hand, when labour is in excess supply and product demand is low, it must ensure that sales receipts are sufficient to cover its wage payments and other variable costs, otherwise it is exposed to a risk of bankruptcy.

In reconciling these goals the firm has limited degrees of freedom, particularly in the short run when the elasticity of substitution between labour and other factors is effectively zero. One strategy is to hold large inventories of the finished product to buffer fluctuations in employment and product demand (when the two are out of step); another is to maintain liquidity by holding large cash reserves or establishing overdraft facilities. In each case the cost of the inventory has to be passed on, in the long run, to customers and employees by increasing the firm's markup over production cost.

Perhaps the most obvious strategy is to be selective in the people to whom the privileges of continuity of employment and product supply are extended. Since the costs of servicing established customers are much lower than the costs of servicing new ones, it seems sensible to discriminate between the two categories. However when the firm has a large number of customers who are served in a very 'public' context, it is difficult to discriminate in this way, although a number of devices are available (e.g. levying a handling charge on non-account customers).

It is much easier for a firm to discriminate in the labour market, for employees are normally fewer in number than customers and the negotiation of the employment contract is more confidential. On economic grounds discrimination with respect to job security should be based on the costs of turnover, which are significantly greater for some categories of worker than others. A major factor is the cost of imparting firm-specific skills to the worker. There is a strong incentive for employers to offer wage stability and job security to skilled and experienced workers at a very low cost to the worker (in terms of foregone average earnings). Unskilled workers must forego proportionately more of their earnings to enjoy the same privileges, since the firm itself gains much less from reducing the turnover of this category of labour.

It can also be argued that unskilled workers have much less incentive to seek wage and employment guarantees. First, the unskilled are generally lower paid, and therefore the degree of insurance offered by unemployment benefit is much greater in relation to their earnings. Secondly unskilled workers are potentially more mobile between industries, and so may have better chances of reemployment at the same wage when made redundant. For the same reason they may believe that they can rely on counter-cyclical public works programmes to provide suitable work in a recession.

This suggests the possibility of a 'dual labour market' in which skilled workers enjoy wage stability and job security while unskilled workers do not. To a certain extent this is borne out in practice. It certainly seems to be true that skilled workers enjoy a greater degree of job security than do unskilled workers. However the differences with regard to wage stability are less apparent. There seems to be a tendency for unskilled workers to stipulate for wage stability, but not to seek employment guarantees. It is difficult to rationalize such behaviour for the following reason.

One of the main preoccupations of a risk-averse worker is a stable wage income. Both wage stability and employment guarantees contribute independently to this, so that neither one is a substitute for the other. But, much more than this, it could be argued that the one is an essential complement to the other. A rational worker should perceive that the introduction of wage stability has implications for employment stability, and vice versa. When wages are stable a short-run profit-maximizing firm faced with fluctuating product demand will substitute employment adjustments for wage adjustments. Thus in the absence of employment guarantees, wage stability will only be obtained at the expense of employment instability.

There appear to be two main reasons why unskilled workers will stipulate for wage stability without employment guarantees. First, they may believe that the wage-elasticity of the demand for labour is low. In this case the employment instability induced by wage stability may be negligible, so that wage stability contributes to income stability independently of employment guarantees. At the same time the low substitutability of labour in production, which underlies the inelastic demand, means that employment guarantees involve a high degree of risk for the firm. Thus workers may find it cheaper to rely on other forms of insurance against unemployment, such as switching jobs or claiming unemployment benefit. Consequently, workers rely on firms for wage stability, and look elsewhere for insurance against unemployment.

Another possibility—hinted at by Keynes—is that workers attach more importance to the preservation or improvement of wage differentials than they do to the stability of wage income. Consequently, trade unions allow money wage rates to be changed only after detailed, and often protracted, negotiations. Although they may permit spontaneous increases in the money wage, they consider that any fall in money wages (either absolute, or relative to some norm) would constitute a serious erosion of differentials, to be resisted at all costs. In such cases trade unions may be willing to forego a secondary objective, such as employment guarantees, in order to attain their primary objective of maintaining and improving differentials.

The preceding analysis has sought to explain why, in the short-run, prices may be maintained fixed in the product market and wages maintained fixed in both the skilled and unskilled labour markets. The goodwill motive establishes a link between price stability and quantity commitments in the product market, and between wage stability and employment commitments in the labour market. The analysis predicts that in the product market, output is always set to meet demand and that in the market for skilled labour, employment is always set to meet supply. Only for unskilled labour is employment set at the short end of the labour market.

3.9 Classical overemployment

This section examines some of the implications of quantity commitments for unemployment. It is important to recognize that under conditions of generalized excess supply, the existence of demand commitments in the product market is of no consequence, since firms are demand-constrained anyway. Quantity commitments are relevant only in the labour market, where they imply that firms will not reduce the employment of skilled labour. It follows that the incidence of unemployment is entirely on unskilled labour. If skilled workers are willing and able to transfer to unskilled work, then the aggregate volume of employment may be unaffected by the existence of selective employment commitments. The only effect will be on the composition of employment: skilled workers will retain employment whereas unskilled workers become unemployed. Thus aggregate unemployment remains unchanged: only the distribution of employment alters.

Quantity commitments in the product market have implications for unemployment only when there is an excess demand, rather than an excess supply, of the product. This is the case where there is unemployment due to too high a real wage. A simple example of this was analysed in Section 3.4. This example is reworked below invoking quantity commitments. To retain the simplicity of the analysis it is assumed that in the short run the supply of skilled

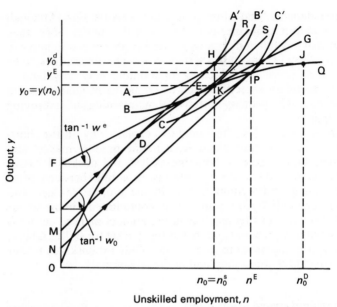

Figure 3.9 *Overemployment equilibrium with quantity commitments in the product market*

labour is fixed. Since by assumption their money wage is also fixed, the employment of skilled workers is a fixed charge on the firm.

For a firm maximizing profit subject to quantity commitments in the product market, and with no employment commitments to its unskilled workers, the optimal strategy is to set the employment of unskilled workers so that with the most efficient feasible deployment of the skilled workers the output is just sufficient to meet demand. In *Figure 3.9* the curve OQ shows the relation between the employment of unskilled workers, n, and output, y, conditional upon a given level of skilled employment, $\bar{n}_S$. The form of the curve depends upon what restrictions are placed upon the utilization of skilled labour—whether, for example, skilled workers are willing and able to perform jobs normally performed by the unskilled.

So far as the representative household is concerned, its wage income will now contain a fixed lump sum component derived from skilled work. This income may be treated analogously to profit, since both are derived from the utilization of fixed factors. In *Figure 3.9* the line FG represents the new household budget constraint. The intercept OF measures Π^h, the total quasi-rent anticipated by the household, made up of profit and income from skilled labour. The slope measures the wage of unskilled labour.

Household preferences for consumption and unskilled work are represented by an indifference map made up of curves such as AA', BB' and CC'. The entire map is conditional upon the amount of skilled labour already being supplied. Full employment equilibrium is at E, where there is equality between demand and supply both for unskilled labour and the product. It should be evident that the formal analysis of employment determination is unchanged by the introduction of fixed endowments of skilled labour with guaranteed employment.

The existence of demand commitments when the real wage is too high leads to overemployment and not unemployment. Referring to *Figure 3.9*, suppose that the real wage is fixed initially at $w_0 > w^e$, as indicated by the slope of the line LR; the anticipated quasi-rent is OL. With output set at the short end of the market, the constrained equilibrium would be at D, below the full employment equilibrium E. However, *ex ante* households are in equilibrium at H with consumer demand y_0^d and unskilled labour supply n_0^s. If firms endeavour to meet this demand they will wish to produce at J. However, at J unskilled labour demand n_0^D exceeds supply n_0^s, and the best that firms can do is to employ all the unskilled labour available; thus they produce at K, with $n_0 = n_0^s$, $y_0 = y(n_0)$. The quasi-rent generated, OM, is less than that anticipated by the households, OL. Next-period households will wish to increase their supply of unskilled labour in order to make good the shortfall of income. Equilibrium will eventually be achieved at P, when household expectations of quasi-rent have been revised down to ON, unskilled employment is n^E, and the output y^E is just sufficient to meet household demand. Comparing E and P shows that employment is now above, rather than below, the full employment level. Firms are employing unskilled labour up to a point where its marginal product is well below the real wage, so that they can produce sufficient output to retain consumer goodwill.

This analysis indicates some important qualifications to the view that unemployment can be attributed to an excessive real wage, and so by implication it casts doubt on the effectiveness of policies which seek to reduce unemployment by cutting the real wage. Some further qualifications are considered in the following section.

3.10 Profit expectations and unemployment

This section is concerned with the way in which household profit expectations influence employment. Household profit expectations are important because they influence the household's perception of its budget constraint, and thereby affect its product demand and labour supply.

The formation of expectations

In GE theory and in the disequilibrium theory literature it is assumed that household profit expectations always adjust to equality with firms' planned profits. However the mechanism by which households learn of firms' prospective profits is not spelt out in detail. Various mechanisms are considered below, and it is shown that all of them are unsatisfactory.

(1) Households could predict current profit from past profit. However, in a changing economic environment, there is no method of prediction which guarantees complete accuracy.

(2) Households could infer profits from the prevailing prices of the firms' inputs and outputs. However this inference requires a knowledge of the production function. Knowledge of the production function is usually derived from a knowledge of technology, which is specialized with firms and is indeed often protected as a trade secret. Furthermore, when firms face quantity constraints, it would be necessary to know what the constraints are and how they are likely to modify the firms' production plans.

(3) Managers could publish forecasts of profit for shareholders' benefit. However, in order to fulfill their primary role of maximizing profit, managers need to know only the increment in profit associated with each strategy and not the absolute level of profit generated by the optimal strategy. Thus the preparation of profit forecasts is an additional managerial function, involving resource costs which will ultimately be borne by the shareholders. Shareholders will wish to trade off the increasing cost of preparing profit forecasts in greater detail against the diminishing returns to greater accuracy. Thus even if profit forecasts are prepared, it is unlikely that they will be a completely accurate reflection of the profits implied by firms' production plans.

(4) It could be argued that the existence of a stock market, in which rights to profit (equities) are traded, would enable firms' expectations to be communicated to households. The price of equity would reflect firms' planned profits, and even if a household did not actively trade in the market, it could learn equity prices easily through the financial news media.

However it is households, as the owners of firms, and not the managers, who set the price of equity. Thus the valuation of equity will reflect households' expectations, not those of managers. Only if the managers of firms are involved in insider trading will there be a tendency for the valuation of firms to be brought into line with their managers' own expectations. The rewards to insider trading are undoubtedly great, and schemes for employee-ownership may well encourage it. But the obstacles to insider trading are in many cases even greater—one is its illegality in most countries. When the deterrents to insider trading are effective, equity prices simply reflect household expectations: households can learn nothing from them about managerial expectations.

(5) Another possibility is to invoke Walras' auctioneer. If the auctioneer were to quote not only a trial wage but also an associated trial profit figure, then both firms and households would necessarily have the same perception of profit.

But modifying the role of the auctioneer in this way implies a change in the behaviour of firms. They would now be motivated to set labour demand and product supply, not to maximize profit, but merely to realize the target profit figure. The outcome would be the same only if the auctioneer calculated the target figure so that it was always consistent with firms' maximizing efforts. This involves a significant extension of the role of the auctioneer. Not only does he adjust trial prices according to notional excess demands, he also calculates the profit implied by these prices and communicates it to households. But since his primary role in initiating price adjustments has already been rejected, it is only consistent to reject this secondary role too.

(6) Finally it is necessary to dispose of a fallacious argument based on a confusion of *ex ante* and *ex post* variables. It is undoubtedly true that what firms generate as profit is equal to what households receive as profit income. In the context of national income accounting this is an identity (provided that retained profits and capital gains are treated consistently). But what households receive as profit after a given set of transactions has been completed is not the same as what households anticipate profit to be when deciding how much to transact at prevailing prices.

If household profit expectations do not automatically adjust to firms' planned profits, how then are they determined? It seems reasonable to assume that, other things being equal, expectations adjust adaptively—and therefore with a lag—to levels of profit realized by firms. However it is consistent with the tenor of Keynesian theory that expectations are also susceptible to exogenous

changes induced by opinion and rumour about business prospects—
in particular about the quantity constraints likely to be experienced
by firms.

Exogenous profit expectations

The role of exogenous profit expectations is analysed in *Figure 3.10*.
Like *Figure 3.9* it refers to a non-monetary economy in which skilled
labour is a fixed factor; it is assumed that both households and firms
perceive correctly the skilled wage and the level of skilled
employment. The role of profit expectations in a monetary economy
is considered in Section 3.11.

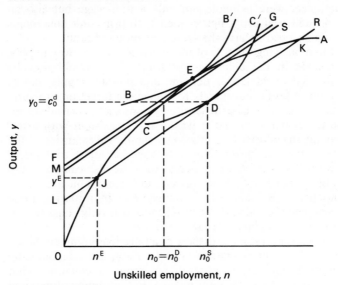

Figure 3.10 *Unemployment with exogenous profit expectations*

Suppose that there is an exogenous reduction in expected profit
from OF, the full employment level, to OL. This shifts down the
budget constraint perceived by the household from FG to LR. The
household is now in equilibrium at D, reducing planned consumption
to c_0^d and increasing unskilled labour supply to n_0^s. Firms are now
demand-constrained. Their profit-maximizing strategy is to produce
at H, where their demand for unskilled labour is reduced to n_0^D. With
employment set at the short end of the unskilled labour market,
$n_0 = n_0^D$, and so there is unemployment among the unskilled. Profit
falls from OF to OM; the direction of the change agrees with that
anticipated by the households, but the magnitude is much less.

If profit expectations do not adjust, then the household budget constraint remains LR. Households cannot be in constrained equilibrium if they are off this perceived budget constraint. Since firms cannot be in equilibrium off the production frontier, there can only be constrained equilibrium at an intersection of the budget line and the production frontier. As shown in *Figure 3.10*, there are two possible intersections, one at J and the other at the extreme right, at K. However, since households never enter into quantity commitments, they can never be in equilibrium at any point above or to the right of D. Thus K is excluded, and the only possible equilibrium is at J. This constrained equilibrium will be reached by a deflationary process in which households repeatedly cut back consumer demand because of a tightening employment constraint, while firms cut back employment because of a tightening sales constraint. Thus when profit expectations are totally inelastic output falls to y^E, profit falls to OL and unemployment rises to $u^E = n_0^s - n^E$.

The constrained equilibrium is characterized by the equality of household expectations of profit and realized profit. Output and employment are determined by the need to adjust firms' realized profit to the level anticipated by households. Thus the conventional direction of causation is reversed: instead of expectations adjusting to realized profit, realized profit adjusts to make expectations self-fulfilling.

Comparison with Barro and Grossman

When the analysis is compared with the Barro and Grossman theory of Section 3.5, certain parallels are obvious. The exogenous fall in expected profit has the same effect as an exogenous increase in money prices, namely it reduces aggregate demand and leads to an excess supply in both goods and labour markets. The similarity is apparent from GWL (equation (12)): the Barro and Grossman approach sets $\pi^h = \pi^f$ but sets $z_m > 0$, while the profit expectations approach sets $z_m = 0$ and sets $\pi^h < \pi^f$; these are just alternative ways of accommodating generalized excess supply (z_y, $z_n < 0$) on the real side of the economy. In either case a constrained equilibrium is attained through a reduction in real income, whose immiserizing effect either eliminates the demand for additional money balances, or brings realized profit into line with expectations. However there are important differences between the models too.

In the Barro and Grossman model the existence of money is crucial to the entire analysis, while the profit expectations model applies to a non-monetary economy as well as to a monetary one. The exogeneity of profit expectations is a consequence of the delegation of production decisions by the owners (the households) to the managers, and the restricted flow of information back from the management to the owners. Thus demand deficiency due to inappropriate profit expectations can be attributed to the specialization of the ownership and management functions. It is not money, but the prevailing form of capitalist organization, which makes possible demand-deficiency unemployment in this model[24].

In the Barro and Grossman theory the existence of unemployment depends crucially on money wage and money price rigidities. If both money wages and money prices are flexible the economy will adjust to full employment. In the profit expectations theory wage and price rigidities are not required for unemployment. When profit expectations are exogenous equilibrium can be achieved only when profits have fallen to the level anticipated by households. If household expectations are incompatible with the full employment level of profit then there is no way in which the economy can adjust to full employment, even though wages and prices are flexible.

Implications for wages policy

This result has important implications for wages policy. Indeed it is possible to strengthen the result still further, and show that in certain circumstances wage adjustments may be counterproductive. Under certain conditions unemployment will be exacerbated by a reduction in the real wage, and may be reduced (though not eliminated) by an increase in the real wage.

Suppose to begin with that changes in the real wage have no effect on household profit expectations. *Figure 3.11* illustrates an initial state of unemployment D. In Section 3.4 (*Figure 3.3*) this was said to represent unemployment due to too high a real wage. Implicit in this view is that household profit expectations are always consistent with firms' planned profits. If the real wage is reduced firms' profits will increase and the economy will adjust to full employment at E.

But if household profit expectations remain unchanged when the real wage is reduced then the perceived household budget line, instead of becoming tangential to the production frontier OA at a point further to the right, will rotate about the intercept H. The new budget line will be HK instead of HJ, and household equilibrium will move down to L. However L cannot be an equilibrium because firms are producing within the production frontier. Employment will therefore contract and a downward multiplier process will bring the economy to equilibrium at M, the point of intersection between the budget line HJ and the production frontier OA. Unemployment at M is higher than at D even though the real wage is lower.

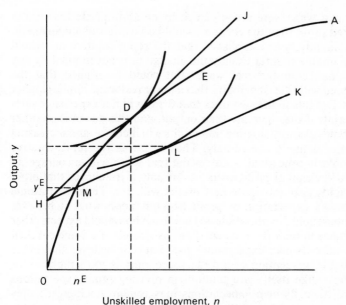

Figure 3.11 *Effect of a real wage cut on unemployment*

A further application of wage cuts would reduce employment even more. Only an increase in the real wage back to its original level will restore employment. An even higher increase would make any sort of equilibrium impossible so long as profit expectations remained at OH. Thus focusing on the unemployment equilibrium at L shows that a reduction in the real wage will reduce employment, whereas a moderate increase in the real wage will increase it.

This proposition is reminiscent of underconsumptionist arguments. Typical of these arguments is that profit income is not fully converted into aggregate demand; that is, profit income constitutes a leakage from the circular flow of income. While these theories correctly view the role of profit as central, their analysis is almost invariably impaired by a failure to distinguish properly between *ex ante* and *ex post* variables, and between endogenous and exogenous variables. The present theory argues that profit expectations are exogenous and that unemployment equilibrium is achieved only when output and employment have adjusted so that realized profit is equal to expected profit. Only when stated in this form is the argument logically sound.

However the assumption that profit expectations are invariant with respect to the real wage may be questioned. If every reduction in the real wage were accompanied by an appropriate increase in expected profit then the economy would adjust to full employment. It has already been established that the representative household will be unable to infer exactly the change in profit implied by any given change in the real wage. But could be argued that the household will at least perceive that a lower real wage implies higher profits. But this in turn assumes that firms will not experience sales constraints if they increase their output, and this depends on other households also anticipating that profits will increase, and increasing consumer demand accordingly. Thus so far as the representative household is concerned, a cut in the real wage will encourage an upward revision of profit expectations only if it believes that other households also anticipate that profits will rise. Thus the rational household's expectation of profit depends upon what it believes other households' expectations to be. If each household expects other households to raise their expectations as a result of a wage cut then it will raise its own expectations too. But if it believes that other households' perception of the macroeconomy is too simplistic, or that they—like itself—are cautious in revising profit expectations upward, then its own expectations may remain unchanged; they may even be revised downward. Thus *prima facie* the case for supposing that real wage cuts will enhance profit expectations is very weak.

3.11 Profit expectations in a monetary economy

It is often suggested that money is somehow a source of instability in the economy. The analysis in Sections 3.5–3.7 shows that this is so only insofar as money wages or money prices are inflexible. When wages and prices are flexible money is effectively neutral as regards economic stability.

This result is strengthened quite remarkably when profit expectations are exogenous. In this case money may actually be a stabilizing influence on the economy. Unemployment which would occur in the absence of a monetary asset may be mitigated or eliminated altogether when a monetary asset exists.

When profit expectations are exogenous in a monetary economy, it is important to distinguish two types of constrained equilibrium. The first is where realized profit adjusts to expected profit, and all markets for labour, product and money are in equilibrium. The second is where the labour and product markets are in equilibrium, and the excess supply of money balances exactly compensates for households' overestimation of realized profit. The first case may be termed a full equilibrium, the second a limited equilibrium. Given the behavioural assumptions on which the present analysis is based, a limited equilibrium, once attained, will perpetuate itself, and there will be no tendency to adjust from a limited equilibrium to a full equilibrium (should such an equilibrium exist).

The concept of a limited equilibrium may be illustrated by considering the case in which both money wages and money prices are flexible. Suppose that there is an exogenous reduction in household profit expectations to below their full employment level. This leads to a reduction in planned consumption, and also to a reduction in the demand for money balances and an increase in labour supply. At the initial wages and prices this creates normal excess supplies of product, labour and money balances. However since money is a circulating medium the excess supply of money balances will not be perceived. The reaction in the product and labour markets will therefore be to bid down the money wage and the money price in order to restore equilibrium. This increases the real value of money balances and so encourages households to run them down by increasing their consumption relative to labour supply. Equilibrium is achieved when the reduction in consumption due to lower anticipated income is exactly compensated by the increase in consumption generated by the running down of money balances. Each household finds that its unanticipated profit income exactly makes good the planned reduction in money balances induced by the lower price level. The equilibrium real wage is virtually the same as it was to begin with, and output and employment are maintained close to their initial levels too.

This example shows that with wage and price flexibility the existence of money serves to stabilize income with respect to exogenous changes in profit expectations. Changes in profit expectations generate fluctuations in prices but not in income or employment.

Suppose now that the money wage is fixed. In this case it is readily shown that, whether or not prices are flexible, pessimistic profit expectations will generate a contraction in income and employment. The impact is similar in most respects to that of an exogenous reduction in aggregate demand; the impact is greater the lower the degree of price flexibility. However the impact will be less than it would be in a non-monetary economy because as real income falls, household's demand for real money balances falls, and the planned reduction in money balances stimulates consumption to some extent. In other words, the marginal propensity to consume out of income is now less than unity, instead of being equal to unity (as in the model of Section 3.10). As a result of this the contraction in output is reduced, and so realized profit does not fall as low as expected profit; equilibrium is achieved when realized profit exceeds expected profit by an amount equal to the excess supply of money. This corresponds to a higher level of income and employment than would be achieved in the absence of money.

3.12 Conclusions, and implications for future research

This chapter has expounded the disequilibrium approach to unemployment and has suggested a number of developments of it. The main points emphasized in the exposition are as follows.

(1) The disequilibrium approach is based on a rejection of Walras' auctioneer and the recontracting mechanism. It is recognized at the outset that transactors respond not to notional excess demands but to realized excess demands. The absence of recontracting is almost universal: it applies to the market for bonds as well as the markets for goods and labour. Non-recontracting cannot therefore account for differences between markets in the speed with which they adjust. This requires a theory of price stability, to explain why in some markets transactors respond to realized excess demand by adjusting quantity rather than price.

(2) No single theory of price stability is entirely satisfactory. Statutory intervention in the form of wage and price controls is only intermittent in most market economies. The goodwill theory suggests prices and skilled wage rates may be inflexible, but does not adequately explain why unskilled wage rates should be so. In this context it is difficult to improve on the suggestions and hints given by Keynes.

(3) The Barro and Grossman theory of generalized excess supply is based on two key behavioural assumptions, only one of which is usually made explicit. The first of these is that money wages and money prices are rigid. The second is that, because money circulates as a medium of exchange, households do not perceive quantity constraints on the supply of money. It is for this reason that an excess demand for money is not checked by quantity rationing in the money market, but only by the immiserizing effect of a contraction in the circular flow of income.

(4) Both the IS/LM model and the Keynesian model of money wage rigidity can be derived by applying disequilibrium concepts to an intertemporal model of household behaviour.

The main developments of the theory are as follows.

(5) The goodwill theory of price stability is shown to have important implications for quantity determination. When goodwill is not a factor, quantity is set at the short end of the market. When goodwill is a factor, price is set by the firms, quantity is set by the households, and firms respond to whatever households demand or supply. Goodwill affects unemployment in two main ways. First, goodwill in the product market means that a high real wage which is associated with an excess demand for output may lead to overemployment rather than unemployment. Secondly, goodwill in the labour market implies that the incidence of unemployment will be much greater among unskilled workers than among the skilled.

(6) The importance of information costs in markets, which underlies the rejection of recontracting, is parallelled by the limited flow of information to households about the profit implications of firms' production plans. When household profit expectations are exogenous, pessimism about profits can lead to a form of unemployment which real-wage adjustments cannot cure. Worse than this, orthodox low-wage policies may actually exacerbate unemployment. This result is reminiscent of the policy implications that Keynes claimed to derive from his *General Theory*. However the mechanism referred to above has a much closer affinity to underconsumptionist thinking than to Keynesian theory.

One of the attractions of disequilibrium theory is that there remains scope for a great deal more work to be done, and that much of this work promises to be of immediate practical relevance. A lot of the work done so far has been taxonomic, describing the various regimes that are obtained from different permutations of excess demands and excess supplies in a multimarket economy. For example, this chapter would have been even longer had it not confined itself to those regimes most obviously associated with unemployment. There are many other regimes to explore, though hopefully research will be concentrated on those most likely to occur in practice.

An important subject, only briefly touched on here, is the impact of future quantity constraints on current behaviour. In fact some of this work has already been done in the course of developing dynamic disequilibrium models. For example, the accelerator theory of investment can be given a disequilibrium interpretation using the concept of expected quantity constraints. Ultimately it should be possible to recast much of conventional Keynesian dynamics in a disequilibrium framework, and so provide it with rigorous microeconomic foundations.

A good deal of work also needs to be done on the foundations of disequilibrium theory itself. The theory of transactors' response to realized excess demand needs to be put onto a more rigorous footing, with the market adjustment process being modelled in greater detail. Theories of entrepreneurship and trading with small numbers provide indications of how this might be done. Experimental economists have gained some insights into this process by simulating market adjustments under controlled conditions. In a particular market it is not only the price or the quantity which adjusts; rather both adjust but at different speeds. The theory of market adjustment must predict how market characteristics influence the relative speeds of adjustment, and how the interaction of the two kinds of adjustment affects the final outcome.

More also needs to be learnt about the dynamics of the circulation of money. Progress here has been restricted not so much by lack of research effort as by the inherent difficulty of the subject. Some kind of breakthrough in this area is probably necessary before the dynamics of disequilibrium can be fully understood.

Notes

1. For a concise presentation of GE theory see Simpson (1975). The definitive work is Arrow and Hahn (1971).
2. A very simple presentation of the neoclassical approach is given by Miller and Upton (1974). The theory of the labour market is discussed in some detail by Alchian (1971) and in particular by Mortensen (1971). An advanced treatment of neoclassical macroeconomics is given by Sargent (1979).
3. The 'classical' economists referred to by Keynes are called 'neoclassical' by historians of economic thought, so that the 'neoclassical' school referred to above becomes neo-neoclassical. Keynes' view of classical macroeconomics appears to have been based chiefly on Pigou (1933) and Robbins (1934). The more eclectic approach of the classical school is emphasized by Solow (1980).
4. See Simpson (1975).
5. See Green (1964).
6. See Flemming (1973).
7. See Fair (1969) and Feldstein (1967).
8. Strictly speaking, therefore, the real value of money balances should be normalized with respect to the volume of transactions. However this would introduce additional complications to the analysis. It is reasonable, though, to assume instead that the

utility of money balances depends on their ratio to planned consumption c^{d}; then

$$u = u^*(c^{\mathrm{d}}, n^{\mathrm{s}}, m^{\mathrm{d}}/c^{\mathrm{d}}) = u(c^{\mathrm{d}}, n^{\mathrm{s}}, m^{\mathrm{d}})$$

so equation (14) remains valid.

9. This point has received considerable emphasis from the Austrian school of economists; see for example, Kirzner (1973, 1980).

10. However, for examples of internal markets which use such a process see Coase (1937) and Williamson (1975).

11. See Walras (1874) and Edgeworth (1881). The asymptotic equivalence of the two procedures for large numbers of traders is demonstrated by Hildebrand and Kirman (1976).

12. See, for example, Bacharach (1976, ch. 6).

13. For further details see Grossman (1974) and Weintraub (1979).

14. See, for example, Howard (1980) and Latham (1980).

15. This is the Clower demand, as opposed to the Dreze demand which is the demand consistent with the expected quantity constraints in *all* markets; see Clower (1965) and Dreze (1975). The strategic aspect of quantity signalling seems to have eluded some critics of the Clower demand, notably Svensson (1980).

16. Though of course some workers are discouraged; see Bowen and Finegan (1969).

17. See Barro and Grossman (1971, 1976) and Buiter and Lorie (1977). The synthesis was based on Clower (1965) and Patinkin (1965). A similar approach has been developed by Malinvaud (1977, 1980). For useful survey papers see Drazen (1980) and Muellbauer and Portes (1978). For a critique of the policy implications derived from the analysis see Hildebrand and Hildebrand (1978).

18. See Keynes (1936, ch. 2, p. 19).

19. Full details are given in Casson (1981), which also offers background material on other parts of this chapter.

20. For this reason applications have focused on consumer rationing in socialist economies (Howard, 1980) and on prices and incomes policies in market economies (Webb, 1979).

21. For theories of voluntary price-stickiness see Barro (1972) and Negishi (1979).

22. This is the essence of the time-state-preference theory of contingent future markets. A simple explanation is given in Hirschleifer (1970, ch. 9) and a more advanced statement in Debreu (1959, ch. 7).

23. See Azariadis (1975, 1976) and Baily (1974). For a critique of this approach see Akerlof and Miyazaki (1980). See also Chapter 2 of this book.

24. It remains true however that firms must exchange their output with final buyers before distributing the proceeds of the sale as wages and profits. If output could be distributed directly to owners and employees as payment in kind, then there could be no such thing as an oversupply of output, and hence there could be no demand-deficiency *per se*. The need to exchange the product before distributing the proceeds arises because in the real world each firm specializes in producing just one or two goods while households consume a wide variety of goods. Only if households diversified their work and their shareholdings between firms in accordance with their consumption preferences would the need to exchange the final product disappear, and this would clearly be inefficient as it would prevent specialization of work according to comparative advantage.

Given that the output has to be exchanged, it may well minimize transaction costs to exchange it for money. However it is not the use of money itself which causes the problem in this case, merely the need for exchange, which is logically prior to the use of money.

References

Akerlof, G. and Miyazaki, H. (1980). The implicit contract theory of unemployment meets the wage bill argument. *Review of Economic Studies* **47**, 321–338

Alchian, A. A. (1971). Information costs, pricing and resource unemployment. In *Microeconomic Foundations of Employment and Inflation Theory*, by E. S. Phelps *et al.* London; Macmillan

Arrow, K. J. and Hahn, F. H. (1971). *General Competitive Analysis.* Edinburgh; Oliver and Boyd

Azariadis, C. (1975). Implicit contracts and underemployment equilibria. *Journal of Political Economy* **83**, 1183–1201

Azariadis, C. (1976). On the incidence of unemployment. *Review of Economic Studies* **43**, 115–125

Bacharach, M. (1976). *Economics and the Theory of Games.* London; Macmillan

Baily, M. N. (1974). Wages and employment under uncertain demand. *Review of Economic Studies* **41**, 37–50

Barro, R. J. (1972). A theory of monopolistic price adjustment. *Review of Economic Studies* **39**, 17–26

Barro, R. J. and Grossman, H. I. (1971). A general disequilibrium model of income and employment. *American Economic Review* **61**, 82–93

Barro, R. J. and Grossman, H. I. (1976). *Money, Employment and Inflation.* Cambridge; Cambridge University Press

Bowen, W. G. and Finegan, T. A. (1969). *Economics of Labour Force Participation.* Princeton, N.J.; Princeton University Press

Buiter, W. and Lorie, H. (1977). Some unfamiliar properties of a familiar macroeconomic model. *Economic Journal* **87**, 743–754

Casson, M. C. (1981). *Unemployment: A Disequilibrium Approach.* Oxford; Martin Robertson (in preparation)

Clower, R. W. (1965). The Keynesian revolution: A theoretical appraisal. In *The Theory of Interest Rates* (ed. by F. H. Hahn and F. Brechling). London; Macmillan

Clower, R. W. (1967). A reconsideration of the microfoundations of monetary theory. *Western Economic Journal* **6**, 1–9

Coase, R. H. (1937). The nature of the firm. *Economica N.S.* **4**, 386–405

Debreu, G. (1959). *Theory of Value.* New Haven; Yale University Press

Drazen, A. (1980). Recent developments in macroeconomic disequilibrium theory. *Econometrica* **48**, 283–305

Dreze, J. (1975). Existence of an exchange equilibrium under price rigidities. *International Economic Review* **16**, 301–320

Edgeworth, F. Y. (1881).*Mathematical Psychics.* London; C. Kegan Paul

Fair, R. C. (1969). *The Short-run Demand for Workers and Hours.* Amsterdam; North-Holland

Feldstein, M. (1967). Specification of the labour input in the aggregate production function. *Review of Economic Studies* **34**, 375–386

Flemming, J. S. (1973). The consumption function when capital markets are imperfect: The permanent income hypothesis reconsidered. *Oxford Economic Papers* **25**, 160–172

Green, H. A. J. (1964). *Aggregation in Economic Analysis.* Princeton, N.J.; Princeton University Press

Grossman, H. I. (1974). The nature of quantities in market disequilibrium. *American Economic Review* **64**, 509–514

Hildebrand, K. and Hildebrand, W. (1978). On Keynesian equilibria with unemployment and quantity rationing. *Journal of Economic Theory* **18**, 255–277

Hildebrand, W. and Kirman, A. P. (1976). *Introduction to Equilibrium Analysis.* Amsterdam; North-Holland

Hirschleifer, J. (1970). *Investment, Interest and Capital.* Englewood Cliffs, N.J.; Prentice–Hall

Howard, D. H. (1980). *Disequilibrium in a Controlled Economy.* Farnborough, Hants; Lixington Books

Keynes, J. M. (1936). *The General Theory of Employment, Interest and Money.* London; Macmillan

Kirzner, I. M. (1973). *Competition and Entrepreneurship.* Chicago; University of Chicago Press

Kirzner, I. M. (1980). *Perception, Opportunity and Profit.* Chicago; University of Chicago Press

Latham, R. (1980). Quantity-constrained demand functions. *Econometrica* **48**, 307–313

Malinvaud, E. (1977). *The Theory of Unemployment Reconsidered.* Oxford; Basil Blackwell

Malinvaud, E. (1980). *Profitability and Unemployment.* Cambridge; Cambridge University Press

Marshall, A. (1961). *Principles of Economics,* 9th edn (ed. by C. W. Guillebaud). London; Macmillan

Miller, M. H. and Upton, C. W. (1974). *Macroeconomics: A Neoclassical Introduction.* Homewood, Illinois; Irwin

Mortensen, D. T. (1971). A theory of wage and employment dynamics. In *Microeconomic Foundations of Employment and Inflation Theory,* by E. S. Phelps *et al.* London; Macmillan

Muellbauer, J. and Portes, R. (1978). Macroeconomic models with quantity rationing. *Economic Journal* **88**, 788–821

Negishi, T. (1979). *Microeconomic Foundations of Keynesian Macroeconomics.* Amsterdam; North-Holland

Patinkin, D. (1965). *Money, Interest and Prices,* 2nd edn. London; Harper and Row

Pigou, A. C. (1933). *The Theory of Unemployment.* London; Macmillan

Robbins, L. (1934). *The Great Depression.* London; Macmillan

Sargent, T. J. (1979). *Macroeconomic Theory.* London; Academic Press

Simpson, D. (1975). *General Equilibrium Analysis.* Oxford; Basil Blackwell

Solow, R. M. (1980). On theories of unemployment. *American Economic Review* **70**, 1–9

Svensson, L. E. O. (1980). Effective demand and stochastic rationing. *Review of Economic Studies* **48**, 339–355

Walras, L. (1874). *Elements of Pure Economics.* English edition (1954) (ed. by W. Jaffé). London; Allen & Unwin

Webb, R. H. (1979). Wage–price restraint and macroeconomic disequilibrium. *Federal Reserve Bank of Richmond Economic Review* **65, No. 3,** 14–25

Weintraub, E. R. (1979). *Microfoundations.* Cambridge; Cambridge University Press

Williamson, O. E. (1975). *Market and Hierarchies.* New York; Free Press

4

The measurement of different types of unemployment

4.1 Introduction[1]

This chapter examines the possibility of dividing aggregate unemployment into separate and clearly distinguishable categories. The major purpose of categorizing the unemployed is to provide information that will help the policy-maker devise more effective methods of reducing unemployment. The effectiveness of government action in dealing with unemployment depends crucially upon a thorough understanding of the nature of unemployment. This provides the rationale for attempting to distinguish between different types of unemployment.

Interest in categorizing the unemployed gained momentum with the publication of the *General Theory* by J. M. Keynes in 1936. Although this placed considerable emphasis on the deficiency in the aggregate demand for goods and services, this was considered to be only one of several possible causes of unemployment. In a Treasury memorandum in 1942, Keynes suggested the following five-fold categorization of the unemployed[2]:

(1) a hard core of unemployables;
(2) seasonal unemployment;
(3) unemployment caused by workers moving between jobs;
(4) unemployment caused by either a skill or a geographical mismatch between unemployment and job vacancies;
(5) unemployment caused by a deficiency in aggregate effective demand for labour.

This classification lies at the heart of the method of categorizing the unemployed that is discussed and evaluated in this chapter. This method is referred to in the literature as the $U-V$ method since it relies on unemployment and vacancy data.

The $U-V$ method divides unemployment into three main components: a demand-deficient component, a frictional component, and a structural component. The approach can be extended by dividing the structural component into three further categories: a geographical component, an occupational component and a mixed occu-pational/geographical component[3].

A number of other attempts have been made to categorize the unemployed using the post-Keynesian distinction between demand-deficient unemployment and unemployment caused by other factors. In a regional analysis of unemployment in Great Britain, Brechling (1967) attempted to measure the extent to which each region's unemployment was related to fluctuations in national unemployment and how far it could be explained by the underlying regional unemployment trends. Work along similar lines has been undertaken for sub-regions in the North West by Campbell (1975). However, this chapter is concerned with the more widely used $U-V$ method of classifying unemployment, and not with the other post-Keynesian methods.

In Section 4.2, the theoretical foundations of the $U-V$ method are examined. A numerical example is used, in Section 4.3, to demonstrate the way in which the $U-V$ method measures the various categories of unemployment. This is followed in Section 4.4 by an empirical analysis of unemployment in Great Britain for the period 1963–1979. Finally, the main problems faced by the $U-V$ method are discussed in Section 4.5. These problems are of a serious nature and the estimates provided in this chapter indicate only broad orders of magnitude of the various types of unemployment. A substantial gap still remains between the estimates provided by the $U-V$ method and the kind of accurate, finely-disaggregated categorization that would be most useful to policy-makers. The $U-V$ method, however, continues to have considerable potential for further development.

4.2 The theoretical basis of the $U-V$ method

The $U-V$ method of categorizing the unemployed stems from the work of Dow and Dicks-Mireaux (1958) who showed that unem-ployment and vacancies exhibited a distinct inverse relationship during the 1950s.

Two quite distinct routes can be taken to derive the $U-V$ relationship. Hansen (1970), for example, begins with a simple classical labour market characterized by 'well-behaved' demand and supply functions for labour. He then argues that the presence of various frictions leads to the simultaneous existence of unemploy-ment and vacancies irrespective of whether there exists excess demand or excess supply in the labour market. Even when the demand for labour greatly exceeds supply, unemployment will exist because some workers will be in the process of changing their jobs

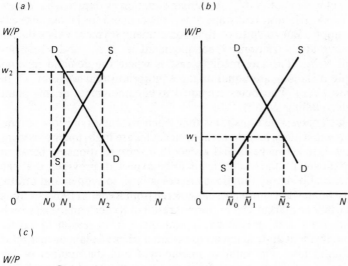

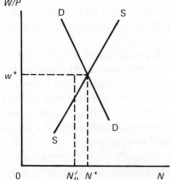

Figure 4.1 *The demand for labour, the supply of labour, unemployment and vacancies in a simple classical labour market.* DD = *demand for labour;* SS = *supply of labour;* N = *employment;* W/P = *real wage*

or because new workers are entering the labour force. Similarly, vacancies will exist even when the supply of labour greatly exceeds demand. This situation is depicted in *Figure 4.1*, which shows a simple classical labour market in which the real wage is a major determinant of the demand for and supply of labour. At the 'high' real wage of w_2 in *Figure 4.1(a)*, the demand for labour is N_1 and the supply of labour is N_2. The level of employment is not, however, at N_1 since employers still have vacant jobs to fill because of labour market frictions, with the result that the actual level of employment is at N_0. With employment at N_0, there exist N_0N_1 vacant jobs and unemployment of $N_0 N_2$. A similar situation is depicted in *Figure 4.1(b)*. At the 'low' real wage of w_1, the demand for labour exceeds the supply. But in spite of this, some unemployment exists due to labour market frictions. Unemployment is $\bar{N}_0 \bar{N}_1$, and vacancies equal $\bar{N}_0 \bar{N}_2$. The intermediate case is where the demand for and supply of labour are equal at the equilibrium real wage of w^* in *Figure 4.1(c)*. Vacancies are equal to unemployment at this point (both equalling $N_0' N^*$).

This analysis demonstrates that when vacancies are low, unemployment is high; and that when vacancies are high, unemployment is low. Hansen suggests that a smooth inverse relationship between unemployment and vacancies is to be expected, provided that the demand and supply functions are not subject to sudden and erratic shifts. Somewhat similar results emerge from Reder's (1969) analysis of the labour market. An important result of Reder's analysis, which differs from that of Hansen, is that there is no reason to expect unemployment and vacancies to be equal when the labour market is in equilibrium. The number unemployed and the number of job vacancies are the outcome of different forces and will be equal, in a situation of labour market equilibrium, only by chance. This problem is discussed later, in Section 4.5.

An alternative derivation of the U–V relationship is available. A smooth inverse relationship between unemployment and vacancies can be obtained from the assumption that the demand for labour is determined by the planned level of output. The driving force behind this Keynesian approach is the proposition that both unemployment and vacancies depend critically upon the effective demand for goods and services. As output rises in response to an increase in the demand for goods and services, employment expands and unemployment will consequently fall. The negative relationship between unemployment, U, and output, Q, is depicted in quadrant A of *Figure 4.2*. Notice that this is a non-linear relationship because, irrespective of the level of output, there will always be some unemployment resulting from labour market frictions. A change in any other determinant of unemployment would cause the entire function to shift its position. These other determinants are assumed to remain unchanged for the present. Vacancies are also assumed to depend upon the effective demand for goods, and this relationship will be positive since employers will search for additional labour as the demand for goods and services increases. A simple linear relationship is assumed in quadrant B of *Figure 4.2*. As with unemployment, the other determinants of vacancies that affect the position of the schedule are held constant.

It is a simple matter to derive the U–V relationship once the unemployment and vacancy functions are known. With output at

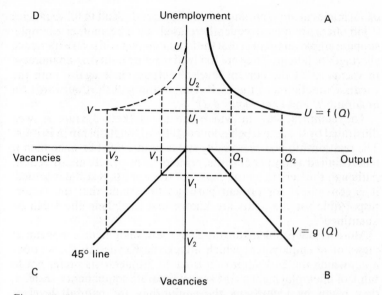

Figure 4.2 *Derivation of the* U–V *relationship using the output-based approach.*

Note *This derivation of the* U–V *function can be transformed into a relationship between the unemployment* rate *and the vacancy* rate *(i.e. expressing unemployment and vacancies as percentages of the workforce) by simply replacing* U *and* V *by their respective rates and by using output relative to some 'norm' such as the underlying trend growth of output*

Q_1, unemployment is U_2 and vacancies are V_1; and similarly for output level Q_2, which is associated with unemployment and vacancies at U_1 and V_2 respectively. The U–V relationship is depicted in quadrant D.

It is worth noting that if either the unemployment function or the vacancy function shifts, the U–V function will also shift. These shifts could occur for a number of reasons. One possibility is that the labour market may become more efficient if information about unfilled vacancies improves. This would cause the unemployment function to shift downwards (in quadrant A of *Figure 4.2*). Working in the opposite direction, a reduction in the cost of searching for jobs (due perhaps to a substantial increase in unemployment benefit) could be expected to shift the unemployment function upwards, as a result of the unemployed spending longer searching for improved job offers. Any such outward shift in the unemployment function necessarily leads to an outward shift in the U–V relationship. Shifts in the vacancy function will also lead to shifts in the U–V relationship. Higher unemployment benefit, for example, may not only raise unemployment but may simultaneously increase the stock of vacancies at any time since it will be more difficult to fill vacancies if job offers are more frequently refused. To take another example, suppose employers expect that the labour market will soon experience shortages of labour. They are likely to react by notifying an increase in vacancies at the current level of output. Once again, both the vacancy function and the $U-V$ relationship will shift outwards (in quadrants B and D of *Figure 4.2*).

The complex way in which labour markets operate is well illustrated by the actual behaviour of the $U-V$ relationship in Britain. The relationship was reasonably stable until 1966, but since then it has exhibited a number of shifts, principally in an outward direction. Although the debate on the causes of these shifts is still not settled, it is convenient for present purposes to assume that the factors responsible for the shifts are known and that their effect can be quantified[4].

More serious problems are raised by the development of monetarist views of unemployment which attack the Keynesian foundations upon which the $U-V$ approach is based. Monetarists prefer not to think of unemployment as the sum of separate components. Instead, they begin by identifying the equilibrium (or natural) level of unemployment. Actual unemployment can differ in the short run from its equilibrium level, but natural market forces (given an adequate degree of wage and price flexibility) will pull unemployment back towards its equilibrium level in the long run. The concept of the natural rate of unemployment and attempts to measure it are considered at length in Chapter 7 of this book[5]. Alternative macroeconomic approaches are examined in Chapter 3.

4.3 The use of unemployment and vacancy data

This section describes how the $U-V$ method can be used to divide the unemployed into different categories. In order to explain the method as simply as possible, a numerical example has been constructed in which there are only three regions and three occupations. Further details are provided in an Appendix to this chapter.

By matching existing unemployment with existing vacancies, it is possible to divide the registered unemployed into five separate categories. The five categories are as follows.

(1) Unemployment due to a deficiency in the aggregate demand for labour, namely demand-deficient unemployment, denoted DD.
(2) Unemployment due to labour market frictions within each labour market, namely frictional unemployment, F.

(3) Unemployment due to a geographical mis-match between the demand for and supply of labour, namely the geographical component of structural unemployment, S_g.
(4) Unemployment due to an occupational mis-match between the demand for and supply of labour, namely the occupational component of structural unemployment, S_o.
(5) Unemployment due to the simultaneous existence of a geographical *and* an occupational mis-match between the demand for and supply of labour, namely the simultaneous occupational–geographical component of structural unemployment, S_{og}.

Total unemployment U is simply the sum of these five categories:

$$U = DD + F + S_g + S_o + S_{og}$$

The demand-deficient component

Demand-deficient unemployment occurs when the aggregate level of demand is 'too low' in the sense that the supply of labour exceeds the demand for labour. The $U-V$ method assumes that the supply of and demand for labour are in equilibrium when national unemployment equals national vacancies. Demand-deficient unemployment therefore emerges only when unemployment exceeds vacancies in the economy as a whole, and will be zero if unemployment is equal to or less than vacancies. Two broad categories of unemployment are therefore identified:

$$\left. \begin{array}{l} \text{Demand-deficient unemployment } (DD) = U - V \\ \text{Non-demand-deficient unemployment} \\ \quad (\text{non-}DD) \qquad\qquad\qquad\qquad = V \end{array} \right\} \text{ if } U > V$$

and

$$\left. \begin{array}{l} \text{Demand-deficient unemployment } (DD) = 0 \\ \text{Non-demand-deficient unemployment} \\ \quad (\text{non-}DD) \qquad\qquad\qquad\qquad = U \end{array} \right\} \text{ if } V \geqslant U$$

A number of examples are illustrated in *Figure 4.3*. In (*a*), it is assumed that $U = 2000$ when $V = 500$ so that $DD = 1500$ and non-$DD = 500$. In case (*b*), $U = V = 1000$ so that $DD = 0$ and non-$DD = 1000$. In case (*c*), $U = 500$ when $V = 2000$ so that $DD = 0$ and non-$DD = 500$.

An interesting and certainly rather odd feature of this method of dividing the unemployed into demand-deficient and non-demand-deficient components is the behaviour of the latter. Non-demand-deficient unemployment is low both in periods of depressed demand and in periods of high demand, reaching its maximum level when

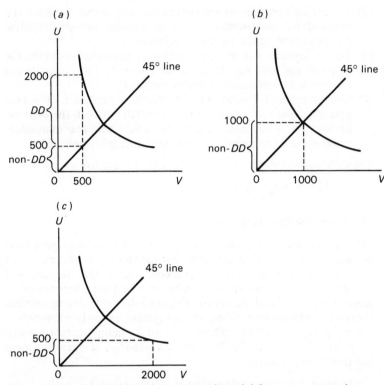

Figure 4.3 *The division of unemployment into a demand-deficient component and a non-demand-deficient component. DD = demand-deficient component of unemployment; non-DD = non-demand-deficient component of unemployment*

unemployment and vacancies are equal. Since non-demand-deficient unemployment arises from various kinds of labour market frictions, it seems reasonable to expect it to fall in response to the increase of new job opportunities during periods of high demand. But the above numerical example reveals that non-demand-deficient unemployment also falls during recessions, this time because of the reduction in vacancies. As vacancies fall during a recession, the mis-match between unemployment and vacancies inevitably declines and an increasing proportion of the unemployed become classified in the demand-deficient category.

An alternative and more plausible interpretation is that non-demand-deficient unemployment does not fall during recessions but merely becomes concealed by the general lack of vacancies, and as a result is wrongly attributed to the demand-deficient component. As demand expands and vacancies once again begin to increase, the mis-match between unemployment and vacancies will reappear. If the U–V method is to be a useful aid for formulating manpower policy, such 'quirks' must be removed from the measurement of the components of unemployment. For example, during a period of expanding demand, the policy-maker requires forecasts of the mis-match that will arise because of structural bottlenecks in the economy. It is therefore necessary to modify the above method. This is done by first identifying the level of unemployment and vacancies at which the labour market is in balance. *Figure 4.4* shows that an equality of unemployment and vacancies occurs when $U = V = 1000$ (as shown by intersection of the 45° line with the U–V relationship). Demand-deficient unemployment is now defined as the excess of unemployment over the level of unemployment *where $U = V$ on the 45° line*. Call this level of unemployment $\bar{U}$. The two components are now given by the following definitions:

Demand-deficient unemployment $(DD) = U - \bar{U}$
Non-demand-deficient unemployment $\quad$ if $U > V$
$\quad$ (non-DD) $\qquad\qquad = \bar{U}$

and

Demand-deficient unemployment $(DD) = 0$
Non-demand-deficient unemployment $\quad$ if $V \geqslant U$
$\quad$ (non-DD) $\qquad\qquad = \bar{U}$

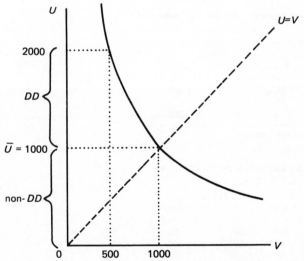

Figure 4.4 *The division of unemployment into a demand-deficient component and a non-demand-deficient component: an alternative approach*

There are difficulties in obtaining an accurate estimate of $\bar{U}$. Many labour markets may never actually experience a situation in which $U = V$, as was the case for males during the period 1963–1979. In such circumstances, estimates of the point at which $U = V$ may be obtained by extrapolating the relationship between unemployment and vacancies[6]. This device can only be applied, however, if the relationship between unemployment and vacancies is stable, or if shifts in the relationship can be adequately explained.

Disaggregation of the non-demand-deficient component

Once the demand-deficient component of unemployment has been measured, the remaining non-demand-deficient unemployment can be subdivided into four separate categories by a simple process of matching unemployment with vacancies. The method is illustrated by the hypothetical example in *Tables 4.1* and *4.2*, which display an unemployment matrix and a vacancy matrix for an economy with three occupations and three regions. For convenience, total unemployment and total vacancies are set at 1000, so that there is no need to estimate the level of unemployment at which $U = V$. This assumption is made in order to simplify the explanation of how the non-demand-deficient components can be enumerated. For simplicity, it is also assumed that there is perfect geographical mobility *within* each of the three regions.

Table 4.1   Unemployment   matrix: a   numerical illustration

| Occupation | | Region | |
	South	Midlands	North
Professional	50	50	100
Skilled	50	50	150
Unskilled	250	100	200

Total unemployment = 1000

Table 4.2 Vacancy matrix: a numerical illustration

| Occupation | | Region | |
	South	Midlands	North
Professional	300	100	100
Skilled	150	100	50
Unskilled	100	50	50

Total vacancies = 1000

Frictional unemployment is defined to exist when unemployment and vacant jobs occur simultaneously in the same occupation *and* in the same region. It is measured by matching the unemployed and the vacancies within each occupational/regional cell. For example, since 50 unemployed persons co-exist with 300 vacancies in the professional group in the South, there are 50 frictionally unemployed persons in this particular cell of the unemployment matrix. A different situation prevails amongst unskilled workers in the North, where only 50 vacancies exist for the 200 unemployed. In this case, only 50 frictionally unemployed exist in this particular cell of the unemployment matrix. Frictional unemployment is therefore obtained by taking the smaller of the two numbers in the corresponding cells of the unemployment and vacancy matrices. *Table 4.3* contains the numbers frictionally unemployed in each occupational/regional cell.

Table 4.3 Frictional unemployment matrix

| Occupation | Region | | |
	South	Midlands	North
Professional	50	50	100
Skilled	50	50	50
Unskilled	100	50	50

Frictional unemployment = 550

The unemployment that remains after the frictionally unemployed have been measured consists of those persons registered as unemployed for whom a vacant job does not simultaneously exist in their own occupation and their own region. Sufficient vacancies exist, but unemployed persons are unable to fill these vacancies either because of an occupational mis-match or because of a geographical mis-match.

Three distinct types of structural unemployment can be identified. If vacant jobs exist in other occupations but within the same region as an unemployed person, the unemployed person is classified in the occupational component of structural unemployment (S_o). If vacant jobs exist in other regions requiring the same occupational skills as an unemployed person, that person is classified in the geographical component of structural unemployment (S_g). Finally, vacant jobs may exist for some of the unemployed persons, but they may be in a different occupational category as well as being in a different region. These persons are classified in the simultaneous occupational/geographical component of structural unemployment (S_{og}).

The three components of structural unemployment can be measured by using a 'matching-up' procedure. First, matrices of 'residual unemployment' and 'residual vacancies' are constructed. The residual unemployment-matrix is obtained by subtracting each cell in the fictional unemployment matrix (*Table 4.3*) from the corresponding cell in the original unemployment matrix (*Table 4.1*). Similarly, the residual vacancies matrix is obtained by subtracting each cell in the frictional unemployment matrix from the corresponding cell in the original vacancy matrix (*Table 4.2*). These two residual matrices are given in *Tables 4.4* and *4.5*.

Table 4.4 Unemployment remaining after frictional unemployment has been enumerated

Occupation		Region	
	South	Midlands	North
Professional	0	0	0
Skilled	0	0	100
Unskilled	150	50	150

Structural unemployment = 450

Table 4.5 Vacancies remaining after frictional unemployment has been enumerated

Occupation		Region	
	South	Midlands	North
Professional	250	50	0
Skilled	100	50	0
Unskilled	0	0	0

Structural vacancies = 450

The total residual unemployment of 450 given in *Table 4.4* consists entirely of structural unemployment since there exist 450 residual vacancies. This structural unemployment of 450 can be subdivided into its three component parts by matching the residual unemployment with the residual vacancies. The geographical component of structural unemployment is obtained by matching the unemployed (within each occupation) with vacancies existing in other regions (within the same occupation). Thus, the remaining 100 unemployed persons in the skilled category in the North are matched with the vacancies for skilled workers in the Midlands and the South. Since the vacancies available for skilled persons exceed the number of skilled persons unemployed, it is necessary to decide how the 100 unemployed skilled persons are to be allocated between the 150 vacancies. The most obvious solution is to distribute the unemployed between the vacancies on a *pro rata* basis. Thus, the 100 skilled persons who are unemployed in the North are matched with 67 of the 100 vacancies for skilled workers in the South and with 33 of the 50 vacancies for skilled workers in the Midlands. Since vacancies only exist in the same occupation for persons in the North's skilled category of unemployment, the geographical component of structural unemployment (S_g) is exactly 100.

Matching unemployed persons with vacancies on a *pro rata* basis is an arbitrary procedure. In particular, it takes no account of the relative costs or benefits of matching the skilled unemployed persons in the North with vacancies in the Midlands and the South. For example, it may be more efficient to match the 50 skilled vacancies in the Midlands with 50 of the skilled unemployed in the North and then match the remaining 50 skilled unemployed in the North with 50 of the 100 skilled vacancies in the South. This would be equivalent to giving the North–Midlands matching a higher probability than the North–South matching of unemployed and vacancies. Unfortunately, little is yet known concerning the relative costs and benefits of matching the unemployed and the vacancies in different regions. There is no obvious alternative to the *pro rata* procedure of matching unemployment and vacancies according to the regional distribution of vacancies.

Having identified the 100 members of the geographical component of structural unemployment (S_g), there remain 350 unemployed persons. These are all unskilled. No residual vacancies exist for unskilled workers in any region, which means that some form of occupational retraining would be necessary if this unemployment were to be removed. The final step is to divide these remaining 350 structurally-unemployed into the occupational category and the simultaneous occupational/geographical category. As can be seen in *Table 4.4*, the remaining 350 unskilled unemployed are dispersed between the three regions. The remaining 350 vacancies are either in the professional category (300) or in the skilled category (50). The 150 unskilled unemployed in the South and the 50 unskilled unemployed in the Midlands can in theory be retrained to take up either the remaining professional vacancies or the remaining skilled vacancies without having to move to another region. These constitute the occupational component of structural unemployment (S_o):

$$S_o = 150 + 50 = 200$$

The last remaining category of unemployment consists entirely of unskilled workers in the North. The elimination of this group would

require both retraining and relocation, for the remaining vacancies
are neither in the unskilled category nor in the North:

$$S_{og} = 150$$

In summary, the following categories of unemployment have been
enumerated:

Demand-deficient unemployment	0
Frictional unemployment	550
Structural unemployment:	
geographical component	100
occupational component	200
mixed occupational/geographical component	150
	1000

4.4 Application of the $U-V$ method to Britain, 1963–1979

Great Britain is fortunate in having detailed statistics for both
unemployment and vacancies stretching back many years. (These
are described in Chapter 8 of this book.) The Department of
Employment collects data on unemployment and vacancies recorded
at Employment Offices and Job Centres. Both unemployment and
vacancy data are available on a quarterly basis by occupation and by
region for Great Britain since 1963. September figures are used
throughout this study in order to minimize the problems posed by
seasonal variations.

Since 1973, unemployment and vacancy data have been available
for 396 occupations and 10 regions. A total of 3960 labour market
'cells' can therefore be identified. Since 1976, it has not been possible
to apply the method to males and females separately, since vacancy
data are now available only for males and females jointly.

The results of applying the method described in the previous
section to the unemployment and vacancy data for Great Britain are
given in *Tables 4.6–4.8* for the period of 1963–1979[7]. Peak year
estimates, such as those for 1965/66 and 1973/74 are more useful
because of the considerable reductions in vacancies during recessions. It can be seen that demand-deficient unemployment was the
predominant component for males even in peak years, frictional
unemployment being the second most important component.
Although structural unemployment was small for males, the
occupational component accounted for 25% of total male unemployment in 1966 and for over 16% in 1973. Both the geographical

Table 4.6 Male unemployment by category: 1963–1975 (in thousands)

Year	Demand-deficient	Frictional	Geographical	Occupational	Occ./Geog.
1963	226.5	53.1	8.0	16.8	0.0
1964	98.5	62.3	10.3	48.2	3.7
1965	61.6	71.6	9.5	51.3	15.5
1966	97.5	72.2	5.4	54.0	0.9
1967	303.3	73.3	6.0	10.7	0.0
1968	325.9	78.5	6.0	10.7	0.0
1969	318.5	81.2	6.2	20.8	0.0
1970	352.2	85.3	5.3	13.5	0.0
1971	562.5	60.8	2.0	3.2	0.0
1972	562.1	78.9	6.5	3.1	0.0
1973	226.8	120.9	19.3	72.0	0.2
1974	315.0	122.1	14.3	50.5	0.0
1975	740.3	76.9	2.5	2.4	0.0

See notes to Table *4.8*.

Table 4.7 Female unemployment by category: 1963–1975 (in thousands)

Year	Demand-deficient	Frictional	Geographical	Occupational	Occ./Geog.
1963	14.1	39.9	15.6	13.7	10.3
1964	0.0	40.1	15.6	9.0	5.5
1965	0.0	38.4	12.2	7.7	1.3
1966	0.0	36.6	10.6	7.8	2.1
1967	0.0	44.7	11.0	13.3	14.5
1968	0.0	43.7	9.2	11.5	7.0
1969	0.0	42.5	8.8	12.1	5.9
1970	0.0	41.8	8.6	14.1	10.6
1971	45.6	37.2	7.6	11.8	2.2
1972	48.4	42.9	10.2	10.7	5.4
1973	0.0	48.1	14.3	17.2	2.0
1974	0.0	50.3	9.0	25.5	15.7
1975	164.8	47.7	2.7	8.2	0.0

See notes to *Table 4.8*.

Table 4.8 Total unemployment by category: 1976–1979 (in thousands)

Year	Demand-deficient	Frictional	Geographical	Occupational	Occ./Geog.
1976	1063.1	136.1	2.0	1.3	0.0
1977	1153.2	153.8	3.6	1.5	0.0
1978	1021.1	216.9	10.6	3.6	0.0
1979	910.0	227.5	17.7	6.3	0.0

Notes
1. The 1963–1972 results are not strictly comparable with the 1973–1979 results since the former are based upon 105 occupational classes whereas the latter are based upon 396 occupational classes.
2. Since 1976, vacancies have not been specified for males and females separately. The division by sex is therefore available only until 1975.
3. Demand-deficient unemployment is measured as $DD = U - V$, if $U > V$; and $DD = 0$, if $V \geqslant U$.

component and the occupational/geographical component were small even during peak years.

The distribution of female unemployment between the five components differed markedly from that experienced by males, the major difference being that demand-deficient unemployment reached zero for females even in many non-peak years. Although this may have been due to a rapid increase in the demand for females during the 1960s, it is possible that the different pattern of female unemployment may have been due to the failure of females to register their unemployment. If this were so, the true level of demand-deficient unemployment would be underestimated by the application of the $U-V$ method to the female unemployment and vacancy data. As far as the distribution of unemployment between the non-demand-deficient components is concerned, the greater relative importance of the geographical and occupational/geographical components for females may partly be a consequence of the low geographical mobility of married women workers.

An interesting extra dimension to the unemployment problem is obtained by examining the relative importance of each component at regional level. *Table 4.9* provides a summary of the regional

Table 4.9 The distribution of each category of unemployment within the GB regions (1973/74 average, September each year)

Regional group	Components of male unemployment (%)					Total unemployment	
	Demand-deficient	Fric-tional	Occupa-tional	Geo-graphical	Occ./Geog.	(%)	('000)
Central	31.6	40.9	26.3	1.2	0.0	100	340.3
Intermediate	69.0	19.9	7.4	3.7	0.0	100	311.4
Depressed	75.9	14.6	3.4	6.2	0.0	100	289.6

Regional group	Components of female unemployment (%)					Total unemployment	
	Demand-deficient	Fric-tional	Occupa-tional	Geo-graphical	Occ./Geog.	(%)	('000)
Central	0.0	69.5	22.8	4.5	3.2	100	61.7
Intermediate	0.0	55.3	29.8	8.9	6.0	100	54.9
Depressed	0.0	38.3	18.7	24.0	19.0	100	65.5

Notes
1. Unemployment in each category is expressed as a percentage of total unemployment in each region.
2. The regional estimates of the various components of unemployment were obtained by extending the method described in Section 4.3. This extension involves the creation of further unemployment and vacancy matrices after the frictional, occupational and geographical components have been enumerated for each region. As explained in Section 4.3, the unemployed are matched with vacancies on a *pro rata* basis.

results. The years 1973/74 were chosen because they are the most recent years during which a peak occurred in the total number of vacancies. The demand for labour has been so low since 1973/74 that the full extent of non-demand-deficient unemployment cannot be assessed because of the scarcity of vacancies. Regions with similar patterns of unemployment have been grouped together so that the regional results can be more easily digested. Three distinct groups are identified: the 'central' regions, consisting of the South East, East Anglia, East Midlands and West Midlands; the 'intermediate' regions, consisting of the South West, the North West, and Yorkshire and Humberside; and the 'depressed' regions, consisting of the North, Scotland and Wales.

For both the intermediate and depressed regions, most of the male unemployment falls into the demand-deficient component. In the central regions, the frictional component is predominant, followed by the demand-deficient component. The situation is different for females. The frictional component is by far the largest single category in all regions, reaching 38.3% even in depressed regions.

Table 4.10 The distribution of each category of unemployment between the GB regions (1973/74 average, September each year)

Regional group	Components of male unemployment (%)				
	Demand-deficient	Frictional	Occupational	Geographical	Occupational/geographical
Central	19.8	57.2	73.1	12.5	12.9
Intermediate	39.6	25.5	18.9	34.4	41.6
Depressed	40.6	17.3	8.0	53.1	45.5
Total (%)	100.0	100.0	100.0	100.0	100.0
(thousands)	542.0	243.0	122.5	33.6	0.2

Regional group	Components of female unemployment (%)				
	Demand-deficient	Frictional	Occupational	Geographical	Occupational/geographical
Central	0	43.6	33.0	11.9	11.0
Intermediate	0	30.9	38.3	20.8	18.7
Depressed	0	25.5	28.7	67.3	70.3
Total (%)	0	100.0	100.0	100.0	100.0
(thousands)	0.0	98.4	42.7	23.3	17.7

Notes
1. Unemployment in each category is expressed as a percentage of GB unemployment in the same category.
2. See note 2 to *Table 4.9*.

This is probably a reflection of the geographical immobility of female workers within each region. If this is so, much of the frictional unemployment for females should be treated as part of the geographical component of structural unemployment.

Finally, it is interesting to examine the way in which national unemployment in each category is distributed between the three regional groups. This is shown in *Table 4.10*. For males, demand-deficient unemployment and the geographical and occupational/geographical components of structural unemployment are heavily concentrated in the intermediate and depressed regions, whereas the central regions have nearly three quarters of the occupational unemployment. The striking feature of the female results is the concentration of geographical and occupational/geographical unemployment in the depressed regions.

4.5 Problems to be overcome

The object of dividing the unemployed into separate categories is to provide the policy-maker with useful information about the nature of the problem so that appropriate policies can be devised. At first sight, the $U-V$ method is an attractive device for achieving this objective since the unemployed can be divided into five distinct categories, each of which suggests a distinct type of policy response. But as with all empirical work of this kind, the method relies heavily upon a number of arbitrary assumptions. This section examines the most vulnerable aspects of the $U-V$ approach and points the way towards the emendment and future development of this technique.

The $U-V$ method begins by assuming that equilibrium in the labour market occurs when total unemployment equals total vacancies. But as pointed out in Section 4.2, there is no sound justification for this assumption. If, for example, the output level of Q_1 in *Figure 4.2* were consistent with a situation of equilibrium in the labour market, the associated levels of unemployment, U_2, and vacancies, V_1, are such that unemployment exceeds vacancies. In practice, these equilibrium values of unemployment and vacancies are unknown. Indeed, the combination of unemployment and vacancies at which the economy can be said to be in equilibrium is likely to change over time owing to shifts in either the unemployment function or the vacancy function. While this does not affect the actual calculation of the components of unemployment, it could make it virtually pointless to analyse changes in the components over time.

Although there have been several attempts to explain the shifts in the U–V relationship since 1966, the problem remains unsolved. Some researchers, such as Maki and Spindler (1975), have argued that one of the major causes of the upward trend in unemployment associated with the outward shifting of the U–V relationship is the increase in unemployment benefit relative to net income. Other researchers, such as Taylor (1972), Feldstein (1973) and Brown (1976), have argued that unemployment has risen because firms have become less willing to hoard labour during recessions than was the case before the mid 1960s. This debate has obvious implications for the U–V method, which relies heavily upon a stable, or at least predictable, relationship between total unemployment and total vacancies. Further progress towards an understanding of this relationship may require a more detailed analysis of the relationship between stocks and flows rather than concentrating entirely on stocks as is the case with the present method. Attention will have to be paid to the flows of workers between various parts of the labour market and the effect of these flows on the unemployment and vacancy stocks[8].

The second serious problem comes from the sequential manner in which the various categories of non-demand-deficient unemployment are calculated. As shown in Section 4.3, the method proceeds by estimating the frictional component, the geographical component, the occupational component and finally the occupational/geographical component *in that order*. It is not obvious at first sight why the individual components of non-demand-deficient unemployment should be calculated in this particular order, though it is possible to seek justification on the grounds that some types of unemployment are easier to eliminate than others and should therefore be the first to be allocated to the available vacancies. Frictional unemployment, for example, is arguably easier to eliminate than the occupational/geographical component of unemployment. Whereas vacancies exist in the same occupation and the same region for the frictionally unemployed, this is not the case for the occupationally/geographically unemployed who happen to be in the 'wrong' occupation and the 'wrong' region simultaneously. But it is not clear that the elimination of the geographical component will always be more efficient than the elimination of the occupational component, as is implied by calculating the geographical component before the occupational component. In some cases, it may be more efficient to eliminate unemployment by retraining workers and matching them with jobs within their own region than by inducing a geographical movement of workers or jobs.

It is easy to demonstrate that a different sequence would give different results. In Section 4.4, estimates of the various components

Table 4.11 The effect of altering the sequence in the calculation of the individual components of unemployment (1973/74)

Components of unemployment	Males		Females	
	Sequence 1 (%)	Sequence 2 (%)	Sequence 1 (%)	Sequence 2 (%)
Demand-deficient	57.6	57.6	0.0	0.0
Frictional	25.8	25.8	54.0	54.0
Structural				
geographical	3.6	0.7	12.8	8.6
occupational	13.0	15.3	23.4	26.5
occ./geog.	0.0	0.6	9.7	10.9
Total	100	100	100	100

Note
Sequence 1 calculates the geographical component of structural unemployment before the occupational component. Sequence 2 does the opposite.

of structural unemployment were produced on the basis of the assumption that it is preferable in all cases to eliminate the geographical mis-match before the occupational and the occupational/geographical components. Suppose, however, that it could be shown that it is preferable in all cases to eliminate the occupational mis-match within regions before the geographical mis-match. It is now necessary to reverse the sequence in which the geographical and occupational components are calculated. The results of reversing the sequence for 1973/74 are given in *Table 4.11*. The relative importance of the geographical component falls whereas the reverse is true for the occupational component.

The sensitivity of the results to changing the sequence is not great, but altering the sequence of the calculation of the components may unfortunately only scratch the surface of this problem. By simply reversing the sequence of two of the categories, it is assumed that the elimination of the occupational mis-match is preferable *in all cases* to eliminating the geographical mis-match. Clearly, this cannot be true. In some cases retraining will be the appropriate policy, while in others migration or industrial relocation policies will be appropriate. A better solution to this problem is to obtain estimates of the most efficient method of eliminating unemployment from any particular cell of the unemployment matrix. This suggests that more information about the efficiency of alternative methods of matching unemployment and vacancies is required. Without this information, the $U–V$ method will continue to be plagued by the problems arising from the arbitrary assumptions that are at present embedded in the sequential nature of the calculations.

The third problem with the method concerns the identification of occupational and regional labour markets. A labour market can be defined as an occupational/geographical entity within which there is perfect labour mobility. Mobility between labour markets is, however, constrained in the short run by frictions: skill requirements prevent the free movement of workers from one occupation to another, and geographical mobility is impeded by a host of factors that can be grouped under the general heading of 'friction of distance'. The categorization of the unemployed therefore suffers from the lack of correspondence between the set of theoretically ideal labour markets and the set of labour markets that are identified by the data. For example, the application of the $U-V$ method in Section 4.4 used unemployment and vacancy data collected for the ten standard regions of Great Britain and for 396 occupational categories for the period 1973–1979.

The division of the aggregate labour market into 3960 separate markets may seem at first sight to provide an adequate disaggregation for the application of the $U-V$ method. It is easily demonstrated, however, that this is not the case. The frictional component is seriously overestimated in practice because of the inadequacy of the geographical subdivision of the data. The ten standard regions of Great Britain are far too large. The Department of Employment defines a travel-to-work area as one within which at least 75% of the area's workers also live. This definition gives rise to 380 separate geographical labour markets[9]. The consequence of defining the geographical limits of a labour market by using the boundaries of the ten standard regions is that a large but unknown proportion of those classified as frictionally unemployed should be counted as part of the geographical or occupational/geographical components of structural unemployment. An unemployed engineer in one part of Scotland is thus classified as frictionally unemployed if a vacancy exists for an engineer anywhere else in Scotland, regardless of the distance between the person's residence and the vacancy. The same problem arises with the occupational disaggregation of the unemployment and the vacancy data. Although 396 occupations are identified, the matching of an unemployed person and a vacancy within the same occupational group may still involve substantial retraining costs because the occupational group includes a range of related but different skills. The problem may be compounded if an unemployed person and a vacancy within an occupational group do not belong to the same industry. On the other hand, a disaggregation that is too fine can also pose problems. For example, if there were substantial mobility between two occupational groups it would be better to treat them as a single occupation.

In the absence of an appropriate disaggregation of unemployment

**Table 4.12 The effect of the level of aggregation on the
relative size of the frictional component (1973/74)**

Number of occupations	Number of regions			
	Males		Females	
	1	10	1	10
1	42.4	41.1	100.0	80.5
18	35.2	31.0	75.8	61.2
396	29.4	25.8	66.8	54.0

Note
Each number in the above table is the percentage of total unemployment
falling into the frictional category.

and vacancies, it is only possible to guess at the effect that such a
disaggregation would have on the results. The sensitivity of the
results to the degree of geographical and occupational disaggregation
is demonstrated in *Table 4.12*. With only one geographical area
(Great Britain) but with 396 occupations, the frictional component
of male unemployment accounted for 29.4% of total male unemployment in 1973/74. The figure falls to 25.8% when ten separate regions
are delineated. The corresponding figures for females are 66.8% and
54.0%. Further disaggregation, to the 380 areas defined by the
Department of Employment, would reduce the frictional component
still further. *Table 4.12* also shows that the frictional component of
male unemployment falls from 41.1% when only one occupation is
identified to 31.0% when 18 broad occupational groups are identified,
and finally to 25.8% when all 396 occupations are identified.

Deciding upon the most appropriate level of disaggregation is a
problem that is not easily resolved. Ten regions is certainly
inadequate and the value of the $U-V$ method would be increased by
moving from the ten regions to the 380 areas defined by the
Department of Employment, even though the methods used to
define these local labour markets are rather *ad hoc*[10]. Moreover, the
geographical extent of local labour markets varies between workers
and between occupations. For instance, local labour markets tend to
be geographically smaller for married women than for other workers.
Too fine a disaggregation would result in the opposite problem, for
if the $U-V$ method were applied to data disaggregated to the local
Employment Office level, frictional unemployment would be
underestimated and structural unemployment overestimated. This
would occur where adjacent Employment Office areas were part of
a common labour market area. Since the size of labour market areas
will also tend to differ between occupations, the method would

produce more useful results if geographical labour markets were delineated for each occupation separately.

Further problems arise from the inaccuracy of the unemployment and vacancy data. It is known that not all unemployed persons are registered as unemployed[11]. This applies to both males and females, though the problem is more severe for females since many unemployed married women have little incentive to join the unemployment register because a large proportion of them are not entitled to unemployment benefit[12]. Little is known about the accuracy of the vacancy data, though it is generally agreed that the true level of vacancies substantially exceeds the recorded level. A survey by the Manpower Services Commission in mid 1977 discovered that only 36% of all unfilled vacancies were officially recorded[13]. This suggests that the vacancy data should be multiplied by a factor of three, a procedure used by Cheshire (1973). The problem with multiplying all vacancies by the same factor is that the extent of the under-recording varies between occupations. For example, the 1977 survey found that 47% of all vacancies for manual workers were recorded compared to 24% for non-manual workers. Moreover, the extent of the under-recording of vacancies varies between regions.

It is interesting to measure the sensitivity of the $U-V$ results to alternative assumptions about the extent of the under-recording. The vacancy matrices for 1973 and 1974 were therefore adjusted upwards, first by a factor of 2 and then by a factor of 3, and the method was then applied to the adjusted data. The results are shown in *Table 4.13*. They demonstrate the dangers of applying the $U-V$ method to data of unknown accuracy. An entirely new picture of the

Table 4.13 The sensitivity of the $U-V$ results to the under-recording of vacancies (1973/74)

Components of unemployment	Males (%)			Females (%)		
	$k=1$	$k=2$	$k=3$	$k=1$	$k=2$	$k=3$
Demand-deficient	57.6	15.1	0.0	0.0	0.0	0.0
Frictional	25.8	37.8	45.7	54.0	69.0	77.3
Structural						
geographical	3.6	3.2	4.3	12.8	15.1	12.0
occupational	13.0	24.7	31.1	23.4	15.9	10.7
occ./geog.	0.0	19.1	18.8	9.7	0.0	0.0
Total	100	100	100	100	100	100

Note
k is the scalar used to multiply the 1973/74 vacancy matrices in order to investigate the sensitivity of the $U-V$ results to various assumptions about the extent to which vacancies are under-recorded.

distribution of unemployment between the five categories is obtained when the vacancy data is adjusted upwards.

A further example of how the inaccurate recording of unemployment or vacancies may have a serious detrimental effect on the application of the method is provided by the possibility that unemployment and vacancies are incorrectly recorded for male labourers. Recorded vacancies for this group are consistently a tiny proportion of the number of registered unemployed male labourers, even during boom years. This could be due either to unemployed males being wrongly categorized as labourers or to the under-recording of vacancies. If vacancies are seriously under-recorded for male labourers, as seems likely, there is good cause to exclude this occupational group from the analysis. When this is done, a completely different picture of the state of the labour market is obtained. The difference between total registered unemployment and total recorded vacancies is substantially lower when male labourers are excluded, indicating a much 'tighter' labour market during periods of high demand than is otherwise observed. This is shown in *Figure 4.5*. The same is not true for females. More surveys of both firms and households are required if accurate adjustment factors are to be obtained.

Finally, it is important to realize that the $U-V$ method does not provide information about all types of unemployment. In particular, seasonal unemployment is not identified by this method.

4.6 Conclusions

The measurement of different types of unemployment is both embryonic and controversial. Whereas some economists would argue that the attempt to divide the unemployed into separate categories is futile and meaningless, others would argue that such attempts are a necessary prerequisite for efficient manpower planning. The latter view has been taken in the present chapter, which has concentrated upon an explanation and evaluation of the $U-V$ method of categorizing the unemployed. While this method undoubtedly faces serious problems in its present form, it could be developed and extended to provide useful information about the nature of the unemployment problem in Great Britain. In particular, it could be developed to produce forecasts of future bottlenecks in the labour market during periods of sustained expansion.

The further development of the method will depend heavily upon two factors. First, it relies critically upon the underlying assumptions

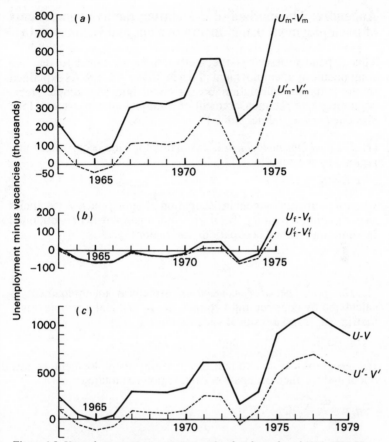

Figure 4.5 *Unemployment minus vacancies: males, females and total 1963–1979.* U = *registered unemployed;* U′ = *registered unemployed excluding labourers;* V = *recorded unfilled vacancies;* V′ = *recorded unfilled vacancies excluding labourers; m, f = males, females*

made about the nature of macroeconomic equilibrium. The definition of macroeconomic equilibrium is intrinsically linked with the concept of labour market equilibrium, which plays such a crucial role in $U–V$ analysis. Secondly, the value of the method relies heavily upon the accuracy of the unemployment and vacancy data. In particular, the reliability of the results is limited by uncertainties concerning the extent of the under-recording of unemployment and vacancies, and by the lack of information on the social costs and benefits of manpower policies. It is suggested here that the potential usefulness of the $U–V$ method in assisting policy formation is substantial enough to justify further research.

Appendix: The method of calculating the five components of unemployment using unemployment and vacancy data

This appendix describes the method used to calculate the five components of unemployment given in *Tables 4.6–4.8*. As explained in the text, the calculation breaks down into five simple steps, beginning with the measurement of frictional unemployment. (See also Gleave and Palmer, 1979.)

(1) *Frictional unemployment* is calculated for each occupation i and region j by the equation

$$f_{ij} = \min(u_{ij}, v_{ij})$$

where u_{ij} = unemployment in occupation i, region j and v_{ij} = vacancies in occupation i, region j. Total frictional unemployment is obtained by summing over all occupations and regions:

$$F = \sum_i \sum_j f_{ij}$$

(2) *The geographical component* of structural unemployment is calculated by constructing two matrices, a residual unemployment matrix, $\{u'_{ij}\}$, and a residual vacancy matrix, $\{v'_{ij}\}$:

$$\{u'_{ij}\} = \{u_{ij}\} - \{f_{ij}\} \qquad \text{and} \qquad \{v'_{ij}\} = \{v_{ij}\} - \{f_{ij}\}$$

The geographical component of structural unemployment is now calculated for each occupation i and region j as follows:

$$g_{ij} = \frac{u'_{ij}}{\sum_j u'_{ij}} \sum_j v'_{ij} \qquad \text{if } \sum_j u'_{ij} > \sum_j v'_{ij} > 0$$

$$= u'_{ij} \qquad \text{if } \sum_j v'_{ij} \geqslant \sum_j u'_{ij} > 0$$

$$= 0 \qquad \text{if either } \sum_j u'_{ij} = 0 \text{ or } \sum_j v'_{ij} = 0$$

Summing over all occupations and regions, the geographical component of structural unemployment is given by

$$S_g = \sum_i \sum_j g_{ij}$$

(3) *The occupational component* of structural unemployment is calculated by constructing two further matrices:

$$\{u''_{ij}\} = \{u'_{ij}\} - \{g_{ij}\} \qquad \{v''_{ij}\} = \{v'_{ij}\} - \{g_{ij}\}$$

The occupational component of structural unemployment, S_0, is now calculated for each occupation i and region j as follows:

$$q_{ij} = \frac{u_{ij}''}{\sum_i u_{ij}''} \sum_i v_{ij}'' \qquad \text{if } \sum_i u_{ij}'' > \sum_i v_{ij}'' > 0$$

$$= u_{ij}'' \qquad \text{if } \sum_i v_{ij}'' \geqslant \sum_i u_{ij}'' > 0$$

$$= 0 \qquad \text{if either } \sum_i u_{ij}'' = 0 \text{ or } \sum_i v_{ij}'' = 0$$

Summing over all occupations and regions, the occupational component of structural unemployment is given by

$$S_o = \sum_i \sum_j q_{ij}$$

(4) *The 'mixed' occupational/geographical* component of structural unemployment, S_{og}, is obtained by allocating any remaining vacancies (after the previous three components have been calculated) to the remaining unemployed:

$$S_{og} = \sum_i \sum_j v_{ij}''' \qquad \text{where} \qquad v_{ij}''' = v_{ij} - f_{ij} - g_{ij} - q_{ij}$$

(5) *The remaining unemployment* after F, S_g, S_o and S_{og} have been enumerated (that is if $U > V$ in aggregate), is attributed to the demand-deficient category:

$$DD = U - F - S_g - S_o - S_{og}$$

Notes

1. We are grateful to Paul Cheshire, Michael Pokorny and Tony Thirlwall for many helpful comments, and to Keith Croston for assistance with the computer programs.
2. See Kahn (1976).
3. See Cheshire (1973), Gleave and Palmer (1979), Hughes (1974), Perlman (1969) and Thirlwall (1969, 1974).
4. Some of the issues are discussed in 'The Changed Relationship between Unemployment and Vacancies', *DE Gazette*, October 1976, pp. 1093–1099.
5. An attempt to measure equilibrium unemployment in the UK has been made by Sumner (1978).
6. Cheshire (1973) fits a log-linear function to the unemployment and vacancy data and then extrapolates to obtain an estimate of the level of unemployment at which unemployment and vacancies are equal.

7. The categories of unemployment given in *Tables 4.6–4.8* were estimated by measuring demand-deficient unemployment as follows: $DD = U - V$ when $U > V$, and $DD = 0$ when $V \geqslant U$. The more widely accepted measure of DD (i.e. $DD = U - \bar{U}$ when $U > V$ and $DD = 0$ when $V \geqslant U$) was not used for two reasons. First, there is the problem of estimating $\bar{U}$. Although methods are available for estimating $\bar{U}$ (*see* Cheshire, 1973; Thirlwall, 1974), the instability of the U–V relationship casts grave doubts on the value of such estimates. Secondly, for years in which $U > V$, it would be necessary to estimate what each cell of the unemployment and vacancy matrices *would* have been if U and V *had* been equal in those years. With 3960 occupational and regional labour market 'cells', this would be a major task. The simpler approach is taken here of drawing conclusions only from peak year estimates (i.e. where U and V come closest to being equal). Fuller details of the method used to obtain the estimates given in *Tables 4.6–4.8* are provided in the appendix to this chapter.

8. See Holt and David (1966), Leicester (1977), and chapter 1, for work on labour market flows.

9. See 'Review of Travel-to-Work Areas', *DE Gazette*, July 1978, pp. 815–816.

10. See Ball (1980).

11. See Evans (1977) for a discussion of changes in the propensity to register during 1961–1971.

12. Hidden female unemployment is discussed in Taylor (1974).

13. The results of the survey are summarized in 'Engagements and Vacancies Survey Results', *DE Gazette*, June 1978, p. 655.

References

Ball, R. M. (1980). The use and definition of travel-to-work areas in Great Britain: Some problems. *Regional Studies* **14**, 125–140

Brechling, F. (1967). Trends and cycles in British regional unemployment. *Oxford Economic Papers* **19**, 1–21

Brown, A. J. (1976). UV Analysis. In *The Concept and Measurement of Involuntary Unemployment* (ed. by G. D. N. Worswick), pp. 134–145. London; Allen & Unwin

Campbell, M. (1975). A spatial and typological disaggregation of unemployment as a guide to regional policy—A case study of NW England, 1959–72. *Regional Studies* **9**, 157–168

Cheshire, P. C. (1973). Regional unemployment differences in Great Britain. *National Institute of Economic and Social Research*, Regional Papers II, pp. 1–40. Cambridge; Cambridge University Press

Dow, J. C. R. and Dicks-Mireaux, L. A. (1958). The excess demand for labour: A study of conditions in Great Britain, 1946–56. *Oxford Economic Papers* **10**, 1–33

Evans, A. (1977). Notes on the changing relationship between registered unemployment and notified vacancies: 1961–71. *Economica* **44**, 179–196

Feldstein, M. (1973). The economics of the new unemployment. *Public Interest* **33**, 3–42

Gleave, D. and Palmer, D. (1979). Spatial variations in unemployment problems: a typology. Paper presented to the European Congress of the Regional Science Association (mimeo)

Hansen, B. (1970). Excess demand, unemployment, vacancies and wages. *Quarterly Journal of Economics* **84**, 1–21

Holt, C. C. and David, M. H. (1966). The concept of job vacancies in a dynamic theory of the labour market. In *The Measurement and Interpretation of Job Vacancies*, National Bureau of Economic Research, pp. 73–110. Columbia University Press

Hughes, J. J. (1974). The use of vacancy statistics in classifying and measuring structural and frictional unemployment in Great Britain, 1958–1972. *Bulletin of Economic Research* **26**, 12–33

Kahn, R. (1976). Unemployment as seen by the Keynesians. In *The Concept and Measurement of Involuntary Unemployment* (ed. by G. D. N. Worswick), pp. 19–34. London; Allen & Unwin

Keynes, J. M. (1936). *The General Theory of Employment, Interest and Money*. London; Macmillan

Leicester, C. (1977). *Flows of Job Seekers through the Unemployment Register*. Institute of Manpower Studies, University of Sussex

Maki, D. R. and Spindler, Z. A. (1975). The effect of unemployment compensation on the rate of unemployment in Great Britain. *Oxford Economic Papers* **27**, 440–454

Perlman, R. (1969). *Labor Theory*. New York; Wiley

Reder, M. W. (1969). The theory of frictional unemployment. *Economica* **36**, 1–28

Sumner, M. T. (1978). Wage determination. In *Inflation in the UK* (ed. by M. Parkin and M. T. Sumner). Manchester; Manchester University Press

Taylor, J. (1972). The behaviour of unemployment and unfilled vacancies: Great Britain, 1951–71. An alternative view. *Economic Journal* **82**, 1352–1365

Taylor, J. (1974). *Unemployment and Wage Inflation*. Harlow; Longman

Thirlwall, A. P. (1969). Types of unemployment with special reference to non-deficient-demand unemployment in Great Britain. *Scottish Journal of Political Economy* **16**, 20–49

Thirlwall, A. P. (1974). Types of unemployment in the regions of Great Britain. *Manchester School* **42**, 325–339

5
Unemployment benefits and incentives

5.1 Introduction

Popular attitudes to unemployment and unemployment insurance in Britain are much influenced by the widespread belief that benefits act as a serious disincentive to work. Such beliefs are scarcely new. Following the 1930 Unemployment Insurance Act, which provided more generous benefits and conditions, Winston Churchill claimed that it had led to 'an avalanche of new claims' (Skidelsky, 1970). Nor were these opinions confined to politicians. As noted by Benjamin and Kochin (1979), economists such as Rueff and Cannan argued that the dole was an important factor leading to prolonged unemployment.

In the postwar period, discussion of the possible disincentive effect of benefits was renewed with the introduction of the Earnings-Related Supplement to unemployment benefit in 1966, and the rise in unemployment after that date. This is well illustrated in the following commentary by Feldstein (1973):

> In October 1966, 1 month after the change in unemployment insurance, British unemployment began rising dramatically. The number of registered unemployed rose from 340 000 in September to 436 000 in October and 543 000 in November. The registered unemployment rate for males rose from 1.6 percent in August to 3.3 percent in January. It is, of course, difficult to know how much of this increase should be attributed to the change in unemployment compensation. Other macroeconomic and tax policies occurred at approximately the same time. It is noteworthy, however, that unemployment rates above 3 percent had been seen only once before in the postwar period (during an unusually bad winter) and that such a rapid rise in the rate of unemployment had not been seen before. Moreover, the male unemployment rate has remained over 3 percent ever since then. The previous relation between the unemployment rate and the vacancy rate ceased to hold after 1966. An examination of the occupational composition of unemployment shows that the proportional rise in

unemployment among skilled manual workers was greatest and among the lower paid unskilled workers (who would benefit less from the earnings-related supplement) was least. Although there are problems in interpreting each piece of data on the British experience, the evidence as a whole clearly indicates that the new method of earnings-related unemployment compensation has raised the level of unemployment.

With the rise in unemployment during the 1970s to levels far above those described by Feldstein, the belief in the disincentive effect has gained great currency. The—largely incorrect—view that the unemployed are better off, receiving benefits and tax rebates, than at work has led many to conclude that unemployment insurance is responsible for a substantial degree of 'voluntary' unemployment.

The aim of this chapter is to review the evidence about unemployment levels and durations, to see how far it supports the popular opinion. Does the existence of unemployment benefit in fact lead to higher unemployment? If so, how large is the effect? What was the impact of the Earnings-Related Supplement and what is likely to be the effect of its abolition?

As a basis for assessing the evidence, the next section sets out a simple analytical framework. Since there is no fully adequate theory of the determination of unemployment, the approach is intentionally eclectic and seeks to sidestep some of the controversies which do not bear directly on the issue in question. It is also restricted in scope in several significant ways. First, it concentrates on the behaviour of *male heads of households* and does not examine in any detail the effects on other workers. This is a serious limitation since, for example, the response of wives to the unemployment of their husbands may be quantitatively at least as important as that of the men. Secondly, it considers only *whether or not a person is in employment* and does not deal with the kind of employment (e.g. whether it is well matched to the person's level of skill), the hours of work, or other dimensions of the job. Thirdly, there is no treatment of the possibility that the unemployment insurance provisions may shift the *demand curve* for labour. It has been suggested that improvement in benefits relative to incomes in work made employers more likely to declare people redundant; in the United States it is argued that unemployment insurance increases the incidence of temporary lay-offs (e.g. Feldstein, 1976).

The empirical evidence reviewed here is of two main kinds. The first, discussed in Section 5.3, is based on aggregate time-series data. In other words, inferences are derived from the observed variations in the overall rate of unemployment (as in the quotation from

Feldstein above). The second, considered in Section 5.4, makes use of cross-section data on individual durations of unemployment. Both sources of evidence have strengths and weaknesses, and the final section weighs the conclusions which can be drawn. It should be emphasized at the outset that the survey of the evidence is not intended to be comprehensive, and that little attention is paid, except in passing, to research for countries apart from Britain.

5.2 Framework for the analysis

The model of the labour market set out here is a simple one; some of the necessary qualifications are set out at the end of the section.

On the demand side of the labour market, it is assumed that there is a structure of jobs on offer, dependent on the state of demand and on technology, and that with each job is associated a specified gross wage. The structure of vacancies is assumed in the short-run to be independent of the supply of labour. Employers try to fill the vacancies with those who apply, either offering them a job or not. There is no attempt to tailor the jobs to the applicants, by making an offer at a lower wage. This feature differentiates the model from that of a perfectly competitive labour market, and it is caused by a variety of factors:

> Equity, custom, internal labour markets, union bargaining agreements, legal constraints, morale factors and difficulties in measuring individual productivity all combine to associate a particular wage with a particular job in any firm. (Nickell, 1979a, p. 1250)

On the supply side, it is assumed that each worker has a *reservation wage* (or a series of reservation wages for different jobs). If when unemployed he is offered a job at a wage equal to, or in excess of, his reservation wage, he accepts. In any period of unemployment he may of course receive no offer of a job, despite any efforts on his part to seek work. When employed, he quits a job when the wage paid falls below his reservation wage: for example, when he becomes aware of better prospects elsewhere, or his benefit income rises. The reservation wage will be adjusted over time, depending for example on the worker's experience in the labour market, changes in taxation, benefits, and wage levels.

Bringing together the demand and supply sides of the market, allowance must be made for the fact that these are not perfectly matched at the micro-level. At any time there are likely to be both vacancies and unemployed people who would accept a job if it were offered to them. The extent of the mis-matching depends on several factors, including the efficiency of employment exchanges, and the availability of information. The resulting level of unemployment is governed by the number of vacancies (dependent in turn on the conditions of demand), the structure of wages offered, the structure of reservation wages, and the extent of mis-matching.

In this simple model, the impact of unemployment benefit and taxation depends on the way they influence the reservation wage. It is quite conceivable that this wage is independent of benefit levels. It may be that employment is preferred to unemployment: '. . . a man works to preserve the respect of his wife, children, friends and neighbours, to fulfil the psychological needs induced by the customs and expectations of a life-time' (Townsend, 1968). No financial advantage to working may therefore be necessary to induce acceptance of a job offer. In contrast, those who argue that there is a disincentive effect take the view that the reservation wage increases with the level of benefits. In its simplest form, this can be modelled in terms of the benefit income, B, and the net of tax wage, Y, with the job offer being accepted if Y exceeds some critical proportion of B. (The proportion may be greater or less than 100%; nothing can be deduced simply from the observation that B is larger than Y.) The ratio of B to Y, referred to as the 'benefit/earnings ratio', or the 'replacement ratio', plays a central role in the empirical studies.

If the reservation wage is not affected by the level of benefits, then that is the end of the matter. Suppose, however, that the reservation wage is an increasing function of B. A rise in benefits consequently means that an unemployed worker is more likely to refuse a job offer (the constraints on making such a refusal are discussed below) or to look less intensively for a job. Whether this change on the supply side is translated into any actual effect on the level of unemployment depends on the conditions of demand. If demand is high then it is possible that he is offered a job with a wage well in excess of the reservation wage, so that small changes in the latter do not in fact affect his decision. Conversely, if demand is low, he may receive no job offer at all, in which case the rise in the reservation wage is again irrelevant. Moreover, it is possible that a rise in the reservation wage has no effect on the overall rate of unemployment even where decisions are affected for some people. If jobs are being rationed, and jobs can be quickly re-offered, then a diminution in the pool of potential workers (i.e. those who would accept) may not have an impact on the employment rate:

Some of those who are now 'voluntarily' unemployed take the place of the 'involuntary' unemployed. The reason why there are N people unemployed can be due to cyclical and structural factors, but which particular individuals are unemployed could be determined by the existence of unemployment benefits and inter-personal differences in tastes and situations. (Sawyer, 1979, p. 136)

To sum up, it is quite possible in theory that the level of unemployment is influenced by benefits. There is however no theoretical necessity that there must be a disincentive effect. It is sometimes suggested that this conclusion is simply an implication of basic price theory (e.g. Grubel and Walker, 1978), whereas it depends on assumptions about individual motivation and about the operation of the labour market. The *existence* of a disincentive effect, and not merely its magnitude, is a matter for empirical demonstration.

The model described above is highly stylized. There is not space here to consider all possible elaborations, but three points in particular should be noted. First, the assumption that a worker is free to accept or reject a job offer ignores the constraints on 'voluntary' unemployment imposed by the social security system. The fact that a person can be disqualified for refusing a job 'without good cause' or for neglecting to avail himself of 'a reasonable opportunity of suitable employment', is not given much weight in the literature, but clearly is a major consideration for both claimants and the government departments. (For discussion of the 'genuinely seeking work test' in the 1920s and 1930s, see Deacon (1976); on present day control measures, see Field (1977) and Fulbrook (1978).) To the extent that such administrative controls are effective, the possibility of a disincentive effect is reduced. Secondly, the effect of unemployment insurance has been discussed in terms of the current benefit level, but workers may take a less myopic view. Future benefit entitlement may influence decisions about whether to seek a job or to accept an offer. This may be particularly important when the operation of the tax system is taken into account. With income tax levied on annual earnings excluding unemployment benefit, a person may calculate the implications for the tax payable over the remainder of the tax year: that is, he may be concerned with the 'marginal' cost of additional periods of unemployment. The interaction of taxation and benefits is quite complex (see Atkinson and Flemming, 1978). Thirdly, the chance of receiving a job offer may be related to the characteristics of the worker (see, for example, Daniel, 1974), including how long he has been unemployed, and the previous offers he has refused. These considerations may in turn affect the worker's decision.

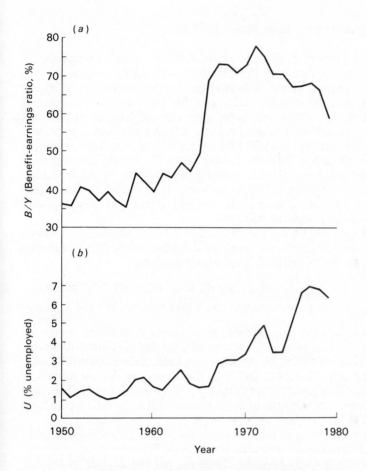

Figure 5.1 *Benefit/earnings ratio and unemployment rate 1950–1979*

(1) The unemployment rate relates to males in Great Britain and expresses the annual average total unemployment (excluding school leavers and adult students) as a percentage of the mid-year estimate of total employees (employed and unemployed).

(2) The benefits earnings ratio is calculated for a married couple with two children, where the husband has average earnings for adult male manual workers in manufacturing and certain other industries, and it is assumed that the wife does not work. The benefit includes Earnings Related Supplement, calculated on the basis of average earnings for the relevant tax year. The figures relate to October of each year.

(Sources (U) *Department of Employment,* British Labour Statistics, 1886–1968, *Table 166, with subsequent data from the Department of Employment* Gazette. (B/Y) *Maki and Spindler (1975,* Table I), Social Security Statistics 1977, Table 46.05, *and the author's own calculations.)*

5.3 Aggregate time-series evidence

One of the bases for the popular beliefs about unemployment insurance is that both the generosity of benefits and the level of unemployment appear to have risen over the postwar period. *Figure 5.1* shows the unemployment rate for men, U, and the ratio of benefits, for a married couple with two children, to average net earnings, B/Y, in October of each year. Both series show a substantial rise over the period 1950–1979 as a whole, although the time path has been rather different. In particular, the benefit/earnings ratio jumped sharply in 1966, with the introduction of the Earnings-Related Supplement (ERS), and has, if anything, declined since then, whereas of course the unemployment rate has increased significantly since the mid 1960s.

Before considering the conclusions (if any) which can be drawn from such changes over time, the definition of the benefit/earnings ratio should be clarified. This ratio is given by

$$\frac{B}{Y} = \frac{\text{National Insurance Benefit (incl. ERS and child benefit)}}{\text{Average gross earnings} - \text{tax} - \text{NI contribution} + \text{child benefit}}$$

Thus in October 1978, average gross earnings, including benefit for two children, came to £83.50, and after tax and NI contributions this was reduced to £67.28. At the same time, unemployment benefit, including child benefit and ERS (calculated on the assumption of average earnings in the relevant tax year), came to £44.41. This gave a benefit/earnings ratio of 66%. Without ERS, the ratio would have been 49%.

In considering changes in the ratio (B/Y), it should be borne in mind that there are several factors at work. The role of unemployment benefit has received most attention, but the decline in the tax threshold has also been a major factor. This is brought out clearly by the figures in *Table 5.1*.

Table 5.1 Changes in the benefit/earnings ratio

	(1) Benefit $(B) \div$ Gross earnings (%)*	(2) Net income $(Y) \div$ Gross earnings (%)*	(1)/(2) (B/Y) (%)
October 1966	60.4	88.1	68.6
October 1978	53.2	80.6	66.0

* Including family allowance/child benefit.

Over the period 1966–1978, the level of benefits fell relative to gross earnings; it was the decline in net income relative to gross that kept the benefit/earnings ratio fairly constant. The ratio depends on the level of child benefit. If in October 1978 this had been set at £4.50 per child, which was the total paid per child under unemployment benefit, for both employed and unemployed alike, then B/Y would have been 62%. It must similarly be noted that there are other elements which should enter the calculation. A more extensive measure of 'total income support' in and out of work would include supplementary benefit, Family Income Supplement, rent and rate rebates, free school meals, free welfare foods, and would allow for work expenses and tax refunds. Finally, it must be remembered that benefits are adjusted at discrete intervals, and the date of up-rating may influence the time path indicated (*Figure 5.1* relates to October of each year). A clear example is provided by 1971 when the benefits were increased on 23 September, compared with 1979, when the increase dated from November. Taking the pre-increase figures for 1971, then the ratio would have been 69% rather than 78% as shown in *Figure 5.1*. Conversely, taking the post-increase figures for 1979 would give a ratio of 66%, rather than 58%.

In terms of the earlier model, the benefit/earnings ratio may be seen as an indicator of the relationship between reservation wages and the wages offered. Other things being equal, this has led to the inference that B/Y and the unemployment rate would move together. It is not however the case that other things do remain equal, as recognized in the quotation from Feldstein given in the Section 5.1. The fact that the two series move together—if only in broad terms—does not mean that one can simply attribute the increase in unemployment to the changing benefit/earnings ratio. To draw any firm deductions it is necessary to construct an adequate model of the determinants of unemployment. Only by examining unemployment at dates which are comparable in other respects, or where the effect of other variables has been allowed for, can one draw conclusions about the response to B/Y.

There are broadly two methods which can be adopted. First, attempts may be made to construct a full-scale model of the determinants of unemployment. Alternatively, this may be short-circuited by trying to relate unemployment to a variable which incorporates the other influences but is itself unaffected by B/Y. The second is the simpler, and is well illustrated by the studies which have sought to explain the changed relationship between unemployment (U) and vacancies (V) since 1966. These studies in effect assume that the demand influences are captured by V, so that '. . . while unemployment has risen very steeply, the vacancy series has remained a better measure of the "true" level of demand pressure' (Bowers *et al.*, 1972, p. 75). For example, Gujarati (1972) fitted a linear–logarithmic relationship between U and V for the pre-1966 period, and used this to measure the deviation of post-1966 unemployment from its predicted level. He concluded that actual unemployment (total male and female) was some 44% higher than predicted (although see the criticism by Foster, 1973); and Bowers *et al.* (1972) estimated that the shift in mid 1971 was about two percentage points.

be attributed to particular changes on the supply side. Gujarati argued that it reflected the Redundancy Payments Act 1965 and the introduction of ERS; but apart from the timing he produced no evidence in support of this assertion. There are several other possible explanations, and these have been discussed by Bowers *et al.* (1972), Bowers (1976), Taylor (1972; 1976) and the Department of Employment (1976). The last adopted a 'constructive' approach to see how far the different factors might in fact have contributed to the shift (taken to be about 300 000 relative to vacancies). The Department first pointed out that many of the unemployed are not receiving ERS, so that the increase in the B/Y ratio applied only to a minority of claimants. Assuming that ERS doubles the length of an individual's spell out of work (which was considered 'likely to be on the high side'), the Department estimated that the resulting increase in the level of unemployment was probably less than 50 000. This is only some sixth of the total shift. (The validity of the underlying assumptions is discussed in the context of the cross-section evidence in Section 5.4.) The Department concluded that '. . . evidence . . . on the numbers receiving these benefits at relevant dates suggests that statutory redundancy payments and earnings-related supplements could have accounted for only a small part of the observed shift' (Department of Employment, 1976, p. 1098).

The first, more ambitious method, via the estimation of a full model of the determinants of unemployment, is illustrated by the work of Maki and Spindler (1975). They estimated an equation to explain the rate of unemployment (U) which incorporated B/Y and two variables designed to capture the structural and cyclical factors. The latter are:

Structural X_{1t} = total labour force multiplied by output per person (i.e. labour supply in efficiency units), expected sign positive.

Cyclical X_{2t} = ratio of GNP to trend (exponential function), expected sign negative.

The results for male unemployment were:

$$\ln U = -2.0 + 1.3 B/Y + 0.00018 X_{1t} - 12.2 \ln (X_{2t}) - 4.6 \ln (X_{2t-1})$$
$$\quad (3.2) \quad (4.9) \qquad (6.6) \qquad (2.9)$$

where the figures in brackets are t-statistics; $\bar{R}^2 = 0.965$, $DW = 1.62$.

The unemployment rate, as in several other studies, is expressed relative to the civilian labour force rather than total employees as in the published statistics. The equation is estimated simultaneously with another equation expressing B/Y as a function of U and other variables.

The precise status of this equation was not made very clear by the authors. It is presumably a reduced form, obtained from a set of labour market equations, but the full derivation from a theoretical model is not given. This makes it difficult to interpret the results, and the question of specification is taken up below. Moreover, it must be remembered that U relates to *registered* unemployment, so that the effect may represent in part an increased propensity to register rather than a lengthening of actual durations. Accepting for the present the equation as it stands, one can calculate the response of U with respect to B/Y. For example, the introduction of ERS raised B/Y from approximately 50 to 70% (see *Figure 5.1*). From the estimated coefficient (1.3), it can be deduced that this would have led to an increase in the unemployment rate of some 30% (i.e. exp (1.3×0.2)). In terms of male unemployment at the end of 1966, this would be some 110 000—or over twice the Department of Employment estimate.

There are a number of criticisms which have been made of the Maki–Spindler results and of their general approach, which has been applied to a wide variety of countries (see Grubel and Walker, 1978). Attention is focused here on three major problems: the specification of the unemployment equation, its interpretation as a reduced form equation, and the appropriateness of the aggregate benefit/earnings ratio.

In commenting on the evidence for Canada, which includes a similar paper by Grubel, Maki and Sax (1975), Diewert (1978) has argued the need for a '... theory of the effect of unemployment insurance which is built up on micro foundations, since the rigorous use of consumer theory in constructing the model to be estimated imposes discipline on the choice of variables to be included as controls'. This sets a demanding standard, but it does point out the essentially arbitrary choice of 'control' variables (X_{1t}, X_{2t}, X_{2t-1}) in the estimated equation. What reason is there to believe that these, and not other possible variables, should be included? The sensitivity of the conclusions reached regarding the influence of the benefits variable has been shown by several authors. The coefficient of B/Y

may be reduced by the introduction of a time trend (Taylor, 1977) or of permanent income (Cubbin and Foley, 1977)[1]. The difficulties are recognized by Spindler and Maki in their reply (1979). Nickell (1979b) has summarized the position as follows:

> ... much of the statistical impact of the replacement ratio in the post-war studies arises because both it and the level of unemployment have risen secularly over most of the last twenty years. The inclusion of any other variable which moves monotonically over time will ... tend to reduce this impact. Given also that the theoretical basis of these equations is weak, we are then left with virtually no statistical or prior criteria for choosing between results. (p. 35)

The second problem is related: the interpretation of the equation as a reduced form. A number of authors have expressed their unease: for example, Helliwell (1978) noted that '... from the point of view of a labour-market economist, or anyone concerned with microeconomic specifications, the use of a reduced-form unemployment equation is intrinsically unsatisfactory. One simply does not know how to work back to the micro-behavioural parameters'. The unemployment relation should indeed be seen in terms of a larger model of the labour market, which considers explicitly employment, hours of work and the supply of labour. Only in such a context can one attempt to explore whether any observed response to variation in B/Y is associated with an increase in labour supply (more workers registering) or with a reduced acceptance of jobs. In the United States and Canada a number of full-scale models of the labour market have been constructed. For instance, Black and Kelejian (1970) estimated a five-equation system covering the demand for man hours, the division of man hours into employment and hours, the determination of average wages, and the supply of labour by primary and secondary workers. A similar approach is adopted in a number of macroeconomic models, including, for example, that of the National Institute (Ormerod and Whitley, 1977).

The appropriateness of the benefit/earnings ratio used by Maki and Spindler has been questioned by several critics. Sawyer (1979) argues, for example, that the appropriate scale prior to 1966 is not the flat-rate National Insurance benefit but the National Assistance scale; the latter was higher and its use tends to reduce the size of the jump in B/Y. In an alternative approach, Taylor (1977) uses a variable for the average benefit actually received. This statistic needs careful interpretation (for example, because of the interaction with National Assistance/Supplementary Benefits), but it has the advantage of avoiding the difficulties which may arise because of the differences in dates of up-rating. As indicated earlier, the variation due to slight differences in timing (e.g. from 69 to 78%) can be large in relation to the variation in the series as a whole.

More generally, the choice of benefit/earnings indicator must be related to the underlying model, and it may be helpful to draw a parallel with other types of aggregate analysis. This is typically justified by reference to an 'average' consumer or household; a procedure which is strictly valid only under strong assumptions but which may be an adequate approximation where the relevant variables change smoothly and where the aggregation is over a representative cross-section of the population. In the present case these conditions are not met. The benefit/earnings ratio varies sharply with earnings and with the duration of unemployment. For a 'representative' worker on £88 per week (including child benefit) in October 1978, the ratio with ERS was 66% (for a married couple with two children). With earnings of £65 a week, the ratio would have risen to 78%; but if there were no entitlement to ERS, then it would have fallen to 52%. In addition, the studies are not concerned with a simple cross-section of the population. By this is meant not just the fact that the unemployed are atypical of the population as a whole, tending to have below-average wages when in work, but also that the B/Y ratio relevant to the analysis is not necessarily that of the representative unemployed. The response to the benefit/earnings ratio depends on the interaction with demand, and on the constraints faced by the individual. If, for instance, it is those with a high B/Y for whom the reservation wage is close to that offered, then it may be reasonable to take the ratio including ERS, even though it is received only by a minority of the unemployed. It may be the more skilled workers for whom the demand exceeds the supply, and hence their decisions which are relevant, not those of the lower paid who make up a greater proportion of the unemployed. What is needed is an indicator of B/Y for the 'marginal' unemployed. Here the micro-economic evidence may be of assistance, and this is the subject of the next section.

5.4 Cross-section evidence

Cross-section studies make use of information on individual unemployment and its relation to the individual's characteristics and position in the labour market. In their most simple form, the studies seek to explain the differential duration of unemployment for individual members of a sample, with one of the explanatory variables being the B/Y ratio. In considering this kind of evidence, it must be borne in mind that one can never hope to explain all the variation in such data. Because of the 'mis-matching' referred to in Section 5.2, the duration of unemployment is a random variable, and even a 'perfect' model will only be able to explain a certain fraction of the variance[2]. What the studies should be seeking to explain, therefore, are the differential probabilities of different individuals remaining unemployed.

There are many factors likely to influence such probabilities: they include age, previous work career, qualifications, family circumstances, and local labour market conditions. These may affect the reservation wage of the individual or the probability of receiving a job offer. This means that any model designed to test for the effect of the B/Y ratio must incorporate these factors. Conversely, their omission may lead to biased estimates of the effect of B/Y. This may be illustrated by the work of Hill *et al.* (1973), who analysed unemployment duration in relation to receipt of ERS. They concluded that this comparison '... produced no evidence in support of the hypothesis, and in fact, in one area, Newcastle, there was a statistically significant tendency for those without earnings-related supplement to remain unemployed the longest' (Hill, 1976). However, as Hill goes on to point out, this comparison is not meaningful since those receiving ERS are not typical of the unemployed. Among other things, they are likely to have better employment records and by definition have been out of work less than 6 months. These features may well make them more attractive to employers. The second point, therefore, is that it is necessary to include in the estimated relationship those factors likely to influence the probability of re-employment.

Among the studies which have attempted to do this (again no attempt is made to give a comprehensive survey) are those of MacKay and Reid (1972) using a sample of redundant workers in 1966–1968, of Lancaster (1979) using a national sample of unskilled unemployed workers in 1973, and of Nickell (1979b) using the 1972 General Household Survey.

MacKay and Reid (1972) carried out a regression analysis of the unemployment experience of 613 male workers declared redundant from 23 engineering plants in the West Midlands. The essential aspects of their results may be summarized in terms of the regression equation:

$$\left\{ \begin{array}{c} \text{Unemployment duration} \\ \text{(including observations} \\ \text{of zero) (mean 11.8} \\ \text{weeks)} \end{array} \right\} \begin{array}{c} \text{DEPENDS} \\ \text{ON} \end{array} \left\{ \begin{array}{c} \text{Personal characteristics (age} \\ \text{55 +, marital status} \\ \text{significant)} \end{array} \right\}$$

$$+ \left\{ \begin{array}{l} \text{Demand characteristics} \\ (\% \text{ vacancies significant}) \end{array} \right\} + \left\{ \begin{array}{l} \text{Search activity (whether} \\ \text{looked for work before} \\ \text{redundancy, employers} \\ \text{contacted, etc.)} \end{array} \right\}$$

$$+ \begin{array}{l} 0.42 \\ (2.0) \end{array} \left\{ \begin{array}{l} \text{weekly unemploy-} \\ \text{ment benefit in £} \end{array} \right\} + \begin{array}{l} 0.005 \\ (1.4) \end{array} \left\{ \begin{array}{l} \text{redundancy} \\ \text{pay in £} \end{array} \right\}$$

Figures in brackets are t-statistics.
Source: MacKay and Reid (1972, Table III)

The effect indicated by the coefficient of the benefit variable is rather smaller than found in the aggregate studies: '... while unemployment benefit may have had some impact in raising the level of unemployment, the small partial regression coefficient does not indicate that workers were "living off the state" for long periods' (MacKay and Reid, 1972, p. 1269). The coefficient implies that a person receiving the maximum £7 ERS (in 1966–1968) would have had a longer expected duration by 2.9 weeks. This is smaller than the hypothetical doubling assumed in the Department of Employment calculation quoted in the previous section, and the overall estimate of the impact of ERS made by MacKay and Reid is correspondingly smaller. Taking an average ERS of £3, they estimate the increased total unemployment to be about 12 000 men. On the other hand, MacKay and Reid include as a separate variable the intensity of job search. Since the effect of benefits is supposed to operate partly through reduced search activity, the total impact may therefore be understated by the coefficient on their benefit variable.

For most of the MacKay and Reid sample, the observations relate to *completed* spells of unemployment. In contrast, the data analysed by Lancaster (1979) relate to 479 workers interviewed twice, some of whom had returned to work by the date of the second interview but others of whom had not yet completed their spell of unemployment. The development of the appropriate estimation technique is described in Lancaster (1979) and Lancaster and Nickell (1979). Lancaster assumes a re-employment probability which is a loglinear function of the benefit/earnings ratio for the individual, of other characteristics, and of duration. He notes the problems which may arise because of unobserved differences in re-employment probabilities, particularly in relation to estimating the effect of duration. Thus individuals with higher probabilities will be less strongly represented at longer durations. Making different assumptions about the extent of such unobserved differences between workers, he concludes that the elasticity of unemployment duration with respect to the benefit/earnings ratio is around 0.6. A rise in the ratio from 50 to 70%, as with the introduction of ERS, would on this basis lead to an increase in average duration of some 22%. This is again considerably less than the doubling assumed in the Department of Employment calculation.

The evidence from the General Household Survey employed by Nickell (1979a, b) is more limited than that available to Lancaster in that it is based on uncompleted spells recorded at a single interview, but it can be used in a similar way to estimate the conditional re-employment probabilities. The data relate to the 426 males in 1972 who had been out of work for more than 1 week and claimed either that they were actively seeking work or that they would have been doing so but for temporary sickness or that they were waiting to take up a job. The B/Y ratio used by Nickell is a more extensive measure including supplementary benefits, rent and rate rebates, Family Income Supplement, free school meals and tax rebates. The results are illustrated by the following estimates of the re-employment probability, p, for a person who has been unemployed s weeks:

$$\ln\left(\frac{p}{1-p}\right) = \text{Quadratic terms in } s$$

+ Personal characteristics (marital status, age, family needs, ill-health)

+ Local demand and other variables

$-1.58B/Y$ [for $s \leqslant 20$] $+0.31\ B/Y$ [for $s > 20$]
  (0.43)   (0.55)

where the figures in brackets are asymptotic standard errors (see Nickell, 1979a, Table I, equation 2).

In the case of the benefit/earnings ratio, Nickell argued that the effect is likely to vary with the duration of unemployment and allowed the coefficient to vary (continuously) at different durations. The likelihood was fairly flat between cut-offs of 15 and 25 weeks but the hypothesis that the coefficient was the same for all durations was convincingly rejected. The implication is that the coefficient is highly significant for durations less than 20 weeks but insignificantly different from zero after that. It is possible that this arises because of unobserved differences between workers, there being a changing 'mix' of unemployed with duration, as noted earlier, but the experiments with different assumptions by Lancaster and Nickell (1979) suggest that this is not the explanation. The overall implications of the estimated coefficient may be seen from the effect of different replacement ratios on the expected duration for a 'typical' man in *Table 5.2*.

Table 5.2 Expected duration of unemployment

Benefit/earnings ratio	Weeks of unemployment
0.4	6.7
0.7	10.5
0.8	12.1
1.0	16.3

Source: Nickell (1979a, Table II)

On the basis of this analysis, and the more extensive treatment of the benefit variable in Nickell (1979b), he concluded that the elasticity of expected duration with respect to the benefit/earnings ratio is between 0.6 and 1.0. In interpreting this, it must be remembered that the B/Y measure is a more extensive one, including other benefits apart from unemployment pay, so that the proportionate impact of a change in unemployment benefit is smaller. For this reason, Nickell himself summarized the results in terms of an elasticity of 0.6, which is the same as that found by Lancaster.

The conclusions from the cross-section evidence in Britain indicate therefore that the effect of benefits on unemployment duration is significant but small in magnitude. In this they seem in close agreement. At the same time, there are a number of possible criticisms. First, the studies described concentrate on the probability of leaving employment once a person has entered. They do not allow therefore for the possible effect on the flow into unemployment. Hence they tend to understate the elasticity to the extent that the propensity to quit increases with B/Y. Nickell (1979b) argued that this effect is of minor importance, on the grounds that the rate of flow into male unemployment has changed little since 1967 and that the General Household Survey shows only about 20% leaving their last job voluntarily. This may be correct, but evidence about reasons for entering unemployment needs careful interpretation, and the conclusion requires confirmation from a study of the incidence of unemployment.

Secondly, one cannot immediately draw conclusions about aggregate unemployment from the estimated individual probabilities of re-employment. As pointed out in Section 5.2, a rise in the reservation wage for one group of workers may simply mean that another group are employed—with aggregate unemployment remaining unchanged. Thus, the introduction of ERS could have led to an increase in the number out of work for less than 28 weeks, but a decrease in longer durations; or it could have led men with a taste for leisure to quit and be replaced by unemployed men with no hobbies. The re-employment probabilities of different individuals are interdependent.

Thirdly, one of the strengths of microeconomic data is that they contain information on individual benefit entitlement, but in practice this information is not complete. For example, the General Household Survey contains relatively little information on the actual unemployment benefits received, and calculations in Nickell (1979a) are based on the assumption that all unemployed received ERS and full NI benefit in the relevant periods. Moreover, the earnings relevant to ERS were calculated from predicted earnings. In his later paper (1979b), Nickell does examine the effect of using actual past earnings and actual current benefits, but it is not apparent that the earnings relate to the relevant period for determining ERS and there is no information on past benefits. It is also assumed in the calculations that the take-up of means-tested benefits is 100%. For benefits such as rent/rate rebates and free school meals, this is a dubious assumption; and for supplementary benefit it is also open to question (the estimated take-up rate by the unemployed in 1975 was 78%—see Supplementary Benefit Commission, 1978). The benefit/earnings indicator may therefore be measured with considerable error, 'and the error may be correlated with relevant unobserved characteristics. For example, those more 'motivated' to search for a job may be more (or less) likely to claim means-tested benefits.

Fourthly, the benefit/earnings ratio used in these studies compares the benefit income with that of a man in work for a full year. However, in deciding on a job offer, an unemployed person may reasonably ask what it is worth to him to start this week rather than next. In this connection the effect of income taxation may be crucial. In a system where the tax base is total annual earnings excluding unemployment benefit, the *marginal* net earnings for an extra week's work may be considerably lower than *average* net earnings. As Atkinson and Flemming (1978) suggested, it may be more appropriate to use a marginal rather than an average benefit/earnings ratio.

Finally, the evidence used by Lancaster and Nickell relates to the early 1970s, when unemployment was considerably below its level at the start of the 1980s. The framework described in Section 5.2 indicated how the impact of the benefit variable might depend on the demand conditions, and it is not clear that the findings can be applied to current conditions. (This applies even more to the results of MacKay and Reid for the mid 1960s.)

5.5 Conclusions

This chapter has reviewed some of the findings about the possible effect of unemployment benefit on the rate of unemployment. The review has not attempted to be comprehensive, concentrating on aggregate time-series and on cross-section studies, and selecting certain of these for special attention. There are a number of other potentially fruitful sources of evidence, including longitudinal studies of the kind being carried out by the Department of Health and Social Security, and the pooling of cross-section data for several years (as in the General Household Survey or the Family Expenditure Survey).

The results may be summarized usefully in terms of the implications for the effect of the Earnings-Related Supplement (ERS), and many of the studies have focused on the consequences of its introduction in 1966. The quotation from Feldstein (1973) in Section 5.1 drew attention to the rise in unemployment after that date, and argued that the introduction of ERS was one of the factors responsible. The time-series analysis by Maki and Spindler (1975) was seen by them as confirming this, and they estimated that the resulting increase in male unemployment was some 110 000. This was more than twice the 'constructive' estimate made by the Department of Employment on the basis of the assumption that the average duration of unemployment for ERS recipients was doubled. Put in reverse, and applied to the abolition of ERS at much higher levels of unemployment, the Maki–Spindler estimated relationship would imply a fall in male unemployment from (say) 1 million to 775 000.

This time-series study has been heavily criticized, and there are several reasons for regarding the findings with considerable scepticism. The specification of the unemployment equation, and its interpretation as a reduced form, raise serious problems. The difficulties of representing the impact of benefits in a single indicator, and of separating it from other trended variables, are substantial. Spindler and Maki themselves agree that '. . . it is probably the case that the insurance-induced unemployment hypothesis has not yet been adequately tested or the magnitude of the effect exactly measured' (1979, p. 159). Indeed, there seems little hope of identifying the benefit effect at all precisely from time-series evidence, and it will at the very least require much more fully-specified models of the labour market.

The cross-section evidence appears to find a significant effect of benefits on individual probabilities of re-employment, but the magnitude is relatively small. Indeed the results of all three studies reviewed indicate that the assumption by the Department of Employment of a doubling of the duration may considerably overstate the impact. Nickell, for example, concluded that ERS would only have increased expected durations for ERS recipients by about a quarter. Again there are problems with the methods employed. In some cases these are intrinsic to the cross-section approach: for example, the aggregation of individual probabilities where these may be interdependent. In other cases, the analysis can be refined: for example, the treatment of the benefit variable and the examination of different demand conditions. The conclusions to be drawn must therefore be qualified, and may need to be modified in the light of subsequent research. There does however seem to be little ground to suppose that the introduction of ERS led to an 'avalanche' of claims or that its abolition will dramatically reduce the level of unemployment.

Writing about the 1930s, Benjamin and Kochin recently concluded that '. . . the army of the unemployed standing watch in Britain at the publication of the *General Theory* was largely a volunteer army' (1979, p. 474). This conclusion is open to question for reasons similar to those discussed in Section 5.3 (their approach resembles that of Maki and Spindler). More importantly, there is at present no strong evidence that there are a large proportion of volunteers among the unemployed watching the monetarist experiments of the early 1980s. It does indeed appear to be a 'conscript' army.

Acknowledgements

This paper is a revised, and shortened, version of a paper prepared at the request of H.M. Treasury in February 1978.

Notes

1. Other writers have argued (e.g. Sawyer, 1979 and Junankar, 1979) that the equation is not stable over the period for which it was estimated, the coefficients having shifted.
2. This point is made clearly in Lancaster (1976) who shows that where the probability of re-employment is constant over time for a person, but differs across individuals, then the R^2 recorded in a least squares regression of duration is strictly less than 0.5.

References

Atkinson, A. B. and Flemming, J. S. (1978). Unemployment, social security and incentives. *Midland Bank Review* (Autumn) 6–16

Benjamin, D. K. and Kochin, L. A. (1979). Searching for an explanation of unemployment in interwar Britain. *Journal of Political Economy* **87**, 441–478

Black, S. W. and Kelejian, H. H. (1970). A macro model of the US labor market. *Econometrica* **38**, 712–741

Bowers, J. K. (1976). Some notes on current unemployment. In *The Concept and Measurement of Involuntary Unemployment* (ed. G. D. N. Worswick). London; Allen & Unwin

Bowers, J. K., Cheshire, P. C. and Webb, A. E. (1970). The change in the relationship between unemployment and earnings increases. *National Institute Economic Review* No. 54, 44–63

Bowers, J. K., Cheshire, P. C., Webb, A. E. and Weeden, R. (1972). Some aspects of unemployment and the labour market 1966–71. *National Institute Economic Review* No. 62, 75–88

Cubbin, J. S. and Foley, K. (1977). The extent of benefit-induced unemployment in Great Britain: Some new evidence. *Oxford Economic Papers* **29**, 128–140

Daniel, W. W. (1974). *A National Survey of the Unemployed*. London; PEP

Deacon, A. (1976). *In Search of the Scrounger*. London; G. Bell

Department of Employment (1976). The changed relationship between unemployment and vacancies. *Department of Employment Gazette* (October), 1093–1099

Diewert, W. E. (1978). In *Unemployment Insurance* (ed. by H. G. Grubel and M. A. Walker), p. 89. The Fraser Institute; Vancouver

Feldstein, M. S. (1973). *Lowering the Permanent Rate of Unemployment*, pp. 47–48. Washington DC; US Joint Economics Committee

Feldstein, M. S. (1976). Temporary layoffs on the theory of unemployment. *Journal of Political Economy* **84**, 937–957

Field, F. (1977). Control measures against abuse. In *The Conscript Army* (ed. by F. Field). London; Routledge and Kegan Paul

Foster, J. I. (1973). The behaviour of unemployment and unfilled vacancies: A comment. *Economic Journal* **83**, 192–201

Fulbrook, J. (1978). *Administrative Justice and the Unemployed*. London; Mansell

Grubel, H. G., Maki, D. and Sax, S. (1975). Real and induced unemployment in Canada. *Canadian Journal of Economics* **8**, 174–191

Grubel, H. G. and Walker, M. A. (1978). *Unemployment Insurance.* Vancouver; The Fraser Institute

Gujarati, D. (1972). Behaviour of unemployment and unfilled vacancies: Great Britain, 1958–1971. *Economic Journal* **82**, 195–204

Helliwell, J. F. (1978). Discussion. In *Unemployment Insurance* (ed. by H. G. Grubel and M. A. Walker), pp. 113–119. Vancouver; The Fraser Institute

Hill, M. J. (1976). Can we distinguish voluntary from involuntary unemployment? In *The Concept and Measurement of Involuntary Unemployment* (ed. by G. D. N. Worswick), p. 172. London; Allen & Unwin

Hill, M. J., Harrison, R. M., Sargeant, A. V. and Talbot, V. (1973). *Men Out of Work.* London; Cambridge University Press

Junankar, P. N. (1979). An econometric analysis of unemployment in Great Britain, 1952–1975. Discussion paper, University of Essex

Lancaster, T. (1976). Redundancy, unemployment and manpower policy: A comment. *Economic Journal* **86**, 335–338

Lancaster, T. (1979). Econometric methods for the duration of unemployment. *Econometrica* **47**, 939–956

Lancaster, T. and Nickell, S. (1979). The analysis of re-employment probabilities for the unemployed. Discussion Paper No. 59. London; Centre for Labour Economics, LSE

Mackay, D. I. and Reid, G. L. (1972). Redundancy, unemployment and manpower policy. *Economic Journal* **82**, 1256–1272

Maki, D. R. and Spindler, Z. A. (1975). The effect of unemployment compensation on the rate of unemployment in Great Britain. *Oxford Economic Papers* **27**, 440–454

Nickell, S. (1979a). Estimating the probability of leaving unemployment. *Econometrica* **47**, 1249–1266

Nickell, S. (1979b). The effect of unemployment and related benefits on the duration of unemployment. *Economic Journal* **89**, 34–49

Ormerod, P. A. and Whitley, J. D. (1977). *National Institute Model 2: The Labour Sector.* National Institute of Economic and Social Research, Discussion Paper No. 10C

Sawyer, M. C. (1979). The effects of unemployment compensation on the rate of unemployment in Great Britain: A comment. *Oxford Economic Papers* **31**, 135–146

Sinfield, A. (1968). *The Long Term Unemployed.* Paris; OECD

Sinfield, A. (1976). Unemployment and the social structure. In *The Concept and Measurement of Involuntary Unemployment* (ed. by G. D. N. Worswick). London; Allen & Unwin

Skidelsky, R. (1970). In *Politicians and the Slump*, p. 167. Harmondsworth; Penguin

Spindler, Z. A. and Maki, D. (1979). More on the effects of unemployment compensation on the rate of unemployment in Great Britain. *Oxford Economic Papers* **31**, 147–164

Supplementary Benefit Commission (1978). *Take-up of Supplementary Benefits*, p. 2, London; HMSO

Taylor, J. (1972). The behaviour of unemployment and unfilled vacancies: An alternative view. *Economic Journal* **82**, 1352–1365

Taylor, J. (1976). The unemployment gap in Britain's production sector 1953–73. In *The Concept and Measurement of Involuntary Unemployment* (ed. by G. D. N. Worswick). London; Allen & Unwin

Taylor, J. (1977). A note on the comparative behaviour of male and female unemployment rates in the United Kingdom, 1951–76. Discussion Paper, University of Lancaster

Townsend, P. (1968). The difficulties of negative income tax. In *Social Services for All?*, p. 108. London; Fabian

6
Unemployment insurance in Britain

6.1 Introduction

Provision of insurance benefits to the unemployed has always been a source of political contention. Yet most discussions of, for instance, the level of benefits, eligibility for benefits and the method of financing the insurance system, have revealed an underlying consensus that the state has an obligation to intervene to provide some sort of unemployment insurance system. It is, however, useful to examine the fundamental motives for state participation in this field by investigating the justifications for intervention put forward by economists. This is undertaken in Section 6.2, which also contrasts some of these theoretical considerations with the actual historical development of state-organized unemployment insurance in Great Britain.

The underlying consensus on the need for state intervention has extended in practice to many of the methods by which the system of state unemployment insurance is organized in Britain. In Britain Unemployment and Sickness Benefits and the state pension are organized through the National Insurance Fund, which is separated from general Exchequer financing of other government expenditure. In addition, there are means-tested benefits, which are financed out of general taxation, for those who are in extra need or are excluded from National Insurance benefits for one reason or another. These underlying institutional arrangements have only occasionally been the subject of critical scrutiny, as in the crisis concerning means-testing of non-contributory unemployment benefits in the 1931 Budget, the infrequent but persistent proposals to merge National Insurance contributions and general taxation, as in the report of the Meade Committee (Meade *et al.*, 1978), and in the 1980 Budget which effectively cast doubt on the viability of National Insurance as a mechanism for providing short-term benefits such as Unemployment and Sickness Benefit at a reasonable level of subsistence. Section 6.3 of this chapter therefore examines the practice of state intervention in Britain in more detail. It describes many of the more important regulations, provides some discussion of the justifications, if any, for these regulations and examines the breakdown of coverage in recent years.

Section 6.4 relates the operation of the British regime of unemployment insurance to the incidence of unemployment in Britain. It describes those who have the highest risk of unemployment and links this experience to one of the main justifications for state intervention put forward in Section 6.2, namely the need to protect high risk individuals. Section 6.5 summarizes the arguments and provides several tentative conclusions for policy that emerge from the analysis.

6.2 The economic analysis of unemployment insurance

Why does the state provide a programme of unemployment insurance? A recent paper by Diamond (1977) lists the following four reasons for the existence of a state organized social security system:

(1) correcting market failure,
(2) redistributing income,
(3) paternalism: that is, compulsory saving,
(4) raising revenue.

These are now considered in turn.

Correcting market failure

The fundamental reason for the existence of insurance is uncertainty. The loss which insurance attempts to cover in the case of unemployment is the loss of earnings when out of work. Now individuals could respond to uncertainty of employment by bargaining for higher wages in those industries most susceptible to unemployment and using the higher earnings as a source of saving to tide them over work interruptions. This response is indeed a feature of those industries characterized by short-term uncertainty, such as building and construction or the docks prior to the move from casual employment.

There are, however, two objections to universal reliance on this method of dealing with loss of income. The first is that there is a social gain from pooling risks through an insurance scheme, rather than relying on individual bargaining, where individuals are risk averse[1]. Pooling risks reduces the total risk, and therefore the risk per insured person[2]. In the second place, uncertainty of employment includes the probability of occasional long periods of general industrial recession, as well as short term interruptions. The probability of such events cannot reasonably be assessed by individuals, making the reliance on individual saving against an uncertain loss of income highly problematic. In practice, this latter uncertainty also makes it difficult to organize an actuarially sound insurance fund, whether private or state-organized, since the insurer needs to know both the likely number of claimants and contributors in order to set contributions at a level which allows the fund to balance[3].

The concern to protect members against loss of earnings, and the social welfare arguments outlined above, led several trade unions and workmen's associations in Britain prior to the 1911 National Insurance Act to provide some form of unemployment insurance[4]. Such schemes, which were largely limited to skilled and craft workers, were characterized by a high replacement ratio (the relation of benefits to earnings) and a relatively short duration of benefits. Such schemes were a classic example of the social gain motive for insurance, since members of individual unions were relatively homogeneous in terms of risk, and thus risk pooling reduced the cost to each insured member. In addition, the provision of unemployment insurance had a socially integrative role as far as the union was concerned, in demonstrating that it was concerned with its members when out of work as well as in work.

There is, however, a fundamental difficulty in the provision of unemployment insurance by a private insurer or even a trade union, and this is the 'adverse selection' problem. In the case of a profit maximizing insurer, it is more profitable to insure those with lower probabilities of unemployment. In practice workers will have varying probabilities of experiencing unemployment, according to their individual characteristics, and those with high probabilities of unemployment may be driven out of insurance coverage either because no insurance is offered or because they will be unable to finance the premium which the insurance market requires. There is therefore a problem of market failure and this is a traditional argument for state intervention.

Having stated the problem as one of market failure, it is useful at this point to consider the question of how much insurance should be provided by the state. Most studies of unemployment insurance have concentrated on a particular problem of optimal provision, that of moral hazard. The existence of a system of insurance against the risk of unemployment is thought likely to affect individual behaviour more than, say, insurance against loss of life or a motor accident. The provision of unemployment insurance will increase the duration of unemployment at the margin by allowing people to be more choosy about which jobs they accept and may even increase the inflow into unemployment since insurance not only directly reduces the income loss while out of work but also reduces net earnings in employment by raising tax rates.

Baily (1978), for example, sets up a two-period model in which workers, who are assumed to be identical, face a probability of layoff in the second period. The state-organized unemployment insurance fund is financed out of taxes levied on wages, and all receipts of the fund are paid out as benefits. Workers who are laid off spend a fraction of the second period unemployed, this fraction initially being assumed to be non-stochastic, although this assumption is later relaxed. During this period workers search for new jobs, and (involuntary) leisure has no utility. Although workers are identical, jobs are presumably not, because the acceptance wage which unemployed workers are prepared to accept is a decision variable. The optimization problem involves finding that level of unemployment benefit where the marginal utility of the loss of consumption resulting from a lower level of unemployment benefit just offsets the deadweight loss from prolongation of spells of unemployment and raising the tax rate needed to balance the insurance fund.

Baily is criticized by Flemming (1978) for his peculiar assumptions concerning the possibility of borrowing by the unemployed. In Baily's model, the unemployed cannot borrow at all against future earnings beyond the second period yet borrowing within the second period to finance consumption during lay-offs is assumed to be costless. Flemming therefore extends Baily's model to deal with various situations of perfect or imperfect capital markets. However, almost in passing, he raises a far more fundamental question for models of this kind which justify state provision of unemployment insurance.

Flemming restricts his analysis to what he calls 'pure' unemployment insurance which he defines as redistribution between people whose income inequality results solely from random incidence of unemployment and not from systematic differences in individual characteristics such as age or skill. Thus, like that of Baily, his model assumes a homogeneous population or subpopulation. To be fair, Flemming is quick to point out that his assumption is of limited realism:

(1) Since homogeneous subpopulations in the general population cannot be identified, even if they exist, any practicable UI scheme will not be 'pure' but will also redistribute in other ways, notably if some individuals are 'unemployment prone'

they will benefit from the redistribution. The impossibility of 'pure' UI may make optimal feasible UI differ from the optimum presented here.

(2) Restriction to a homogeneous population of jobs and workers reduces the motives for the latter to search. Reservation wages play no part in the analysis. In this respect the search model constructed below, in which the unemployed have simply to find a vacancy, is somewhat artificial. (Flemming, 1978, p. 404)

This raises the key problem in relating these models to the existence of systems of unemployment insurance organized by the state. Remember that unlike private insurance schemes or trade union schemes, state involvement in unemployment insurance is predicated on the existence of market failure where population heterogeneity is crucial. Thus models based on population homogeneity are of very limited realism. State involvement in unemployment insurance must therefore be based not on the provision of 'pure' unemployment insurance, in Flemming's sense, but on the premise of explicit or implicit redistribution among individuals with differing probabilities of unemployment. Indeed, as is argued in the next subsection, it is the concern to both accept and at the same time limit the redistributive implications of unemployment insurance provided by the state that underlies many of the political controversies surrounding public involvement in this area in Britain.

One further argument associated with market failure may be noted. It has been suggested by some authors that private insurers fail to assess risks efficiently[5]. The private sector may fail to provide insurance to those who, even if they are not bad risks objectively, are considered so by the insurance industry. Such subpopulations may include people lacking education, racial minorities, single parents and women. If, however, such individuals are not objective bad risks, it is hard to see why it is not in the interest of someone to profitably provide insurance for these groups. The point made by Titmuss may be more subtle, however, and rest on the idea that the risk of 'unemployment-proneness' may be endogenous. Individuals may become bad risks because they are identified as being bad risks[6]. But if this is correct, Titmuss is pursuing a redistributive argument for state involvement rather than a market failure argument.

Finally, it is possible that the state might be able to monopolize unemployment insurance not because the private market fails to provide insurance but because the state sector can operate insurance at lower cost than the private sector due to economies of scale in administration. Diamond argues, in the context of Federal provision of pensions in the United States, that administrative costs in the public sector are indeed lower than in private insurance schemes. Nevertheless this does not seem to be sufficient justification for state intervention. The history in Britain of the development of state involvement in unemployment insurance suggests that although some people, such as Beveridge and Pigou, thought the state could provide insurance at low cost, this argument was never central to the debate about the necessity for state intervention.

Redistributing income

Any system of unemployment insurance redistributes income towards those who are currently experiencing unemployment. However, in a regime of 'pure' unemployment insurance with a homogeneous population facing a random probability of unemployment, there should be no net redistribution other than through the problem of moral hazard. This problem can be dealt with by tying payment of benefits to registration by the individual as available and willing to work. If public insurance exists because of market failure resulting from population heterogeneity, on the other hand, there may well be substantial redistribution from low risk individuals to those who are most 'unemployment-prone'.

This reasoning would suggest that income redistribution is a primary motive underlying the provision of unemployment insurance by the state. Nevertheless, if redistribution towards high risk individuals were the sole aim of unemployment benefit provision, there would be little point in replicating or imitating a private insurance system: the state could simply provide income maintenance to those in most need of financial support. This could be done directly through the tax system or by a separate income maintenance programme. The problem of moral hazard crops up again in the context of an income maintenance programme, but it is not immediately clear why this problem is avoided by introducing an explicit coinsurance element into the programme (that is, an individual contribution to the insurance fund) as opposed to, say, a stringent work test.

As mentioned in Section 6.1, the British system of unemployment insurance is composed of an explicit 'insurance' system, under which employed individuals contribute to a National Insurance Fund and receive Unemployment Benefit when out of work, and an additional income maintenance sector, providing means-tested Supplementary Benefit to those excluded from the National Insurance system or having extra family needs. The history of how this regime of two separate programmes developed is a complex one, which will be described where relevant in ensuing sections. It is interesting at this point to note, however, that the desire to limit redistribution through the National Insurance system is explicit at many points in the legislative development of the scheme. Thus the National Insurance Act of 1911 was seen by its proponents as an extension of the risk pooling activities of trade unions to a wider number of 'scheduled trades'. The view, held strongly by Beveridge and others, that an insurance scheme of this kind implied a contractual relationship between the individual and the state which would be destroyed if there was explicit redistribution towards the 'unemployment-prone', led to the exclusion of trades containing such individuals from the scheme. A long but interesting extract from a speech by Sir Hubert Llewellyn Smith of the Board of Trade to the British Association (Economics Section) in 1910 illustrates this clearly:

1. The scheme must be compulsory; otherwise the bad personal risks against which we must always be on our guard would be certain to predominate.
2. The scheme must be contributory, for only by exacting rigorously as a necessary qualification for benefit that a sufficient number of weeks' contributions shall have been paid by each recipient can we possibly hope to put limits on the exceptionally bad risks . . . armed with [the] double weapon of a maximum limit to benefit and of a minimum contribution, the operation of the scheme itself will automatically exclude the loafer . . . for the same reason it is essential to enlist the interest of all those engaged in the insured trades . . . by associating them with the scheme both as regards contribution and management[7].

This is a classic statement of the traditional principles of insurance: the fear of redistribution driving out the low risks, the existence of coinsurance (contributions) and deductibles (duration limits on benefits) and the attempt to incorporate the insured into administration in order to deal with the problem of moral hazard. It is clear that Llewellyn Smith did not envisage National Insurance as a redistributive scheme and indeed, Beveridge, despairing later in the 1930s with the apparent destruction of the traditional insurance scheme in those years because unforeseen levels of unemployment forced benefits to be extended to unemployed individuals with no contributions, was led to advocate a return to an industrial basis for unemployment insurance, with risk only being pooled within the (less heterogeneous) workers of each industry (Beveridge, 1930, pp. 408–411).

It will be demonstrated in Sections 6.3 and 6.4 below that

redistribution within the current National Insurance regime is severely limited and that the most 'unemployment-prone' are still excluded from benefits. In November 1978, for example, only 38% of the registered unemployed received Unemployment Benefit while over half relied on means tested Supplementary Benefit[8]. In general, an unemployment insurance scheme will redistribute where there are no exclusions from benefit, where low income groups experience highest unemployment rates and where contributions are related to earnings in employment without any upper limit. In practice, unemployment insurance regimes impose substantial limitations on redistribution. In Britain at the present time, redistribution in the National Insurance scheme is limited by regulations concerning the number of contributions for receipt of Unemployment Benefit, limitations on the duration of benefit in single and linked spells and an upper earnings limit on contributions. These regulations and planned amendments to them are described in more detail in Section 6.3.

Finally, it is necessary to point out that the actual redistributive impact of unemployment insurance may be more limited than at first appears, because the actual earnings distribution must be contrasted with the hypothetical distribution that would exist if there were no unemployment insurance. If 'unemployment-prone' individuals were able to bid up their wages when in work to compensate for periods of unemployment, the basis upon which redistribution is measured would be altered.

Paternalism: compulsory saving

It has been suggested that state provision of unemployment insurance may be justified by market failure, but that the consequent redistribution is often curtailed within the state 'insurance' programme (although this is more doubtful when the whole income maintenance programme is considered). However, contributions to a compulsory insurance scheme may also be regarded as a form of forced saving. The justification for using insurance as a form of forced saving rests on two propositions. The first, outlined earlier, is that buying insurance is a more efficient way of dealing with risk than private saving. Even people who are not particularly at risk may be risk averse and try to save larger amounts than are really necessary, given the objective probabilities, in case their worst expected outcome actually occurs. Insurance, however, is a form of contingent saving with premiums based on the average likelihood over the insured populations of the event occurring (Baily, 1978).

This proposition only justifies provision of insurance in some form. The case for state intervention rests on a second proposition, namely that where the population is heterogeneous, a small group of high risk individuals might, despite all the available evidence, refuse to save or insure themselves against the probability of experiencing unemployment. Compulsory insurance, similar to third party motor insurance in Britain, would seem to solve this problem; but this forced saving might have to be provided by the state if the high risk individual were unable to obtain private cover.

It is an empirical question whether the state insurance system actually insures high risk individuals in Britain, although it undoubtedly provides a form of forced saving since contributions to the National Insurance Fund are compulsory for the employed and self-employed. Whether such forced saving is justified depends on whether saving would have been suboptimal in the absence of a state insurance scheme but it is of course impossible to know what this saving would have been. Historically, some measure of saving earmarked for unemployment insurance can be obtained by examining the records of trade unions prior to the 1911 National Insurance Act. Thus in the period 1898–1907, the 100 principal trade unions paid out some £4 000 000 in unemployment insurance benefits from accumulated contributions[9]. Those who were not members of insuring trade unions had to rely on their savings but, despite relatively stagnant real wages at the end of the nineteenth century, the extent of working class saving through unions, mutual associations, cooperatives and insurance companies on provision of health insurance, benefits against old age and disability, funeral expenses and unemployment was remarkable[10].

In the modern context, the assets held by unemployed individuals as a result of past saving form an important issue. The existence of income maintenance programmes reduce the need for such saving, but coverage by state schemes is not universal and was until recently concerned with provision of a subsistence level of income rather than maintenance of earnings. Thus some private asset holding would be expected among unemployed individuals. Few data are available on this subject in Britain: the General Household Survey does not ask questions about saving and the Family Expenditure Survey has a limited definition of saving and does not publish the relevant cross-tabulations. Furthermore, recipients of National Insurance benefits are not required to declare the extent of their assets. However, recipients of Supplementary Benefit, who made up over half the unemployed in November 1978, are required to provide evidence concerning asset holdings. A survey of unemployed men in receipt of Supplementary Benefit in 1974 by Clark (1978) found that 86% of men interviewed had no financial assets whatever and the same author quotes DHSS records (presumably for *all* those unemployed in receipt of SB) as showing that 95% of those who did have savings had less than £150[11]. Although there is an incentive to conceal savings in interviews, it seems clear that the vast majority of those in receipt of Supplementary Benefit, and presumably a substantial, although smaller, proportion of those in receipt of Unemployment Benefit or debarred from Supplementary Benefit, have no savings of any importance.

The conclusions to be drawn from this are that contributions to state insurance have undoubtedly reduced private saving but that it is unclear whether the total level of saving has been higher as a result of state involvement[12]. Furthermore, even if private savings would have been deficient in the absence of state insurance, it is difficult to know whether this deficiency was caused by the refusal of individuals to save optimally (the paternalist argument), by lack of profitable opportunities (market failure) or simply because of low earnings when in work (the redistributive argument).

Raising revenue

National Insurance benefits are financed by contributions which take the form of a payroll tax levied on employers part of which is deducted from the earnings of employees, supplemented by a contribution from the general tax receipts of the central government exchequer. The rates of contribution are reassessed each year so that the outgoings of the National Insurance Fund are roughly balanced by its receipts. Means-tested benefits such as Supplementary Benefit are financed out of general taxation.

It is obvious that were National Insurance benefits such as pensions and Unemployment Benefit to be financed out of general taxation, instead of a separate contributory system, general taxes such as income tax or Value Added Tax would be levied at a higher rate. Nevertheless, National Insurance contributions are simply another form of tax and not an actuarial insurance fund, since current receipts are paid to current claimants, and at first sight it seems somewhat surprising that a separate tax form should be established at all. The explanation of this, although not perhaps the justification for its present continuation, is again historical. The early National Insurance legislation replicated many features of existing trade union schemes which had established separate contributory schemes, and was seen by its proponents as an insurance scheme distinct from general relief of destitution. Contributions were seen as a form of coinsurance to reduce the problem of moral hazard. The distinct character of the National Insurance scheme has been eroded in recent years, however, with the incorporation of the contribution into PAYE and the end of a separate National Insurance stamp.

Payroll taxes are rather an efficient method of raising revenue from the administrative point of view because the elasticity of revenues with respect to changes in the tax rate (in this case, the contributions rate) is near unity. All employers pay insurance contributions and therefore increased contributions can be passed on in the form of higher product prices or lower (increases in) money wages, as the econometric evidence suggests (Brittain, 1972). It is not surprising, therefore, to find that in the early days of such schemes, trade unionists and radicals argued against state contributory insurance on the grounds that the incidence of payroll taxes, unlike other taxes, would be highly regressive, particularly with a flat-rate contribution[13]. Incidence may have changed since then with the incorporation of the vast majority of wage-earners into income tax and the move to graduated National Insurance contributions (albeit with an upper-earnings limit) but a full discussion of tax incidence is beyond the scope of this chapter[14].

In considering the revenue-raising function of an insurance scheme, it is useful to consider the National Insurance Fund in more detail. If the receipts of the National Insurance Fund exceed the payments, the system can be considered as a revenue-raising supplement to general taxation. An excess of receipts to the National Insurance Fund is loaned to the government through purchases of government stocks via the National Debt Commissioners, and this can be used to offset a part of the Public Sector Borrowing Requirement or indeed supplement the budget surplus[15].

The first few years of the National Insurance Fund saw the accumulation of a moderate surplus as unemployment rates just prior to 1914 were below the budgeted rate of 8.6%. The inter-war years saw the National Insurance Fund moving into heavy deficit, relying on borrowing from the government and an exchequer contribution to the Fund of up to 50% of receipts (compared to 15–20% in the post-1945 period)[16]. The statistics for the period 1949–1977 are shown in *Figure 6.1*. These statistics show whether there was a net inflow to, or outflow from, the National Insurance Fund in this period. It is clear that in the early period a moderate surplus was accumulated, that in the 1960s there was a small net outflow and that the accumulated surplus rose sharply in the mid 1970s with a peak inflow of over £900 million in 1977 (all figures are in current prices). In November 1980, the National Insurance Fund stood at around £4500 million which represented over a third of the value of expenditure from the Fund in that year[17].

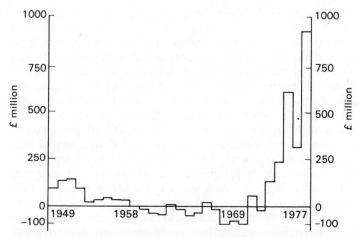

Figure 6.1 *Excess (deficit) of receipts over payments of the National Insurance Fund 1949–1977.* Source *DHSS* Social Security Statistics 1977, *HMSO,* Tables 44.02, 44.04. Note *All prices are current prices*

It might seem paradoxical that the surplus of the National Insurance Fund grew sharply during precisely the period when unemployment rose, since the rise should lead to a fall in the number of contributors and a rise in benefits paid. In fact Unemployment Benefit constitutes a small proportion of expenditure from the Fund, varying from 3% of payments in the 1950s to 7 or 8% in recent years. The major expenditure has been on pensions (60–70%) with Sickness Benefits (and, later, Invalidity Benefits) accounting for about 15%, and administrative costs 4%. Nor has the increase in the surplus stemmed from an increase in the contribution from the exchequer, which has remained roughly constant at 15–20% of receipts, or from income from investments, which had declined to only 2% of receipts in the 1970s.

There are two major reasons for the recent revenue-raising function of the National Insurance Fund. The first is that the Government Actuary, in setting the contributions rate to finance expected payments from the Fund in the course of the year, bases his forecast of inflation on the official government forecast, which has recently underestimated inflation. Thus the total value of earnings-related contributions has been higher than projected[18]. The second temporary cause of the surplus is connected with the introduction of the new earnings-related pension scheme. Although contributions were earnings-related from 1975, no earnings-related pension was paid until 1979 because details concerning contracting-out needed to be resolved.

The period 1975–1979 therefore represented a period of substantial forced saving. It is hard to believe that revenue-raising motives did not indirectly enter into this decision, however, since it could have been possible to adjust contributions gradually in that period. Indeed the government has explicitly used the employers' contribution to the National Insurance Fund as a revenue-raising device and a tool of macroeconomic policy, in the form of the National Insurance surcharge which is received directly by the central exchequer.

Some authorities (e.g. Feldstein, 1974) have argued that the social security programme should accumulate a fund along actuarial lines to finance future payments. The early planners of unemployment and health insurance in Britain treated the two types of insurance quite distinctly, since it was envisaged that health insurance (and pensions) would be characterized by an age pattern of contributions and claims while unemployment incidence was only unequal on a lifetime basis insofar as general economic conditions varied (Gilbert, 1966, pp. 280–281). But as Feldstein points out, the actuarial motive for accumulating a fund, which would require a substantial increase in the level of current contributions, is unnecessary as long as the state has the power to tax earnings. Rather, the argument for accumulating a fund is that it will reduce the future burden of taxes, particularly with an ageing population. Nevertheless neither Britain nor the United States have established an actuarial fund to finance payments to the unemployed, the sick and the elderly, not only because future generations have no current votes in politics, but also because the exact provisions of social security schemes have changed so frequently that the actuarial implications of present legislation vary almost from year to year.

It can be concluded that revenue raising is not an explicit aim of the British insurance scheme although the avoidance of further demands on existing taxes was an important consideration in early controversies. In recent years a substantial surplus has been accumulated, while the budget of 1980 suggests that the government may be moving towards a separation of the financing of short-term benefits from contributions and a reconsideration of the revenue implications of the National Insurance system (see Section 6.5).

Summary

This section has examined the four motives for state involvement in unemployment insurance suggested by Diamond in the context of general social security provision, and some of the literature on optimal provision of unemployment insurance by the state. Elements of all four motives appear to explain certain characteristics of state intervention, but many arguments, notably those of optimal insurance models, fail to provide sufficient justification for state intervention as opposed to private or cooperative provision of insurance. A deeper historical analysis might seek to examine in more detail the form of state intervention in Britain and how the present scheme came about in the face of conflicting interests[19].

The next section examines the operation of the British unemployment insurance system in more detail. It describes the recent breakdown of the 'insurance' part of the programme for provision of benefits to the unemployed.

6.3 The unemployment benefit regime in Britain[20]

Contributions

The 1946 National Insurance Act represented the culmination of the move towards 'insurance' based on a contributory system providing flat-rate contributions and benefits supplemented by a means-tested sector[21]. This section concentrates on the move since then towards earnings-related insurance which was finalized in the Social Security Act 1975. Whereas previously eligibility for benefits, including Unemployment Benefit, had been determined by the *number* of contributions paid in employment, the present scheme requires a minimum *value* of contributions. Contributions are proportional to earnings and the current (1980/81) rates are 6.75% of earnings paid by the employee and 10.2% paid by the employer, between an upper and lower earnings limit (the latter being set at approximately the level of the basic state pension). The year for which the relevant value of contributions is determined is the tax year, and the benefit year is the following calendar year. An individual who is registered as unemployed or sick is credited with a flat-rate Class 1 (employed) contribution at the minimum rate. Class 2 contributors (the self-employed) pay a different rate and are not eligible for Unemployment Benefit.

The move towards earnings-related 'insurance' resulted from a desire to supplement the flat-rate pension by an earnings-related component. This two-tier pension is not applicable to those who have contracted out of the earnings-related tier of the state scheme. Those who have contracted out pay lower contributions, with the 1980/81 rates being set at 4.25% of earnings for the employee and 5.7% for the employer. Finally, employers are currently paying a 3.5% National Insurance surcharge on their contribution, although this surcharge is paid direct to the central exchequer.

Benefits

Prior to 1975, full flat-rate Unemployment Benefit was payable, after 3 'waiting days'[22], if 50 Class 1 contributions had been paid in the appropriate contributions year. Reduced benefit was payable to those with at least 26, but less than 50 contributions. In certain circumstances, benefits could be raised for additional Class 2 contributions but these alone were not sufficient to claim Unemployment Benefit. Since 1975, the requirement for full benefit is that in the contributions year a value of contributions equal to 50 times the rate for the lower limit must be paid. Reduced rate benefit at 75% of the full flat-rate is payable for a value of $37\frac{1}{2}$ times and 50% for 25 times the lower earnings limit. The new scheme is therefore regressive in the sense that higher wage earners require a lower number of actual weeks of employment relative to low wage earners in order to be eligible for full benefits. Nevertheless, overall eligibility will be increased by the 1975 Act so long as the lower earnings limit does not exclude a substantial proportion of low wage earners. There are additional provisions covering new entrants to the labour force and working wives.

Other factors also determine eligibility for benefits. Individuals who are otherwise eligible but on strike, left their job voluntarily or were dismissed for misconduct can be excluded from benefit for up to 6 weeks. These individuals, along with those with insufficient contributions, may apply for means-tested Supplementary Benefit[23]. Few people are, however, affected by these specific exclusions. In May 1977 only 3% of those unemployed on Supplementary Benefit had their claim disallowed for leaving a job voluntarily, and 1% for industrial misconduct, although this regulation may have discouraged some people from registering as unemployed. However, 38% of the unemployed who depended solely on Supplementary Benefit had insufficient contributions (Clark, 1978, p. 388). Unemployment Benefit is also not paid if the individual restricts 'unreasonably' the location or type of job he or she is willing to accept or refuses 'without good cause' to take a job offered, and these regulations have been enforced in periods of high employment when certain regions suffer from a shortage of labour[24].

One exclusion which might usefully be examined at this point is that debarring the self-employed from claiming Unemployment Benefit. The self-employed pay a special rate which is less than the sum of the rates of contributions of the employer and employee and they are eligible for other National Insurance benefits. The rationale for debarring them from Unemployment Benefit is presumably that their notional contribution is lower than the total paid by or on behalf of the wage earner. Nevertheless if employers pass on their

National Insurance contribution in the form of higher prices, the self-employed will share in the incidence of the employer's contribution. If, on the other hand, employers respond to the contribution by paying lower wages than they would otherwise have done, the self-employed do not bear the cost. Unfortunately, studies which indicate that employers are able to shift the burden of National Insurance contributions are unable to discriminate between these two mechanisms. The distinction between notional and effective incidence does, however, suggest that such exclusions have to be justified on other grounds.

If an individual is entitled to Unemployment Benefit he or she will receive it for a continuous period of up to 1 year if he or she remains unemployed. The only limit on eligibility is the linked spells rule. Under this regulation, a person registered as unemployed must have worked for at least 6 weeks immediately preceding the unemployment spell (prior to 1980 the figure was 13 weeks), otherwise he or she will be treated as if the previous and current spells of unemployment were a single spell.

At present, flat-rate benefit may be supplemented, for a period lasting from 2 weeks after the start of the spell for 6 months, by Earnings Related Supplement (ERS) subject to the individual satisfying the basic requirements for National Insurance benefit. The level of ERS is based on earnings in the preceding tax year and is calculated by a complicated formula on a graduated and slightly progressive scale with lower and upper earnings limits which are raised each year. One obvious consequence of basing ERS on income in the previous tax year is that the level of supplement will be rather low in periods of rapid inflation of earnings and prices. Furthermore ERS is calculated by dividing annual earnings by 50 in order to derive a notional figure for weekly earnings. This averaging procedure will reduce the value of ERS paid to anyone with a history of work interruption. Finally, even if the individual is potentially eligible for ERS at the full rate, a further provision limits the total value of benefits including ERS to 85% of previous earnings.

The introduction of ERS in 1966 reflected the shift towards an earnings-related 'insurance' system. Nevertheless, the number of unemployed in receipt of ERS has rarely exceeded a fifth of the unemployed and the government announced in 1980 its intention to phase out ERS by 1982. Two other measures in the budget of that year are of equal significance. One was the proposal to tax short term National Insurance benefits by 1982 or as soon as possible after that date. The second was the decision to raise short term National Insurance benefits, i.e. Unemployment and Sickness Benefit, by less than the rate of Supplementary Benefit, in November 1980. The result of this, coupled with the abolition of ERS, is that many more of the unemployed will in future have to claim Supplementary Benefit to bring their incomes up to the officially designated minimum.

Some welfare aspects of the benefit regime in Britain

In the light of the discussion in Section 6.2, it seems useful to appraise the regulations governing the financing and payment of Unemployment Benefit and other state benefits for the unemployed in Britain in relation to these theoretical considerations. Unfortunately it is not easy to make sense of many aspects of the British benefit regime without detailed knowledge concerning the historical background to the development of the British welfare state and the changing principles and compromises embodied in the legislation. Some of these developments have been described in Section 6.2 and space does not permit further detailed historical investigation. Nevertheless some discussion of the conflicts of principle inherent in the benefit regime is useful at this point.

One important principle is to minimize the deadweight cost of administering benefits. By this criterion, the National Insurance system is more administratively efficient than the Supplementary Benefit Commission, which is responsible for the major means-tested benefit for the unemployed. Operating expenses account for only 4% of the outgoings of the Fund whereas the Supplementary Benefits Commission absorbs 13.5% of its outgoings in administration (Atkinson and Flemming, 1978). Although the National Insurance Fund is less costly to administer, it is still necessary to ask whether a separate Fund for unemployment 'insurance', as opposed to, say, a minimum income administered through the tax system, is strictly necessary[25]. It was explicitly recognized in the early days of unemployment insurance that benefits would be non-actuarially financed out of present contributions, so that, as Mesher succinctly argues

> Future benefits are determined not by levels of past contributions but by what the community at the time considers right.
> (1976, p. 20)

Historically, it was believed that the role of the state in the provision of unemployment insurance should be limited to providing a minimum subsistence benefit and that this should be financed from a separate Fund because a flat-rate benefit financed out of ordinary taxation would be too redistributive. Beveridge also felt that

Once it is admitted in principle that, either under the guise of insurance or in some other form, genuine unemployment can be relieved indefinitely by the simple device of giving money from a bottomless purse, prevention is only likely to go by the board. (1930, p. 294)

Thus although he believed that subsistence benefits might be extended indefinitely so long as the individual remained unemployed, the existence of a separate contributory fund with explicit financial constraints would strengthen the resolve of the government to maintain high levels of employment and so reduce the drain on public funds resulting from substantial payments to the unemployed. For these reasons, a separate state-organized 'insurance' fund was instituted. Nevertheless, once both contributions and, with the introduction of Earnings Related Supplement in 1966, benefits became earnings-related, the need for a separate fund became redundant. As Mesher points out, a consequence of the 1975 Act is that the contributions test has become:

. . . a quagmire of contributions, credits and [after 1975] earnings factors . . . . Contributions will be collected in the same way as PAYE tax, but a distinct fund is retained. This is almost all that survives of the original Beveridge contribution system. A flat rate of contribution irrespective of income was one of the [Beveridge] Report's fundamental principles. (1976, pp. 18, 21)

The 1980 proposals have, of course, further muddied the waters. Earnings-related unemployment benefit is to be phased out so that the benefit regime is composed of earnings-related contributions, similar to but separate from the tax system (except for the upper limit), and the payment of flat-rate benefits which are supplemented by other means-tested benefits paid out of general taxation. The administrative rationale for such a combination of methods of finance and forms of benefit seems unclear.

It was pointed out in Section 6.2 that contributory insurance might be justified as a form of coinsurance in order to limit the problem of moral hazard, and that this principle explained the early incorpo-ration of existing forms of contributory insurance, such as those provided by trade unions. However, one result of the 1975 Act is that few people understand the complexity of rules governing eligibility for benefit, so that the relevance of contributory requirements to the problem of moral hazard is unclear. Furthermore, the problem of moral hazard is essentially concerned with *present* attachment to the labour market and thus the gap between the contribution year and the benefit year means that the relevance of the past contribution period to present entitlement is limited. Finally the existing requirement that individuals must register as unemployed in order to obtain benefit is the simplest, and probably a sufficient, method of limiting 'voluntary' unemployment.

Two other important welfare considerations in examining British provision of unemployment insurance are the redistributive impact of benefits and contributions, which is interrelated with the question of eligibility, and the question of the impact of unemployment insurance on incentives. The latter problem is dealt with in Chapter 5 and is not considered further here[26].

In principle, an unemployment insurance system which pays flat-rate benefit financed out of earnings-related contributions is highly redistributive, in the sense that high risk individuals, who presumably have lower earnings, gain a greater 'return' on their contributions. But, on the contributions side, the redistributive aspect is limited by imposing upper and lower earnings limits on earnings-related contributions. The lower earnings limit may exclude some contributors from accumulating the minimum value of contributions, although the limit is set so low that it is unlikely that many full-time earners are in such a position. The averaging procedure for calculating earnings for ERS has a similar impact. Similarly, the upper earnings limit will limit the deduction from high earners in regular employment, although the limit is set well above average earnings.

On the benefits side, the requirement for a minimum value of contributions allows high wage earners to satisfy eligibility requirements more quickly, and high risk individuals will also be penalized by the limit on the duration of National Insurance benefits and the linked spells rule. Analysis of these provisions requires a more detailed investigation of the incidence of unemployment among the population, and further discussion is postponed until Section 6.4. Finally, it should be noted that a full analysis of redistribution would take account of the financing of Supplementary Benefit out of general taxation which in turn would require a detailed analysis of the incidence of the whole system of taxation.

Eligibility for unemployment insurance in Britain

The most useful way of looking at eligibility for National Insurance benefits and other related benefits is to estimate the probability of an individual receiving the various benefits at any stage of his or her spell of unemployment. Such a study requires detailed information concerning the characteristics of the unemployed, preferably in the form of a longitudinal or cohort study in which the experience of a sample of individuals is traced over a period of time. Unfortunately there is at present no such study available in Britain[27]. The simplest approach is, therefore, to utilize published data on the eligibility of the stock of unemployed for various benefits at particular dates, and these data are illustrated in *Figure 6.2* for the period 1968–1978.

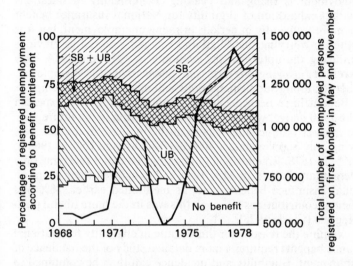

Figure 6.2 *Number of registered unemployed and entitlement to benefit 1968–1978.* (Source: *Department of Employment* Gazette *January 1980,* Table 112. *DHSS* Social Security Statistics 1973, *HMSO*)

Figure 6.2 shows the changes in eligibility, as described on the left hand vertical scale, against the background of changes in the level of unemployment, as depicted on the right hand vertical scale. The period contains one unemployment cycle, with peak unemployment at the beginning of 1972, followed by a major and prolonged period of high unemployment after mid 1976. The proportion receiving no benefit fluctuates between 16% and 28% of the total stock of registered unemployed in this period. In earlier years, the proportion varies inversely with the level of unemployment because at low levels of unemployment average durations shorten and a larger number of the unemployed leave the register very quickly without claiming benefit because of the rule concerning 'waiting days'. However, after 1976 the proportion receiving no benefit rises despite the continued high level of employment. This may be in part because of an 'added worker effect' (such as an increased proportion of wives who are ineligible for National Insurance benefits registering to seek work as a consequence of the rise in male unemployment).

Alternatively the rise may reflect a toughening in the administration of benefits and increased enforcement of exclusions[28].

The proportion in receipt of Unemployment Benefit declines from well over 50% in 1968 to 38% in 1978. The downward trend seems to be steady although it appears to be more pronounced when unemployment is rising and peaking. Lengthening of durations means that exhaustion of eligibility for National Insurance benefit occurs more frequently in periods of rising unemployment, but it is nevertheless worrying that eligibility was not restored to previous levels during the upturn in the economy in 1973 and 1974. This might reflect a growing long term component among the unemployed. Numbers claiming Supplementary Benefit in addition to Unemployment Benefit have been declining, although it might be expected that the 1980 budget will increase this proportion in the future.

The most striking change has been the increase in the numbers receiving only Supplementary Benefit, from around 25% in 1968 to over 40% in 1978. Roughly half of unemployed males receiving only Supplementary Benefit in May 1977 had exhausted their claim on National Insurance benefits, and, as mentioned earlier, 38% had insufficient contributions although this was in the more liberal post-1975 regime (Clark, 1978).

To examine the reasons for this decline in eligibility for National Insurance benefits requires a more detailed study of the incidence of unemployment. Eligibility and incidence can then be combined to answer the question posed in Section 6.2: does unemployment insurance provide insurance to high-risk individuals who would otherwise be excluded and is it thus clearly redistributive?

6.4 The incidence of unemployment in Britain

The concentration of unemployment in Britain

An initial description of the incidence of unemployment would point to several dimensions of the inequality of experience. The regional inequality of unemployment incidence is well known: thus in October 1980, when the aggregate unemployment rate for the United Kingdom was 8.5%, regional rates varied from 5.6% in the South East to 15.6% in Northern Ireland. The duration of unemployment varies widely, for instance among age groups. Using data from the 1972 General Household Survey, Nickell (1979a) shows that the expected average duration of a completed spell of unemployment at that time was 7 weeks for a male aged 20 rising to 17 weeks for a male aged 60 and completed durations for all age groups have risen substantially since then[29]. Such durations illustrate one reason why relatively few of the stock of unemployed on the register are in receipt of Earnings Related Supplement. Substantial numbers of older people have exhausted their claim on ERS, while few of the younger people (who on average leave the register before their claim to ERS expires) are eligible because they lack work experience.

Another important dimension is the uneven incidence of unemployment among those with different skills. In September 1979 there were 1.76 unemployed registered as craftsmen for every craft vacancy in the United Kingdom but over 33 unemployed registered as unskilled for every vacancy as a general labourer[30]. Even in the relatively prosperous Midlands region, there were 41 general labouring unemployed for every vacancy. Unemployment incidence is therefore especially concentrated in depressed regions, among older people and among the unskilled.

The figures are revealing but more information is needed in order to depict eligibility for benefits and thus the coverage of unemployment insurance in Britain. For example, the unemployment rate might rise because durations lengthen so that greater numbers exhaust their claim on National Insurance benefits, or unemployment may rise because the inflow rises, which has uncertain effects on eligibility. Furthermore, the duration of a spell of unemployment is an important indicator of the likelihood of obtaining benefits for all or part of the spell, but does not describe the *total* experience of unemployment of an individual in any period of time. This is determined by the total number of separate spells of unemployment as well as their average duration. Recurrent spells will affect eligibility for flat-rate benefit under the linked spells rule and for ERS under the procedure by which weekly earned income is averaged over all 50 weeks of the tax year.

This total experience of unemployment, or overall inequality of incidence, can be illustrated in the following manner. Every year there are roughly 4.5 million spells of unemployment begun in Britain, and this number remains roughly constant irrespective of the pressure of demand for labour, which thus tends to determine the average length of spells. The working population is composed of approximately 26.5 million individuals. Thus if no individual experienced more than one spell of unemployment in a year, one sixth, or 17%, of the population would experience a spell of unemployment annually. In reality, something like 70% of weeks of unemployment in a single year are experienced by only 3% of the population. By similar reasoning, if unemployment were evenly distributed over a 3 year period, roughly 50% of the population would experience some unemployment. However, in the period 1971–1973, for three cohorts of individuals born in 1923, 1933 and

1943, less than 5% of individuals accounted for 80% of weeks of unemployment (Disney, 1979).

This concentration of unemployment among a small group of individuals could be the result of either an unequal distribution of spell durations composed of some short spells and a few very long spells, or by substantial spell recurrence, or both. Among older age groups, long spell durations are the major cause of concentration of unemployment, with a substantial proportion experiencing spells in excess of 26 and even 52 weeks, as borne out by the evidence of Nickell (1979a), Bowers and Harkess (1979) and others. The point may also be illustrated from work done by Owen (1981). In the period 1970–1974, those aged 55 who experienced more than 52 weeks of unemployment individually accounted for 40% of total weeks of unemployment in that age group whereas among 25 year olds, those experiencing the same durations accounted for only 10% of total weeks of unemployment.

Although the preponderance of long durations among the older unemployed is well known, it is sometimes asserted that the experience of unemployment is much more random among younger people, as evinced by the shorter average durations of spells of unemployment among this group and their higher rate of inflow to the register. This is often taken as evidence of search behaviour and explains limited eligibility for insurance benefits among this age group in terms of lack of initial contributions and voluntary quitting. Although this is partially correct, as indicated by the high proportion in receipt of Supplementary Benefit through insufficient contributions, even among this age group unemployment is concentrated among a small minority. This is due to spell recurrence rather than long durations. The experience of a male cohort born in 1943 during the period 1971–1973 is illuminating. The total number of spells per year as a percentage of the total labour force in this age group is roughly 23%—a higher percentage than the overall 17% mentioned above. Now if individual probabilities of leaving and entering the register were constant, rather less that 1 in 4 of the unemployed in this cohort would experience a *second* spell of unemployment, and less than 1 in 16 a third spell, and so on. The average number of spells per person experiencing unemployment in that year would be approximately 1.3 by this reasoning. The actual average number of spells per unemployed person among that age group is 1.5, suggesting that the risk of a second spell among the younger unemployed is significantly greater that the *average* probability of a first spell among that age group as a whole (Disney, 1979). Thus spell recurrence is also highly concentrated, even within those age groups most likely to experience frequent spells of unemployment.

Some idea of the characteristics other than age of those most prone to spell recurrence may be obtained from *Table 6.1*, which depicts some results from a random survey of the unemployed undertaken by the Department of Employment in June 1976, with a follow-up survey 6 months later. Care should be taken in interpreting results based on a survey of those on the unemployment register as opposed to the population as a whole, since those on the register at an arbitrary date may have different characteristics from the total number that pass through the register. At any point in time the register will contain a relatively larger number of individuals with low probabilities of leaving unemployment, and these individuals may also differ from the average in their probability of leaving

Table 6.1 Spell recurrence among the unemployed according to characteristics in 1976

	Males		*Females*	
	Number in sample	*Average number of spells in past year[1]*	*Number in sample*	*Average number of spells in past year[1]*
(1) by occupation and current duration				
All white collar[2]	2756	1.19	2100	1.29
Up to 13 weeks	1017	1.28	1064	1.33
13 to 26 weeks	603	1.22	475	1.28
Over 26 weeks	1136	1.09	561	1.12
Craft and similar occupations	2273	1.40	128	1.22
Up to 13 weeks	1049	1.58	53	1.39
13 to 26 weeks	497	1.39	36	1.19
Over 26 weeks	727	1.15	39	1.03
General labourers and other manual	9265	1.35	1703	1.28
Up to 13 weeks	3251	1.63	710	1.42
13 to 26 weeks	1690	1.24	386	1.30
Over 26 weeks	4324	1.12	607	1.10
(2) by follow-up survey				
Not left the register 6 months later	6235	1.21		
Found work	4045	1.44		
Left for other reasons	3741	1.39		

Notes:
1. Including present spell.
2. Includes managerial and professional, clerical and related, and other non-manual occupations.
Source: Department of Employment: *Characteristics of the Unemployed*: sample survey, June 1976, unpublished tabulations.

employment and thus their propensity to repeated spells. Nevertheless, the relative ranking of orders of magnitude is probably about right.

Table 6.1 suggests that among men, highest spell recurrence occurs among 'general labourers and other manual' who have been on the register for less than 13 weeks, followed by craftsmen. Spell recurrence is greatest among craftsmen because general labourers tend to stay on the register longer, as can be gauged from the numbers of the sample in each duration category. For women, spell recurrence and the division by spell durations are similar among all occupational categories. Spell recurrence is also higher among those who leave the register quicker, as indicated by the results of the follow-up survey.

In summary, incidence of unemployment is unequally distributed. Long spell durations are borne by older workers, by the unskilled and by those in regions with higher rates of unemployment. Spell recurrence is not just confined to the young, but is prevalent among unskilled general labourers and male craftsmen. The total experience of unemployment, taking into account both spell durations and spell recurrence, is unequally concentrated for all age groups, with older people experiencing longer spells and younger people extensive spell recurrence. These results provide some information with which to answer the question posed at the end of Section 6.3 concerning the coverage of the state system of unemployment insurance.

The relation between incidence and eligibility

The last part of Section 6.3 outlined a plausible explanation for changes in eligibility by linking eligibility to variations in the aggregate demand for labour. It was argued that as unemployment rises durations lengthen and a smaller proportion of the unemployed are debarred from benefits by the regulation concerning 'waiting days'. Indeed, in so far as the composition of the inflow changes, with more involuntary registrants relative to voluntary quits, eligibility for National Insurance benefit might temporarily increase. However as durations lengthen at the peak of unemployment, a growing number of the unemployed become ineligible for Earnings Related Supplement with durations exceeding 28 weeks, and Unemployment Benefit with durations exceeding 52 weeks. This, perhaps coupled with a tightening of administrative attitudes towards claimants in such periods, explains the decline in eligibility for National Insurance benefits at the present high levels of employment.

Nevertheless, these factors alone cannot explain the low coverage of Unemployment Benefit. Suppose the rate of outflow of individuals from the register was 5% weekly, implying an average duration of a spell of unemployment of around 20 weeks. In this case only 7% of the unemployed would remain on the register after 52 weeks. The operation of such a process alone does not appear to explain the high proportion of individuals who are ineligible for National Insurance benefits, as illustrated in *Figure 6.2*.

There are two ways in which this conflicting evidence can be reconciled. The first is that an observation of the stock of unemployed at points in time, such as *Figure 6.2*, introduces a measurement bias. If the average duration of a spell of unemployment is calculated by counting the unemployed at successive points in time, rather than by tracing an individual cohort over time, there is an above-average probability of observing long-duration individuals in successive counts. This leads to the familiar proposition that the measured uncompleted spell durations of the currently unemployed are usually longer than the average completed durations[31]. It obviously follows from this that if long-duration individuals are observed more often in the unemployment counts underlying *Figure 6.2*, and if these individuals are likely to have exhausted their claim on National Insurance benefits, then the proportions ineligible in *Figure 6.2* will be biased upwards.

The second point is more important. Underlying the proposition of a constant outflow is the implicit notion that the population is homogeneous and that the probability of leaving the register is independent of the duration of unemployment. In practice the *aggregate* probability of leaving the register is observed to decline over time and a greater proportion of the unemployed are observed to be in long-duration categories, and thus ineligible for National Insurance benefits, than a model with constant outflow rates would imply. It is possible that the probability of leaving the register does indeed decline over time, that is, that the probability is related to duration, but it is also possible that some 'sorting' process exists by which the population is divided into different subgroups with constant but differing probabilities of leaving the register[32]. Those subpopulations with 'better' labour market characteristics leave the register, on average, more quickly leaving a residual of unemployed labour which experiences a high incidence of unemployment.

It is, in this author's view, the latter 'sorting' process which largely explains the fall in the aggregate probability of leaving the register. Lancaster and Nickell (1980) try to separate the effect of duration from individual characteristics in explaining this decline. They find that as more individual characteristics are added to their model, the importance of the duration-related variable declines. In other words, it is individual characteristics rather than length on the register which are the major explanation of probabilities of leaving the register.

The previous part of this section suggested precisely which subpopulations are in practice likely to suffer from a high risk of unemployment and thus to be deprived of National Insurance benefits. The chief subpopulation is the class of unskilled and general labourers. *Table 6.1* demonstrated that they formed a large proportion of the unemployed, experiencing longer than average durations and also, perhaps surprisingly, a high incidence of spell recurrence. They may be deprived of Unemployment Benefit under both the 52 weeks limit on duration and the linked spells rule. They will almost certainly be regarded by unemployment offices as individuals who can be directed into any available low paid jobs and thus most likely to come up against the clauses concerning refusal to take jobs 'without good cause' and restricting 'unreasonably' the location or type of job when these clauses are infrequently applied. Furthermore, the choice of job which high risk individuals can get is limited, and unemployment shifts these individuals down the occupational ladder into even lower paid jobs (Metcalf and Nickell, 1979).This produces a stratum of workers who are most marginal in employment, being the first to lose their jobs when aggregate demand for labour slackens. Their jobs require longer periods to produce the requisite value of contributions and earnings sufficient to obtain Earnings Related Supplement and have disadvantages which induce voluntary quitting and the possibility of being debarred from National Insurance benefits for up to 6 weeks.

No other subpopulation has such a combination of characteristics. Younger people may be unable to obtain National Insurance benefits under the linked spells rule and the minimum requirement for contributions. Older workers and workers in depressed regions may exhaust their claim for Unemployment Benefit due to long durations. Women may be deprived by having insufficient contributions through having opted out, and may be debarred from Supplementary Benefit if they have a working husband. Nevertheless the unskilled subpopulation bears much of the brunt of unemployment.

It is useful to mention the impact of the linked spells rule, which is not generally discussed in policy debates concerning the un-employment insurance regime in Britain. The evidence in the earlier part of this section showed that around one third of the unemployed experienced a previous spell of unemployment in the year and might be penalized by this rule. A simulation analysis of a heterogeneous population suggests that roughly one third of the unemployed are likely to have experienced a previous spell of unemployment within 13 weeks of the present spell and 17% within 6 weeks of the present spell (Creedy and Disney, 1981). They may therefore be affected by this rule. These proportions are not very sensitive to changes in the outflow probability or the joint distribution of inflow and outflow probabilities. In the light of this, and the absence of such a rule in the unemployment insurance regimes of most other countries[33], there seems little justification for its continued existence[34].

The last, and most important, question raised by this analysis concerns the justifications put forward for state provision in Section 6.2. Two arguments appear to be of immediate relevance: market failure and the scope for redistribution. The analysis of incidence suggests that many of those most prone to unemployment, namely the unskilled and general labourers, older people, those with a propensity to change jobs and those in depressed regions, are least likely to obtain private insurance in the absence of state unemployment insurance. But it is clear that many of them are unable to obtain benefits under the National Insurance scheme. Redistribution to these individuals is limited because although they pay contributions while in work, the regulations governing the payment of National Insurance benefits coupled with the interaction between work interruption and low earnings, limit the amount of insurance benefits paid to them[35]. Such redistribution as occurs appears to be due to the existence of a separate income maintenance programme from the 'insurance' scheme, namely Supplementary Benefits. The rationale for a National Insurance Fund which does not adequately insure high risk individuals and leaves the redistribution aspect of benefit provision to a separate means-tested sector is unclear.

6.5 Conclusions

An examination of the case for state provision of unemployment insurance in Section 6.2 pointed to four reasons for its existence: correcting market failure, redistributing income, paternalistic compulsory saving and raising revenue. Models of optimal insurance which assume a homogeneous population fail to provide a rationale for state intervention in the particular context of market failure.

An assessment of the contributory and benefit aspects of the unemployment insurance regime in Great Britain in Section 6.3 suggested that most rules and regulations were designed to limit redistribution, with the consequence that many unemployed had to turn to the means-tested Supplementary Benefit sector for support. Historically, the National Insurance system, financed by contributions separated from general tax revenues, had served the function of providing social security without imposing a burden on general taxation and had indeed in recent years raised substantial revenues for the government exchequer. Nevertheless, the change in the basis for contributions in 1975, putting the system on roughly the same revenue-raising basis as income tax, the failure of the Fund to provide 'insurance' to over 60% of the unemployed, and the 1980 budget which phased out the earnings-related component of Unemployment Benefit and reduced the value of short-term National Insurance benefits in real terms, suggests that a distinct National Insurance system for the provision of unemployment insurance has become less justified.

Section 6.4 suggested that the incidence of unemployment in Britain is highly unequal and that distinct subgroups of the labour force, notably the unskilled, bare the brunt of unemployment. The lack of eligibility for National Insurance benefits was explained by this concentration of the experience of unemployment among a relatively small group. It was argued that historically these subgroups had been unable to obtain private or trade union insurance cover prior to the introduction of state insurance, and that the failure of state unemployment insurance to provide benefits to these individuals casts doubt on the market failure and redistributive arguments as explanations of state intervention in Britain.

The official unemployment insurance system is now in some confusion. The distinct character of the Beveridge scheme with its emphasis on a contributory flat-rate method of financing subsistence benefits has been eroded by the introduction of an earnings-related component on the one hand and the increasing reliance on means testing on the other. Reform of the system involves posing the question of whether there is anything worth salvaging in the idea of National Insurance. The distinct character of British unemployment insurance after 1911 was that it incorporated the contractual obligations implicit in earlier schemes in order to provide a self-financing system from which contributors would have the right to a guaranteed minimum income. However, the scheme has been unable to deal with periods of high unemployment, as in the 1930s when the National Insurance scheme was frequently bailed out by the central exchequer, and in the 1970s when eligibility for National Insurance benefits declined steadily. It is hardly surprising that a scheme which limits redistribution by a flat-rate contribution prior to 1975 and an upper earnings limit on contributions since then is unable to deal with the extremely unequal incidence of unemployment which is a characteristic of the British labour market.

There are several directions which a reformed system of

unemployment insurance could take in Britain. The first, which appears to be the direction of the post-1979 Conservative government, is to move towards a system of means-tested benefits for those unemployed who are deemed by administrative officers to be in need. Such a regime would place the major burden of support on existing means-tested benefits such as Supplementary Benefit. The idea of concentrating resources on the needy is superficially appealing but has several drawbacks. Familiar problems include administrative inefficiency, low take-up and the problem of coordinating many different benefits to avoid high marginal tax rates. However, if the implication of such a shift of priority is the destruction of a separate contributory 'insurance' system against unemployment, it is reasonable to question the necessity for a separate insurance 'fund' into which contributions are paid. It should be explicit in such circumstances that the sole function, if any, of the National Insurance Fund is to finance the state pension and other long term benefits if Unemployment Benefit is to be reduced to a minor role (perhaps along with Sickness Benefit).

An alternative strategy would take the opposite direction by strengthening the existing National Insurance system. In effect, such a 'Back to Beveridge' scheme would revert to flat-rate contributions and benefits and would require a liberalization of the regulations, notably in reducing the value of contributions required to satisfy eligibility, extending the duration of National Insurance benefits and abolishing the linked spells rule. Unfortunately, as Beveridge understood, sufficient contributions to finance benefits could only be accumulated if the government were committed to a policy of full employment. Otherwise contribution requirements would have to be minimal in order to increase eligibility to levels that justified the continuation of a separate contributory 'insurance' scheme.

The final direction of reform, which is perhaps the most appealing other than on grounds of cost, is to merge National Insurance contributions into the general taxation system and provide income to the unemployed, as well as to other low income groups, via an integrated scheme such as a negative income tax or a guaranteed minimum income. Such schemes have been discussed extensively[36]. Administratively, the idea is appealing now that National Insurance operates through PAYE, although it should be pointed out that since National Insurance contributions are not presently exempt from other taxes on incomes, the resulting income tax rate might well be higher that the sum of the present tax rate and the rates of National Insurance contributions. Such a merger would also have redistributive implications in relation to the incidence of taxes and benefits, although the resulting abolition of the present ceiling on earnings-related contributions would probably add to the progressiveness of the tax structure. On the side of benefits paid to the unemployed, a scheme such as a negative income tax is also a form of means testing, but nevertheless such a reform would eliminate the explicit selectivity and resulting stigma of reliance on discretionary benefits. Whether taxpayers and successive governments committed to public expenditure cuts would be amenable to such a radical reform is, of course, doubtful but nevertheless it would represent a large step away from the present inconsistent and inequitable treatment of the unemployed.

Notes

1. Where individuals prefer insurance with a premium m, which protects against loss of earnings, to facing without insurance a probability distribution of earnings loss with mean m. See Pauly (1968).
2. This results from the Law of Large Numbers (see Pauly, 1968).
3. In the case of state-run insurance, the government can of course attempt to control the economy in such a way as to reduce the demands on the insurance fund and so reduce the probability of high loss. Beveridge insisted that such intervention was necessary for an insurance fund to succeed.
4. For the early history of social security in Britain and other countries, see Gilbert (1966) and Rimlinger (1971).
5. See Titmuss (1968, Chapter 15) and (1974, Chapters 7 and 8).
6. The analogy is with the arguments of dual labour market theorists, who suggest that workers in the secondary labour market take on the characteristics, such as high turnover rates and absenteeism, with which their position is associated.
7. Quoted by Beveridge (1930), p. 265.
8. Department of Employment *Gazette* January 1980.
9. Beveridge (1930, p. 224). But two-thirds of trade unionists received no benefits and only one-quarter of manual workers were in trade unions in this period. Interestingly, there was clearly some redistribution within the trade union between contributors and beneficiaries: in the London Society of Compositors in the period 1904–1907, for instance, 56% of the total spent on unemployment benefit was expended on 9% of the membership (*ibid.*, p. 145).
10. Some evidence is revealing on this question. According to Gosden (1973), the 1872 Royal Commission on Friendly Societies (which normally provided health insurance and funeral

benefits) reported the existence of 32 000 societies with 4 million members, 8 million registered beneficiaries and funds of approximately £11 million (p. 74). Note that most societies operated on a pay-as-you-go basis in the mid nineteenth century and thus the turnover of funds was far greater. Total funds of all provident institutions at the beginning of the twentieth century totalled £400 million (Gosden, 1973, p. 259). In addition, industrial insurance companies at the end of the nineteenth century had 30 000 000 funeral benefit policies outstanding, employed 100 000 men to sell insurance and funeral benefits, mostly in working class neighbourhoods, and held a face value of policies in 1910 of £285 million. The Prudential, the largest insurance company, was the largest private owner of freehold property in the United Kingdom, the largest shareholder of Bank of England stocks, and of Indian and colonial government bonds and stocks (Gilbert, 1966, pp. 318–320).

11. Under the rules introduced in 1975, the value of an owner-occupied property plus any other capital amounting in total to £1200, is ignored altogether in calculating a claimant's resources.

12. Critics of existing state insurance schemes have emphasized this. See Feldstein (1974). However Burns (1941, p. xiv) points out that a contributory 'insurance' system which pays guaranteed benefits irrespective of private saving will reduce savings by less than a means-tested system.

13. See Gilbert (1966, p. 270) and, for France, Rimlinger (1971, pp. 61–62).

14. A recent discussion is contained in Kay and King (1978). See also Creedy (1981).

15. A surplus of the Fund is generally invested initially in tap Treasury bills but subsequently reinvested in long or medium dated stocks. The portfolio is largely determined by the Treasury although before the Second World War the Unemployment Insurance Statutory Committee generally had an independent purchasing policy. See Prest (1975, p. 210).

16. See Beveridge (1930, pp. 271–294) and Burns (1941).

17. *The Times*, 28 Nov. 1980. Other statistics are taken from *Social Security Statistics*. Attempts were made in the 1950s to establish a National Insurance (Reserve) Fund, composed originally of monies left from the pre-1946 schemes. Investments were added to this Reserve Fund in 1953 and 1956, probably because of concern about the actuarial implications of changes in the age structure of the population. However, after the passing of the 1975 Social Security Act, assets were transferred to the National Insurance Fund.

18. The proportion of earnings-related to flat-rate contributions gradually rose after 1961, when a graduated pension was introduced. Since 1975 all contributions are earnings-related.
19. At the risk of pulling a Marxist rabbit out of the hat at this stage of the present discussion, an interesting attempt on these lines is that of Ginsburg (1979).
20. Throughout this chapter [and book], reference is made to Great Britain. Northern Ireland social security is administered separately but the provisions are largely identical. However, many of the statistics used here refer to Great Britain rather than the United Kingdom.
21. For an analysis of this scheme see George (1968).
22. Prior to 1971, benefit was reimbursed for these 3 days if the individual was unemployed for longer than 2 weeks.
23. Since 1971, persons not eligible for Unemployment Benefit because of 'industrial misconduct' or 'voluntary unemployment' may have their Supplementary Benefit reduced for up to 6 weeks by 40% of the relevant scale rate.
24. Specific cases are discussed in Mesher (1976).
25. This question is discussed in more detail in Meade *et al.* (1978) and Creedy (1981).
26. It is worth pointing out, however, that many previous studies of the relation between unemployment insurance and incentives in Britain have ignored the question of eligibility for benefits. The importance of this omission is illustrated by the last part of Section 6.3 (pp. 168–170).
27. However, Creedy and Disney (1981) attempt to estimate eligibility for National Insurance benefits in this way by combining a simple model of probabilities with some of the available empirical evidence. See Section 6.4.
28. There has recently been some controversy concerning the division of functions between the Manpower Services Commission, which administers Job Centres, the Department of Employment and the Department of Health and Social Security as to whether this division is (1) administratively efficient, in terms of finding employment, especially the for long-term unemployed, and (2) able to minimize the voluntary prolongation of spells of unemployment.
29. Nickell (1979a, p. 1261). Bowers and Harkess (1979) give completed durations for males in January 1977 of 16 weeks for those aged 18–25 and 45 weeks for those aged 55 and over. Comparable figures for January 1972 were 9.5 weeks for those aged 18–25 and 38.6 for those aged over 55 (women were 7.6 and 24.2 respectively). These average durations are longer than those

of Nickell but his durations are standardized for individual characteristics.

30. Department of Employment *Gazette* (Vol. 87, No. 11, November 1979, pp. 1114–1117). The term 'general labourer' may be a catch-all for individuals not registered under other categories, but it might be expected to include a high proportion of unskilled individuals.

31. For methods of calculating completed spell durations see for instance, Nickell (1979a, b).

32. Salant (1977) provides a clear exposition of this point.

33. Blaustein and Craig (1977, Table 8) describe the main provisions in several industrialized countries.

34. The rule also applies in the case of linked spells of sickness and had the positive motive of avoiding the need for requalification for benefit (waiting days) in the case of linked spells. However the 1980 budget has introduced 'waiting days' for each spell composing the linked spell so that the rule simply penalizes those with a high risk of spell recurrence. The conclusion in the text is therefore reinforced by this change in the regulations.

35. This is also true when eligibility for the earnings-related component of the state pension is considered.

36. See, for instance, Meade (1972), Meade *et al.* (1978) and Creedy (1981).

References

Atkinson, A. B. and Flemming, J. S. (1978). Unemployment, social security and incentives. *Midland Bank Review* (Autumn), 6–16

Baily, M. N. (1978). Some aspects of optimal unemployment insurance. *Journal of Public Economics* **10**, 379–402

Beveridge, W. I. (1930). *Unemployment: A Problem of Industry* (New Edition). London; Longmans

Blaustein, S. J. and Craig, I. (1977). *An International Review of Unemployment Insurance Schemes*. Michigan; Upjohn Institute for Employment Research

Bowers, J. K. and Harkess, D. (1979). Duration of unemployment by age and sex. *Economica* **46**, 239–260

Brittain, J. (1972). *The Payroll Tax for Social Security*. Washington, D.C.; The Brookings Institution

Burns, E. M. (1941). *British Unemployment Programs 1920–1938*. Washington, D.C.; Committee on Social Security, Social Science Research Council

Clark, M. (1978). The unemployed on Supplementary Benefit: living standards and making ends meet on a low income. *Journal of Social Policy* 7, 385–410

Creedy, J. (1981). *Pensions in Britain*. Cambridge; CUP for NIESR

Creedy, J. and Disney, R. (1981). Eligibility for unemployment benefits in Great Britain. *Oxford Economic Papers* 33 (forthcoming)

Department of Health and Social Security. *Social Security Statistics*. London; HMSO (various issues)

Diamond, P. A. (1977). A framework for Social Security analysis. *Journal of Public Economics* 8, 275–298

Disney, R. (1979). Recurrent spells and the concentration of unemployment in Great Britain. *Economic Journal* 89, 109–119

Feldstein, M. (1974). The optimal financing of Social Security. Discussion Paper No. 388, Harvard Institute of Economic Research

Flemming, J. S. (1978). Aspects of optimal unemployment insurance: search, leisure, savings and capital market imperfections. *Journal of Public Economics* 10, 403–425

George, V. (1968). *Social Security: Beveridge and After*. London; RKP

Gilbert, B. B. (1966). *The Evolution of National Insurance in Great Britain*. London; Michael Joseph

Ginsburg, N. (1979). *Class, Capital and Social Policy*. London; Macmillan

Gosden, P. H. J. H. (1973). *Self-Help: Voluntary Associations in Nineteenth-Century Britain*. London; Batsford

Kay, J. A. and King, M. A. (1978). *The British Tax System*. Oxford; Clarendon Press

Lancaster, A. and Nickell, S. (1980). The analysis of re-employment probabilities for the unemployed. *Journal of the Royal Statistical Society*, Series A 143, 141–152

Meade, J. E. (1972). Poverty in the welfare state. *Oxford Economic Papers* 24, 289–326

Meade, J. E., et al. (1978). *Structure and Reform of Direct Taxation*. London; Allen & Unwin

Mesher, J. (1976). *Compensation for Unemployment*. London; Sweet and Maxwell

Metcalf, D. and Nickell, S. (1979). *Occupational mobility in Great Britain*. London; London School of Economics, Centre for Labour Economics Discussion Paper No. 60

Nickell, S. J. (1979a). Estimating the probability of leaving unemployment. *Econometrica* 47, 1249–1266

Nickell, S. J. (1979b). The effect of Unemployment and related

Benefits on the duration of unemployment. *Economic Journal* **89**, 34–49

Owen, S. (1981). Do the faces in the dole queue change? *Government Economic Service Occasional Paper* (forthcoming)

Pauly, M. V. (1968). The economics of moral hazard: comment. *American Economic Review* **58**, 531–537

Prest, A. R. (1975). *Public Finance*, 5th Edition. London; Weidenfeld and Nicholson

Report on Social Insurance and Allied Services (The Beveridge Report) (1942). London; HMSO, Cmnd. 6406

Rimlinger, G. V. (1971). *Welfare Policy and Industrialization in Europe, America and Russia.* New York; John Wiley

Salant, W. W. (1977). Search theory and duration: A theory of sorts. *Quarterly Journal of Economics* **91**, 39–57

Titmuss, R. M. (1968). *Commitment to Welfare.* London; Allen & Unwin

Titmuss, R. M. (1974). *Social Policy.* London; Allen & Unwin

Wages, prices and unemployment

7.1 Introduction

The study of the interrelationship between the rate of unemployment and the rate of change of the average price level or of the average (real or money) wage level has played a major role in post-war economics. Two basic schools of thought emerged during the 1950s[1]. The neo-Keynesians held that inflation was caused by the existence of an 'inflationary gap' which was the consequence of excess demand for goods and services, while the cost-push school contended that inflation was caused by independent cost pressure on the price level, often attributed to trade unions[2].

This chapter considers attempts made to test these alternative views which have conflicting policy suggestions for dealing with inflation. The main concern is to examine the wide variety of phenomena relating to the Phillips curve. The discussion follows the convention that any relationship which has the rate of change of money wages as the dependent variable is referred to as a 'Phillips curve'. A narrower view is that the strict Phillips curve is restricted to the case in which percentage unemployment and its rate of change are the independent variables and the functional form is non-linear.

In considering any particular study it is necessary to examine whether, for example, wage rates or earnings are used (and whether these rates are weekly or hourly), whether the data are quarterly or annual, how the unemployment series is dealt with, what combination of explanatory variables are used, whether all the variables are current or whether some are lagged, the functional form of the specification, and the time period covered. These important details are, however, provided in the Appendix so that the text can concentrate on the main issues raised and on the conclusions of these studies.

Section 7.2 examines the theory suggested by the original Phillips (1958) paper and then considers the possible breakdowns or extensions of this relationship, focusing mainly on the role of trade unions, the effects of incomes policies and the role of expectations.

7.2 The Phillips curve

The main empirical question raised by the recognition of a link between labour costs and prices is whether a predictable relationship between unemployment and wage changes exists, and if so, what form it takes.

The first substantial contribution in this direction was by Phillips (1958). As this has stimulated so much further study it is worth considering in some detail. Phillips suggested that the rate of change of money wage rates can be explained by the rate of unemployment and the rate of change of unemployment. He initially examined annual UK data for 1861–1913 and observed a non-linear relationship which he described by

$$\dot{w} = a + bU^c \tag{7.1}$$

where U is a measure of the excess supply of labour and $\dot{w}$ is the rate of change of the price of labour[3]. In order to estimate a, b and c Phillips proceeded in a somewhat unorthodox manner, presumably because he preferred to obtain approximate estimates of the (as he saw it) correctly specified relationship rather than accurate estimates of an approximated relationship as later workers have done.

He grouped the unemployment data into six classes and took the average value of the rate of change of money wages and of percentage unemployment in these classes. Thus he reduced the number of observations he was dealing with from 53 to 6. Writing equation (7.1) in log–linear form

$$\log (\dot{w} - a) = \log b + c \log U \tag{7.2}$$

he proceeded to use the four observations where $\dot{w}$ was positive to estimate b and c, by an ordinary least squares approximation, assuming $a = 0$. He then adjusted the resulting curve to fit the remaining two observations and hence estimated a. The fitted curve was

$$\dot{w} + 0.900 = 9.638 U^{-1.3} \tag{7.3}$$

and is shown in *Figure 7.1*.

However, Phillips states that he would prefer to have estimated a relationship of the form

$$\dot{w} = a + bU^c + h(1/U^m) \, dt/dU \tag{7.4}$$

to take full account of his belief that the rate of change of unemployment is a vital constituent, but adopted his method for convenience. He stated that provided the final term is trend free, his estimation procedure is satisfactory.

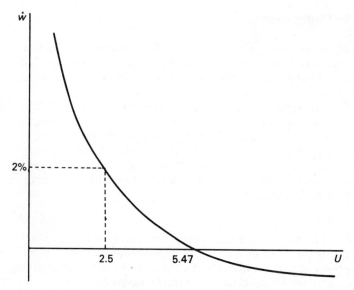

Figure 7.1 *The original Phillips curve*

The averaging method is important as there is rather more of a problem than Phillips formally concedes. His main problem is that should his preferred relationship (7.4) prove to be the correct specification then by ignoring the final term and using his log–linear specification for all observations he has both a multiplicative and additive error on the form (7.1). The additive error is due to the fact that the number of years when unemployment was increasing was approximately equal to that when unemployment was decreasing. Thus, by his averaging procedure he has removed, or at worst made insignificantly small, the additive stochastic term and so his estimation from the four points will give unbiased estimates of 7.4[4].

Having estimated his curve relating money wage changes and unemployment, Phillips then observed the effect of the rate of change of unemployment, using the time path of the scatter diagram between the two variables. He noted that this time path takes the form of loops around the regression curve and observed 6½ cycles of 8 years duration over the period 1861–1913. He further noted that when unemployment is falling the points were above the curve, indicating wages rising faster than average. When unemployment rose, the points were below the curve, showing wages rising more slowly than the expected rate for each level of employment. From this he concluded that the rate of change of unemployment was an important determinant of the rate of change of money wages. In addition, Phillips considered one other factor, the rate of change of retail prices, as having an effect. The effect of this variable occurred only in very special cases mainly due to large (greater than 13%) rises in import prices.

Having found the relationship for the period 1861–1913, Phillips then applied this curve to the periods 1913–1948 and 1948–1957. In both cases he found that it fitted the points fairly well, but the loops appeared to change direction for the post-war period.

He then drew several tentative conclusions about the role of unemployment in explaining variations in money wages. He stated that '. . . the rate of change of money wages can be explained by the level of unemployment and the rate of change of unemployment, except in or immediately after these years in which there is a sufficiently rapid rise in import prices to offset the tendency for increasing productivity to reduce the cost of living'. In addition, his interpretation of the results indicates that, in the absence of rapid increases in import prices and with productivity increases of 2% per year, the price level would remain stable with an unemployment rate of $2\frac{1}{2}\%$[5].

It is clear that Phillips was concerned with the statistical regularities he had found and he provided no more than a smattering of theoretical foundation. Thus it would appear that both demand-pull and cost-push protagonists could view the results as support for their philosophy. Economic policy had become a matter of choosing the most preferred point on the trade-off between inflation and unemployment and designing policies to get there.

7.3 Criticisms and extensions of Phillips

First, it is worth noting some contemporary views. Routh (1959) criticized Phillips' data, the construction of the variables and the estimation procedure used. He claimed that they compounded to exaggerate the closeness of the relationship while assuming away the effects of lags and expectations. Knowles and Winston (1959) found the stability and the simplicity of the relationship unlikely in view of the many institutional changes that had taken place over the period considered and in addition noted that a wide range of wage inflation had been comparable with many different unemployment rates. Further, they criticized Phillips' interpretation of the loops, and suggested that a rationale could be made for the loops being either clockwise or anticlockwise. In the face of so much qualitative change, the quantitative performance required a great deal of explanation and a theoretical base was urgently required.

Lipsey's theoretical base for Phillips

A sounder theoretical base was provided in the United Kingdom by Lipsey (1960) and in America by Samuelson and Solow (1960). This section will concentrate on the work of Lipsey, who suggested a theoretical foundation for Phillips' observed relationship and estimated the relationship using standard techniques.

Lipsey began by examining the behaviour of wage rates in a single labour market. He suggested that the rate of change of wages should be related positively to the level of excess demand in the labour market while unemployment should be related negatively to excess demand. From these two relationships there must be an inverse relationship between wage inflation and unemployment.

Considering this is more detail, the analysis begins by looking at excess demand in say the jth labour market, shown in *Figure 7.2*. From this it is clear that the equilibrium wage rate is w_j^{*6}. However, if the wage rate is below w_j^* then there will be excess demand for

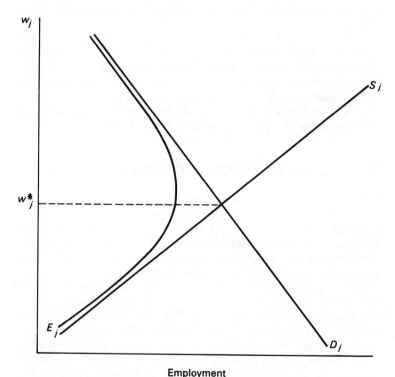

Employment

Figure 7.2 *Employment and wages in a single labour market*

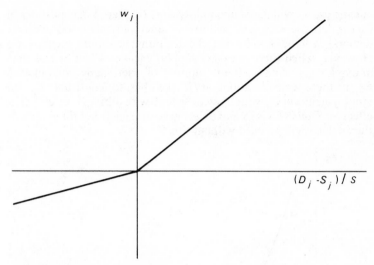

Figure 7.3 *A linear reaction function*

labour and, provided the demand and supply curves are stable over time, upward pressure on the wage rate causing it to rise to w_j^*. Lipsey considered the speed of the reaction of the wage rate, and postulated that

$$\dot{w}_j = f[(D_j - S_j)/S_j] \qquad (7.5)$$

where D_j is the demand for labour in market j, and S_j is the supply of labour in market j. He then considered a simple linear form of this relationship:

$$\dot{w}_j = \alpha[100(D_j - S_j)/S_j] \qquad (7.6)$$

Thus the higher the percentage excess demand, the greater is the rate of increase of wages. When considering excess supply, Lipsey suggests that wages fall more slowly than they would rise in response to an equivalent excess demand. This relationship is illustrated in *Figure 7.3*.

Note that the analysis implies that in equilibrium (where labour supply is equal to labour demand) the rate of change of wages in the market is zero. This conflicts with Phillips' empirical result that zero wage change relates to a positive rate of unemployment. This may be resolved by returning to *Figure 7.2*, observing the curve E_j and using the fact that unemployment is only an approximate measure of excess demand. If it is assumed that there is no structural unemployment, then when the market is actually in equilibrium vacancies, V_j, will equal unemployment, U_j. Hence in conditions of excess demand vacancies will exceed unemployment, so the excess demand will be $V_j - U_j$ and the frictional unemployment is U_j. However, when there is excess supply, vacancies will be less than unemployment and V_j is the number of frictionally unemployed. From these considerations it is possible to construct E_j, the employment curve, which is consistent with Phillips' result[7]. The effect on *Figure 7.3* is to move the curve to the left but for simplicity the analysis will proceed without this.

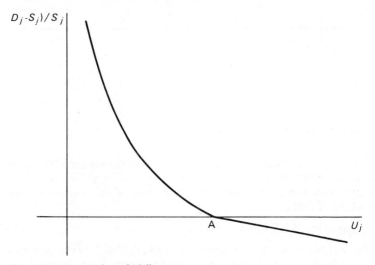

Figure 7.4 *Lipsey's derived Phillips curve*

The measurement of demand is, unfortunately, extremely difficult in practice and from the above it is apparent that a better measure will require vacancy and unemployment data. In this case $(V_j - U_j)/S_j$ may be regarded as a reasonable approximation for $(D_j - S_j)/S_j$. However, Phillips had no reliable data for vacancies for the period considered and as Lipsey was rationalizing Phillips' procedure, aggregate unemployment was used as a proxy measure.

Following Lipsey, the relationship between excess demand and unemployment is non-linear to the left of the point A in *Figure 7.4* but linear to the right. The linear segment arises because in that section there is an excess supply of labour, and it is assumed that unemployment directly reflect excess demand. Where vacancies equal unemployment, the wage rate is w_j^* and excess demand is zero, with unemployment at A. In the case of the segment to the left of A, vacancies exceed unemployment because excess demand is positive, implying that frictional unemployment will vary in a non-linear and inverse way with excess demand.

There are now two relations

$$\dot{w}_j = \alpha[100(D_j - S_j)/S_j]$$

and

$$U_j = f[(D_j - S_j)/S_j]$$

and combining these will produce a Phillips type of relationship.

Aggregation over labour markets and Lipsey's empirical work

Having derived his result for a single labour market, Lipsey proceeded to aggregate to the macroeconomic level to facilitate comparison with Phillips[8]. Although the idea of the formulation is to allow a test at the aggregate level, there are no clues given as to the possible identity of the individual markets, and it is by no means clear how separable these individual markets actually are. For example, what is meant by unemployment in a given market? Furthermore, in the Lipsey analysis demand and supply in a given market are functions of the wage rate in that market only, and interdependence with wage rates in other markets is ignored. These problems form only the tip of the iceberg but it is apparent that the problem of using microeconomic theory for an explanation of aggregates is plagued with difficulties. The connection between the aggregate Phillips curve and any microeconomic structure is liable to be very complex.

The basic assumptions of the Lipsey aggregation are threefold and encompass most of the above objections. First, it is assumed that there is considerable non-linearity in the relationship between wage changes and unemployment; secondly, that there exist reasonably isolated labour market sectors, with wages responding to unemployment in each; and thirdly that unemployment rates between different sectors are sufficiently uncorrelated.

For the purpose of exposition, Lipsey assumed that there are only two labour markets, each of which operates in the manner of the previous section with an insignificant amount of mobility between the markets. In aggregate

$$U = (U_i + U_j)/2$$
$$\dot{w} = (\dot{w}_i + \dot{w}_j)/2$$

where subscripts i and j refer to separate markets.

Clearly if $U_i = U_j$ then $\dot{w}_i = \dot{w}_j$ and the aggregate 'reaction' function is the same as the two separate ones. The only interest occurs if $U_i < U_j$ and for this case reference is made to *Figure 7.5*. The average unemployment rate is U^* and on inspection it can be seen that the average rate of increase of money wages will be greater than that predicted from U^*. The rate of increase of wages in market i is greater than the rate of decrease in market j, which results directly from the non-linearity of the curve. Clearly the analysis could be

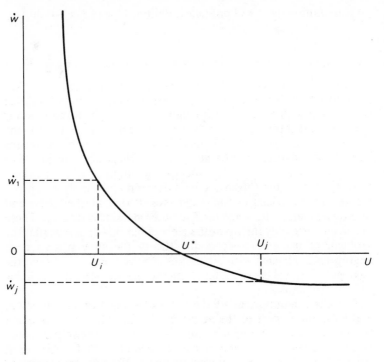

Figure 7.5 *Aggregation over two labour markets*

extended to cover cases where all markets have an excess demand for, or supply of, labour. What is apparent is that the greater the difference between $\dot{w}_i$ and $\dot{w}_j$ then the greater will be the discrepancy between U and U^* and so it is not only the unemployment rate but the distribution of unemployment which determines the location of the Phillips curve. It follows that the macroeconomic function will be to the right of the microeconomic one and the degree of displacement will be determined by the amount of inequality[9].

Given the position of the macroeconomic function, Lipsey turned to Phillips' second hypothesis that the rate of change of unemployment was also a crucial determinant of the rate of change of money wages. This was used to explain the 'loops', and was tied by Phillips to expectations[10]. However, Lipsey deals with this phenomenon in terms of the relationship between the dispersion of unemployment rates between separate markets and the aggregate relationship postulated for a complete cycle. If there were a systematic variation in the inequality of unemployment between different sectors of the economy over the course of a cycle, a systematic variation in the degree of displacement of the observed data from the structural aggregate relationship would result. This will generate an anticlockwise loop round the Phillips curve, given the additional assumption that the dispersion of unemployment is greater in the upswing of the cycle than in the downswing.

Thus the Lipsey hypothesis is not dealing with a causal relationship between $\dot{w}$ and U but one of the form

$$\dot{w} = f(U, \sigma_u) \tag{7.7}$$

where σ_u is the dispersion of unemployment. The relationship

$$\dot{w} = f(U, \dot{U}) \tag{7.8}$$

which was used by Lipsey can only appear due to another relationship between σ_u and the phases of the cycle, represented by $\dot{U}$[11]. Given this unsatisfactory position it is worth outlining an alternative explanation proposed by Hines (1969), before returning to the empirical results found by Lipsey.

Hines examined the 'tightness' of the labour market using the analysis of unemployment and vacancies discussed above. If unemployment and vacancies are related in a non-linear way, then when excess demand rises vacancies will rise more quickly than unemployment. Thus if unemployment is used as a proxy for excess demand there will be a bias in the measurement. This is because for any level of unemployment employers will bid harder for labour when unemployment is falling than when it is rising. Hence, assuming this bidding is successful, it will reduce unemployment in periods of excess demand by less than it reduces vacancies, and so produce the Phillips loops. Thus $\dot{U}$ is a reasonable approximation for the level of excess demand.

Returning to Lipsey's analysis, he used the following specifications

$$\dot{w}_t = a + bU_t^{-1} + cU_t^{-2} \tag{7.9}$$

and

$$\dot{w}_t = a + bU_t^{-1} + cU_t^{-4} \tag{7.10}$$

Using the same annual data as Phillips, equation (7.9) is used for the years to 1913 whereas equation (7.10), which displays much sharper curvature, is used for the later years to 1957. Lipsey subsequently added $\dot{U}$ and $\dot{p}$ as measures of the rate of change of unemployment and prices respectively, to test their effect as further explanatory variables.

For the 1862–1913 period, Lipsey tested

$$\dot{w}_t = f(U_t)$$
$$\dot{w}_t = f(U_t, \dot{U}_t)$$

and

$$\dot{w}_t = f(U_t, \dot{U}_t, \dot{p}_t)$$

A typical result is

$$w_t = -1.21 + 6.54U_t^{-1} + 2.26U_t^{-2} - 0.619\dot{U}_t + 0.21\dot{p}_t \qquad R^2 = 0.85$$

Lipsey gives squared partial correlation coefficients for U:0.78; $\dot{U}$:0.50; $\dot{p}$:0.17. This implies that variation in U explains 78% of the variance in $\dot{w}$, while $\dot{U}$ removes 50% of the variance not already associated with U and $\dot{U}$; and so on.

He concluded that there is a significant relation between the rate of change of money wages and the level of unemployment and its rate of change, but he rejected the hypothesis that the cost of living enters with a threshold effect, and the partial correlation between $\dot{w}$ and $\dot{p}$ shown above is very weak. However, when the model is fitted to the period 1923–1957, the basic equation described above continues to perform reasonably well. But a look at the squared partial correlation coefficients is enlightening. For 1923–1939, 1948–1957

$$\dot{w}_t = 0.74 + 0.43U_t^{-1} + 11.18U_t^{-4} + 0.038\dot{U}_t + 0.69\dot{p}_t \qquad R^2 = 0.91$$

and the squared partial coefficients are U:0.38; $\dot{U}$:0.30; $\dot{p}$:0.76.

Clearly the variables U and $\dot{U}$ are less significant in explaining the variance in $\dot{w}$, and it would appear that the period is described by a wage–price spiral, rather than by a strict Phillips curve. The other striking feature is the sign of the coefficient on $\dot{U}$. It is now positive which suggests that Phillips loops have changed direction.

This analysis therefore leads from the strict Phillips curve to the wider range of general 'Phillips-type' models referred to in Section 7.1. The greater dependency on prices suggests a wider aspect than Phillips considered. Before turning to these studies some final comments on Phillips' and Lipsey's work are in order. A short discussion of work which immediately followed the initial analysis then introduces issues considered in later sections.

Interpretations of Phillips and further empirical results

In Phillips' original paper no distinction was drawn between the short-run curve and a long-run curve. This is apparent because it is difficult to imagine $\dot{U}$ being kept at zero in the short run and so maintaining unemployment at a constant level would imply a long-run Phillips curve. In addition, it is impossible to slide along the Phillips curve to change the terms of the inflation–unemployment trade-off because $\dot{U}=0$ at each point along it and movement necessitates $\dot{U}$ being non-zero. Thirdly, because it is not directly related to a time-series it is not possible to obtain predictions of future $\dot{w}$. Thus Desai (1975) has concluded that, '. . . the shape of the Phillips curve is not invariant from one period to another'. Given these facets of Phillips' work, it must be concluded that it is the change of nature which Lipsey imposes—by looking at a standard time-series regression model—which has allowed for the possibility of alternative specifications.

However, much of this interpretation requires a great deal to be read into Phillips' paper. Others have argued that the procedure adopted by Phillips was merely an aid to computation and his plotting of a locus with $\dot{U}=0$ was for convenience only. On this basis, Gilbert (1976) re-estimated the original Phillips specification using non-linear numerical techniques and found that if all the points were used '. . . the equation that Phillips first suggested as approximate (equation (7.3)) does appear superior to obvious alternatives even though this was not apparent from his method of estimation'.

This statement requires a little illumination. Gilbert initially examined the Lipsey equation for 1861–1913 and compared this with equations (7.1) and (7.4). He found that the exclusion of the last term in (7.4) induced a certain amount of bias because of the non-linearity but he also found poor Durbin–Watson statistics in all specifications. This may be due to the omission of explanatory variables or it may be that the specification of the variables induced spurious autocorrelation of the residuals. Assuming the latter to be the case Gilbert redefined the rate of change variables

$$\dot{w} = (\log W_t - \log W_{t-1}).100 \tag{7.11}$$

and similarly for $\dot{U}$.

The use of these definitions then improved the Durbin–Watson statistics. Gilbert thus concluded that Phillips' original specification was marginally better than that of Lipsey. What must be noted here is that although the claim of the Lipsey specification to statistical superiority was therefore ill-founded, the importance of Lipsey's contribution is in its time series aspect and the attempt to provide some underlying theory. However, both Phillips' and Lipsey's studies suffer from their use of annual data. Their choice was necessary because of data limitations but the rate of change variable requires more 'delicate' treatment to deal with short lags.

The overall effect of Lipsey's study was to cause a proliferation of studies based directly on it to be carried out for other countries, but at this stage one further fact should be clarified. Throughout this chapter attention has been focused on the relationship between unemployment and the rate of change of money wages, whereas the normal practice is to refer to price inflation. What is needed to rectify this apparent anomaly is to relate $\dot{w}$ to $\dot{p}$. One possibility is to assume that prices are determined by taking variable costs and adding to these a fixed percentage mark-up to cover fixed costs and a margin for profit. Another is outlined by Lipsey (1979) who assumes that all factor incomes increase at the same rate as wages and, if productivity is also exogenous, the rate of change of wages less the rate of change of productivity is equal to the rate of change of prices. The true relationship between $\dot{w}$ and $\dot{p}$ is of course more complex than this but what is apparent is that the change from $\dot{w}$ to $\dot{p}$ does not affect the nature of the Phillips curve as a 'reduced form'[12] but does expose the possible inadequacies of a single equation approach.

What is abundantly clear from Lipsey's results for the later periods is that the monocausal explanation of the change in money wages provides poor explanation of the data[13]. However, the more general model with unemployment as a proxy for excess demand, the rate of change of unemployment as a proxy for the distribution of excess demand, and using the rate of change of prices as an additional variable, provides a good fit. The single wage equation approach therefore appears to be inadequate, and recourse must be made to models using more than one equation.

Klein and Ball (1959), for example, used a four-equation model and quarterly data for the period 1948–1956. They introduced a 'political factor' (using a dummy intercept term) which showed that after 1952 the rise in money wage rates was $2\frac{1}{2}\%$ higher than in earlier years. Their other findings were in broad agreement with Phillips and Lipsey and the use of a dummy intercept variable suggested that government intervention with an incomes policy by the Labour Government of 1948–1951 had been significant. However, all the studies so far mentioned have ignored two specific problems. One, which has been touched on already, is the appropriate measure of excess demand, and the other is the effect of cost-push elements in the form of trade union influence and firms' reactions to profitability. The second problem will be considered in detail in

Section 7.5. The first was initially examined by Dicks-Mireaux and Dow (1959) who used an index of excess demand for labour based both on unemployment and vacancies[14]. Their results and those of the later study by Dicks-Mireaux (1961) confirmed the importance of price changes and the excess demand for labour in explaining wage changes. This was the forerunner of other studies which considered the applicability or suitability of unemployment as a satisfactory measure of excess demand and some references to this work are made in the final section of this chapter.

Although a number of particular problems remained unanswered it may nevertheless be said that until the middle 1960s the existence of a trade-off between unemployment and inflation was generally accepted. However, the experience from 1966 has produced a change in this simple view. There has been a worldwide rise in wage and price levels, and in the UK this explosion has occurred when unemployment has also been rising. This simultaneous move in the same direction of variables which were thought to be 'tradeable' has led to fundamental reconsideration of the explanation previously discussed.

7.4 The role of expectations

The most influential criticisms of the Phillips curve, by Friedman (1968) and Phelps (1968), follow the excess demand tradition. Friedman argues that real wages, rather than money wages, respond to excess demand, in which case money wages will respond to both excess demand and the expected changes in prices. Then

$$\dot{w}_t = f(U)_t + \dot{p}_t^e, \qquad f'(U) < 0 \tag{7.12}$$

where $\dot{p}_t^e$ is the proportional rate of change of prices expected for time t. An expected increase in the price level implies that people will compensate by increasing their wage aspirations by the same proportion. In addition, the Friedman hypothesis implies that a 'natural' rate of unemployment may be defined that is consistent with any steady rate of inflation[14]. This may be examined using *Figure 7.6*.

Assume that the economy is initially at equilibrium with wage and price stability, and that there is a constant rate of productivity growth, $\dot{r}$, and unemployment of U_0. If the government decides that U_0 is unacceptably high and U_1 is preferred, it can be achieved by suitably increasing aggregate demand. Because of feedback to factor markets, an excess demand for labour is created. The economy can then be seen as being at B on the original Phillips curve, and $\dot{w}_1$ will

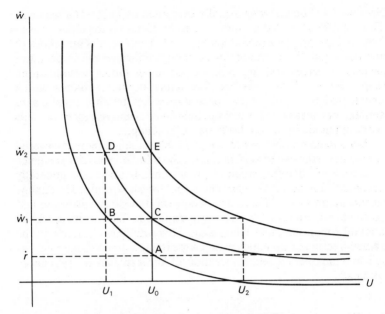

Figure 7.6 *Derivation of the Phillips–Friedman long-run Phillips curve*

be the rate of wage inflation. Factor prices will rise at a rate $\dot{w}_1 - \dot{r}$ and this will feed back into the formation of price expectations. Provided that adjustment of expectations is not instantaneous there will be some time before individuals have fully adjusted to the new level. However, while this adjustment is taking place individuals tend to overestimate the real value of wage offers and, because their reservation price has fallen, unemployment declines to U_1. But as workers come to learn the value of their money wages, some leave the labour market causing unemployment to increase towards U_0 at the same time as expected inflation approaches actual inflation[15]. Workers recognize that wage increases equivalent to $\dot{w}_1$ are needed to keep up with current and expected inflation and will adjust to point C with unemployment back at U_0.

Any further attempts to move unemployment would mean movement along a new Phillips curve and the process described above would be repeated. The position would move from C to D to E and expectations would be $\dot{w}_2 - \dot{r}$. Having considered attempts to lower unemployment, it is necessary to consider the result of attempting to reduce the rate of inflation within this framework. Assume the economy is at E and the government manages to reduce the rate of wage increase to $\dot{w}_1$. For some time price expectations are

$\dot{w}_2 - r$, and unemployment rises to U_2 as workers underestimate the real wage. As inflationary expectations are eventually revised downwards unemployment falls back to U_0. The long-run Phillips curve is therefore the vertical line through U_0, which is defined as the 'natural' unemployment rate. Any rate of inflation is compatible with this level of unemployment. In equilibrium there is no trade-off between the rate of change of money wages and unemployment, due to the fact that all workers have adjusted to inflation which thus has no effect on the level of unemployment.

It can easily be seen that the crux of the argument hinges on the assumption that the coefficient on $\dot{p}_t^e$ in equation (7.12) is unity. This can be seen as follows[16]. If

$$\dot{w}_t = f(U)_t + k\dot{p}_t^e \qquad 0 < k \leqslant 1$$

and it is assumed for simplicity that

$$\dot{p}_t^e = \dot{p}_{t-1},$$

then

$$\dot{w}_t = f(U)_t + k\dot{p}_{t-1}$$

Further, if

$$\dot{p}_t = \dot{w}_t - \dot{r}_t$$

then

$$\dot{w}_t = f(U)_t + k\dot{w}_{t-1} - k\dot{r}_{t-1} \qquad (7.13)$$

and in equilibrium

$$\dot{w}_t = [f(U)_t - k\dot{r}_{t-1}]/(1-k) \qquad (7.14)$$

In the world of Phelps and Friedman $k = 1$ and so the only way to reduce unemployment is to raise the rate of change of productivity; whereas a trade-off exists with $k < 1$. Attempts to measure k will be considered below[17].

Having outlined the basic theory it is now possible to examine the empirical work relating to the different approaches. This chapter concentrates on the main issues rather than providing an exhaustive survey of empirical studies. Further details are, however, provided in the appendix.

7.5 The role of trade unions

The view that wages may be significantly affected by bargaining between unions and employers has led to a desire to incorporate the role of unions into the theory of wage change. There have been two main approaches to the problem: the first is the introduction of variables to the wage equation which are meant to reflect bargaining power, while the second involves an exposition of the bargaining process. The latter approach is exemplified by Johnston (1972) and the later empirical work (Johnston and Timbrell, 1973)[18]. Examination of the role of trade unions in econometric studies of wage inflation in the United Kingdom has been limited, and attention will be focused here on the work of Hines (1964, 1968, 1969, 1971), and the criticisms by Purdy and Zis (1973, 1974).

The use of variables to reflect bargaining power

Hines' early work (1964) challenged the notion of a simple short-run trade-off between inflation and unemployment. His basic hypothesis was that the rate of change of money wages depends crucially on trade union 'pushfulness'[19]. This variable was approximated using the rate of change in the percentage of the labour force unionized, $\dot{T}$, and the level of union membership, T. The reasoning behind this is that when unions are militant they attempt to improve membership and increase wage demands. Hines' initial study reported a three-equation system in which $\dot{w}, \dot{p}$ and $\dot{T}$ are simultaneously determined[20].

$$\left.\begin{array}{l} \dot{w}_t = a_0 + a_1\dot{T}_t + a_2T_t + a_3\dot{p}_t + a_4\dot{p}_{t-1} + a_5U_{t-1} \\ \dot{p}_t = b_0 + b_1\dot{w}_t + b_2\dot{m}_{t-1/2} + b_3\dot{r}_t \\ \dot{T}_t = c_0 + c_1T_{t-1} + c_2\dot{p}_t + c_3\dot{p}_{t-1} + c_4D_{t-1/2} \end{array}\right\} \qquad (7.15)$$

where $\dot{m}$ is the rate of change of import prices, and D is a profits variable.

The model was fitted to annual data for the period from 1921 to 1961 (excluding war years). The unionization variables were found to be very significant, whereas unemployment was insignificant. Other equations using only the unionization variables provided further support for Hines' hypothesis[21].

In later papers Hines found support using both annual data (1968) for the period considered by Phillips (1958) and quarterly data (1971) for the post-war period. For this second study Hines changed the specification of his union variable to a proportionate rate of change.

A sizeable and mainly critical literature has grown up from Hines' result. This seems to have evolved from incredulity about the hypothesis, given the fact that variations in union membership in the United Kingdom since the war have been very small[22]. The most persistent attack on Hines has been by Purdy and Zis (1973, 1974) who initially redefined some of the variables. They calculate $\dot{T}$ using the percentage of potentially unionizable labour force rather than the whole labour force. They also consistently use annual data, claiming that Hines' quarterly data were dubious, being based on annual data and quarterly interpolations. Hines' method leads to a bias in the coefficients on $\dot{T}/T$ and $\dot{T}$ (and their 't' statistic) due to underestimation of the variance of both variables over time.

In addition, they calculate wages and prices consistently. Hines defined

$$\dot{w}_t = 100[(W_t/W_{t-1}) - 1]$$

and

$$p_t = 100(P_{t+1} - P_{t-1})/2P_t$$

while Purdy and Zis defined all rates of change in a similar manner to the Hines price variable. Re-estimation of the 1971 model (Purdy and Zis, 1973) using these data suggested that the statistical significance of unionization is less than Hines claimed. Although this variable is still significantly different from zero, the relative effects are at least ten times less in Purdy and Zis than Hines[23]. Given the considerations about the quarterly data and the fact that Hines' annual model is very close to that of Purdy and Zis it may be felt that Hines overstated his case. What is particularly strange is that if $\dot{T}$ represents militancy at the aggregate level then it would be expected that the Purdy and Zis measure would perform better. As this is not the case some alternative interpretation of the variable is perhaps necessary.

Purdy and Zis decomposed $\dot{T}$ into $\dot{T}_m$, the change in density which has come about from activities which Hines termed as militant and $\dot{T}_e$, the change in union density arising from labour force reallocation. They found that the 'militancy' variable had a slight effect in the inter-war period but that the effect was insignificantly different from zero in the post-war period. Since the reallocative variable was also not significantly different from zero, they concluded that overall $\dot{T}$ is not an important determinant of post-war inflation.

This was later criticized by Thomas (1977), who used the same definition of union activity as Hines but defined wage and price variables following Purdy and Zis. His results for the pre-war period from 1892 support Hines but he was unable to deal with the post-war period because of multicollinearity[24]. He suggested that unionization affects both the position and the shape of the Phillips curve by causing an anticlockwise rotation. As unionization increases the response of wage changes to variations in unemployment is reduced, and in addition there is an upward shift of about three percentage points. Unfortunately the results are equivocal for the post-war period and there is an inclination to follow Parkin's (1978) suggestion that changes in unionization provide little explanation of post-war inflation in the UK.

It is then necessary to consider alternative measures of union influence. There are, for example, the subjective measures of Dicks-Mireaux and Dow (1959) and the dummy variable approach of Klein and Ball (1959), but this section will examine only the role of strikes. There is of course a problem of causality, since union militancy (measured by strikes) may be both a cause and an effect of wage inflation. A further problem is that strike frequency data provide a poor index of union militancy. For example, strikes often result from a breakdown in negotiations, so that the figures may simply reflect employers' resistance. Strikes also have a distinct seasonal pattern, with high incidence in the first quarter, a peak in March or April, falling to a trough in July and August, rising to a secondary peak in September or October and falling markedly in December.

There are, as may be expected, conflicting empirical results, some of which arise from differences in models and in the specification of variables[25]. A further problem is raised by the lack of a sound theoretical underpinning, so that there are different expected signs on the strike variable as well as the doubtful line of causality which has already been noted[26]. Thus the correlation between wage changes and strikes is really all that is available, and it is to be expected that this will be greater in quarterly and semi-annual models than in annual models if data are not seasonally adjusted (Godfrey, 1971; Godfrey and Taylor, 1973; Taylor, 1972, 1975). With these conflicting results attention must be given to the pure bargaining models of wage determination.

Bargaining models

Johnston's model (1972) is used to illustrate this approach, and is based on the fact that firms seek to minimize the expected cost of both the settlement and the strike, given an initial wage claim[27]. His model also uses an estimate of the relationship between the probability of a strike and a pre-strike wage offer, and an estimate of the length of strike needed to secure acceptance of a given wage offer. The sequence of events is that the firm receives a claim from the union, Δw^c, which it discounts to Δw^{rc}. From this information the firm makes an offer which will be accepted with probability $1 - \Pi$ and rejected with probability Π. The process ceases if the offer is accepted, but otherwise the firm must make new wage offers as the strike continues. It will make offers which it thinks will end the strike at minimum cost, and will make an offer only if no settlement or shutdown is reached[28]. Johnston then uses the following specification

$$\Delta w = \Delta w^{rc} + f(i, w/(e-1), \Pi, b) \qquad (7.16)$$

where Δw = the size of the wage settlement
i = firm's rate of time discount
$w/(e-1)$ = current rate of profit per worker; w is the current wage rate and e the elasticity of demand for the product
b = parameter relating additional cost imposed by strike length

Δw is positively related to all the above variables but is negatively related to the rate of discounting used by the firm.

The model was estimated by Johnston and Timbrell (1973), who assumed that Δw^{rc} depends on inflation expectations (which is proxied by either $\dot{p}_{t-1}$ or $\dot{p}_{t-1}^2$) and either a catch-up variable, c, which measures the extent to which real wages have cumulatively fallen behind an assumed target growth rate[29], or a three-year moving average of the proportionate rate of change of the ratio of net to gross wages (denoted $\dot{\lambda}^c$). Further, the variables i, $w/(t-1)$ and b are regarded as being constant, as is Π in most of the work. In fact when Π was used it was on the assumption that it depends on the number of strikes. An additional variable n/N was used, which reflects the fraction of the labour forcing settling a wage claim in the period considered, in this case a year. Thus the model used for empirical study was

$$\dot{w} = h(\dot{p}^e, \dot{\lambda}^c \text{ or } c, n/N, \Pi) \qquad (7.17)$$

Results were presented for two annual samples, 1952–1971 and 1959–1971, from which several interesting results emerge. It is clear that n/N gives no aid to the explanation of wage changes, and the introduction of $\dot{\lambda}^c$ takes away the explanatory power from $\dot{p}^e$ (however measured). When the catch-up variable, c, is used in conjunction with $\dot{p}^e$, the former is not significant but the coefficient on the expectations variable is not significantly different from unity. This point will be taken up later when the empirical work on expectations is considered directly[30]. Johnston and Timbrell also compared their model with the expectations augmented Phillips curve and showed the latter to be unsatisfactory with a poorer fit and the wrong slope.

A second study with a similar thesis was carried out by Henry, Sawyer and Smith (1976). They set out to test the hypothesis that trade unions attempt to achieve a rise in money wages consistent with a target rate of increase in real net earnings. Their model is an extension of an earlier one by Sargan (1964)[31] and also includes the pressure of demand as an independent variable. The estimating equation was

$$\dot{w}_t = \delta_0 + \delta_1 \dot{p}_{t-1} + \delta_2 \ln U_{t-1} + \delta_3 \ln (NE_{t-1} - \dot{p}_{t-1}) + \delta_4 t \qquad (7.18)$$

where NE is net earnings and t is a time trend.

The equation was estimated using quarterly data from 1948–1974. Although Henry, Sawyer and Smith claimed that their model performed better than a Phillips–Lipsey model and an expectations augmented Phillips model and a Hines model, a glance at the estimated coefficients raises serious doubts. The only statistically significant variable is the time trend and the overall fit is not very good. Furthermore the Durbin–Watson statistic indicates first order serial correlation, which implies overstatement of the significance of variables.

It is therefore concluded that Johnston and Timbrell have so far produced the most satisfactory explanation. The following section considers how government intervention in the form of incomes policies may affect the Phillips-style trade-off.

7.6 The effects of incomes policies

Inflation inevitably produces pressure for various forms of controls over prices and wages. This has not only been true of the United Kingdom: international organizations such as the OECD have repeatedly urged the applications of wage–price controls. The question of whether these controls are desirable is beyond the scope of this chapter; this section examines two basic methods which have been used in an attempt to measure the impact of controls and guidelines for the United Kingdom. The first method deals with the controls using dummy variables, whereas the second, following Lipsey and Parkin (1970), uses separate equations for wage and price changes and involves the examination of residuals from the fitted equations.

The use of dummy variables

The initial work on dummy variables stemmed from the 'political' intercept dummy used by Klein and Ball (1959). Although their study did not strictly deal with incomes policies but rather with the political party in power these two factors were synonymous for the period considered. The principle behind the approach is as follows. Consider a wage equation of the form

$$\dot{w}_t = \alpha_0 + \alpha_1 U_t + \alpha_2 \dot{p}_t \tag{7.19}$$

The first step is to employ a single intercept dummy to give

$$\dot{w} = \alpha_0 + \alpha_1 U_t + \alpha_2 \dot{p}_t + \alpha_3 D_t \tag{7.20}$$

where D assumes a value of unity when a policy is in operation and a value of zero at other times. The next step is to estimate the equation and examine the coefficient on the dummy variable. A significant negative coefficient would be taken to indicate that a prices and incomes policy moves the wage equation in the 'desired' manner, whereas a coefficient that is not significantly different from zero suggests that the policy does not operate successfully.

It should be noted here that there is no need for the dummy variable to be just of the unit/zero type. If the view is taken that the reduction in the intercept occurs progressively, implying that the effectiveness of the policy changes with the length of time it remains in force, then a dummy variable could be constructed with varying weights.

Neither of the above methods distinguishes different types of incomes policy. The dummy variables are the same regardless of whether direct policy measures or merely 'guidelines' are being used. Further distinctions may, however, be made by using several intercept dummies. This method has been used to attempt to distinguish between voluntary policies (which operated in the years 1948–1950 and 1965) and policies using direct control.

The general view of this method is that policy operates to reduce the intercept of the wage equation but to leave the slope coefficient unaltered, producing a parallel shift in the curve. However, intercept and slope dummies could be used, in which case

$$\dot{w}_t = \alpha_0 + \alpha_1 U_t + \alpha_2 \dot{p}_t + \alpha_3 D_t + \alpha_4 (D_{1t} U_t) + \alpha_5 (D_{2t} \dot{p}_t) \tag{7.21}$$

where the Ds are defined in any of the ways described above (though the unit/zero type is the most common). Having estimated the coefficients on the dummy intercept and slope variables, if at least one is negative and none is positive and significantly different from zero then it is concluded that the policy is effective.

Each of the above methods was used in early studies. Although there was little consistency between studies in the magnitude of the effects, they did suggest that prices and incomes policies may be effective in shifting the wage equation. But no effects were obtained for the price equation. In all these studies one major problem became apparent. This was the difficulty of deciding whether an incomes policy was being used, and in particular how long the effect lasted. Indeed, this problem haunts all empirical studies of these policies.

Separate equations and the examination of residuals

The study by Lipsey and Parkin (1970) stimulated a proliferation of work in this area and embodies a totally different approach from that described above. Their study arose from a general dissatisfaction with the use of shift dummies, and doubts about the appropriateness of their use in a price equation.

They felt that the underlying assumption of a reduction in gross margins during incomes policies is unsatisfactory, since it is doubtful whether such a reduction would be prolonged in the face of a desire ultimately to restore gross profit margins[32]. Furthermore, even an insignificant coefficient on the dummy variable does not rule out the possibility of reduction in profit margins for at least a portion of the period for which the dummy is inserted.

The model used by Lipsey and Parkin consisted of the following wage–price model

$$\left.\begin{array}{l} \dot{p}_t = a_0 + a_1 \dot{w}_{-r} + a_2 \dot{m}_{-s} + a_3 \dot{q}_{-t} \\ \dot{w}_t = a_4 + a_5 \psi(U)_{-u} + a_6 \dot{p}_{-v} + a_7 S_{-w} \end{array}\right\} \qquad (7.22)$$

where r, s, t, u, v and w are lags in quarters,

  $\dot{m}=$ the proportionate rate of change of import prices
  $\dot{q}=$ the proportionate rate of change of output per head
  $S=$ some measure of trade union aggressiveness

The price equation is derived from the argument that the market value of final output relates to the value of labour input, the value of imported materials, the value of other inputs and residual profit. Other simplifying assumptions are that the cost of other inputs is a constant proportion of measured costs and that firms aim for a constant proportionate mark-up, which together imply that profits are a linear function of output price. Combining these assumptions with that of a constant import factor and that expectations are based on past experience, the price change equation can be derived by differentiating with respect to time. The wage equation follows directly from the earlier work by Lipsey (1960), with the addition of a union aggressiveness measure.

The examination of these equations is really the preliminary part of the investigation which determines whether policies have produced some shift in the wage and price equations. Two sets of time series data are used: the first covers successive quarters of periods during which a policy was in force; the second covers quarters when no policy operated. Using these two sets of data, the equations are estimated separately for 'policy-off' and 'policy-on' periods. A standard F-test is used to examine the differences between the intercepts and the slope coefficients in the two equations. The null hypothesis specifies that the true 'policy-off' and 'policy-on' equations have identical intercept and slope coefficients. If this is not rejected then it can be concluded that the prices and incomes policies were ineffective. However, if the null hypothesis is rejected, it is necessary to examine the effects of the shifts, and at this stage the examination of 'residuals' is carried out[33]. The estimated 'policy-off' equation is used to calculate the rate of increase of money wages or prices that would be expected in a particular period if the policy had not been in force. Each of the calculated values is then subtracted from the corresponding observed rate of increase to obtain the residual. If the average of such residuals is negative, it is concluded that the policies achieve their objective; the actual rate of increase of wages or prices is less than would have been the case without them.

The variables used by Lipsey and Parkin referring to rates of change were calculated using the Phillips–Lipsey definitions, while unemployment was calculated as the following moving average over three quarterly periods.

$$U_t' = (U_t + U_{t-1} + U_{t-2})/3$$

Union aggressiveness was measured by the percentage of the labour force unionized. In addition, they examined lags of various lengths on the independent variables, using the coefficient of determination as the criterion for selection; but found that only the import variable required a lag of any kind. Ordinary least squares approximation of the wage equation gave the following results for the period 1947(3)–1967(2)[34].

'Policy-off'

$$\dot{w}_t = 6.672 - 2.372U_t' + 0.457\dot{p}_t + 0.136\dot{T}_t \qquad R^2 = 0.856$$
$$\quad\;\;(5.79)\quad (3.64)\quad\;\;\;(6.25)\quad\;\;\;(0.07) \qquad DW = 0.231$$

'Policy-on'

$$\dot{w}_t = 3.919 - 0.404U_t' + 0.227\dot{p}_t + 3.764T_t \qquad R^2 = 0.138$$
$$\quad\;\;(2.77)\quad (0.56)\quad\;\;\;(0.93)\quad\;\;\;(1.16) \qquad DW = 0.724$$

where the figures in parentheses are t statistics.

From these results it would seem that incomes policies have weakened the relation between the rate of change of money wages and unemployment, and have weakened the effect of prices on wages. However, the measure of union aggressivenesss appears to have improved, although it is still not significantly different from zero. For 'policy-on' periods, R^2 is not significantly different from zero and it can be seen also that there is significant serial correlation. It appears that the forces which previously explained the wage equation have been replaced and that unions now have a greater influence.

The F-tests of the structural stability of the policy-off and policy-on equations and of the hypothesis that the equations are the same were rejected[35]. Examination of residuals revealed that only the 1948–1950 policy had a restraining effect, but that the other policies gave positive residuals. They therefore concluded that incomes policies had not worked. These results were strengthened by subsequent work by Parkin (1970) which dealt with price expectations rather than with prices. He concluded that '. . . the trade-off is effectively broken by incomes policy and replaced by a constant average rate of increase in money wages which is independent of the level of unemployment.'

Criticisms of the Lipsey–Parkin model

Not surprisingly these results provoked a series of comments. In addition to the obvious problem that it may not be feasible to treat all incomes policies alike, there is the problem that the policy-off periods, even if correctly identified, may not be similar. Sumner (1972) divided the policy-off period into two subsamples, 1959(4)–1955(4) and 1957(1)–1961(2). He found that the relationship between wage changes and price changes collapsed, although the wage–unemployment trade-off remained stable. If the policy-off equation is not stable, then assessing the effects of incomes policies using the Lipsey–Parkin method of extrapolation is not valid. This also leads to the much greater problem that if the model involves simultaneous equations, the estimation technique should take account of the simultaneity. Furthermore, prediction should be made using the reduced form. When Wallis (1971) and Godfrey (1971) allowed for the simultaneity and the serial correlation they found that all the variables of the model lost their significance. All that remains is the correlation between $\dot{w}$ and $\dot{p}$[36].

Hines (1971) attempted to refute the total collapse view, and interpreted his results as suggesting that the determinants of the system are the same whether or not an incomes policy is in force. The difference is that the overall effect is as desired for the policy-on periods. This was further investigated by Parkin, Sumner and Jones (1972), using the reduced form of Hines and Lipsey and Parkin's models and their findings suggest that the magnitude of the effect is insignificant whether it is believed that there is a breakdown or not.

In this case the major interest of Hines' study is that it gives further insight to the role that definitions of variables play in changing equations. This can be seen by comparing his results with those of Lipsey and Parkin in the Appendix to this chapter.

A return to dummy variables

Returning to the use of slope and intercept dummy variables, Godfrey (1971) found no support for any policy shift in the functions. Burrows and Hitiris (1972) reinforced this view for the price equation, but they obtained inconclusive results for the wage equation. Their approach did not reveal a change in the slope coefficient on the unemployment variable. More importantly they also found that the wage equation coefficients are very sensitive to the specification of the variables[37]. Furthermore, their wage equation did not 'collapse' but they could find no effect of incomes policies on the overall rate of wage increase, although they suggest that the time profile may have changed.

It would seem, therefore, that incomes policies have been largely ineffective in controlling the rate of wage and price changes in the United Kingdom. All of the models discussed above use a price change equation based on mark-up pricing and a wage change equation which is based on either bargaining or neoclassical theories. However, using a neoclassical wage and price model Sherrif (1977) found that intercept dummies for 'announcement' and 'continuation' effects of the policies produced encouraging results, whereas no significance could be found using the standard approach. All of this suggests that more careful attention to the underlying theory is needed before satisfactory results concerning incomes policies are likely to be obtained.

The studies discussed in this section have all attempted to assess the possible effects of government intervention on the 'trade-off' between unemployment and inflation represented by the Phillips curve. However, following the discussion of expectations in Section 7.4, it is necessary to examine whether such a 'trade-off' does exist in the long run. The absence of a 'trade-off' implies a very limited role for government intervention, which at best may only affect the movement of the economy when out of equilibrium.

7.7 The long-run trade-off between unemployment and inflation

It was shown in Section 7.4 that the issue of whether there is a long-run trade-off is based solely on whether, in either a price or wage expectations-augmented Phillips curve, the coefficient on the rate of change of expectations is unity. There are basically two approaches which may be used. The first involves direct estimation of an equation such as

$$\dot{w}_t = f(U)_t + k\dot{p}_t^e \qquad 0 < k < 1 \tag{7.23}$$

and testing whether the coefficient k is significantly different from unity. However, this can be done only if data on price expectations are available. Otherwise the second approach must be used, which requires an assumption that expectations are formed according to some strict rule. An example of such a rule is the first order adaptive scheme

$$\dot{p}_t^e - \dot{p}_{t-1}^e = \theta(\dot{p}_{t-1} - \dot{p}_{t-1}^e) \tag{7.24}$$

The model is then completed by the addition of a third equation

$$\dot{p}_t = \dot{w}_t - \dot{r}_t$$

The Solow model

The pioneering empirical work relating to the United Kingdom did not, however, follow this formulation. This was by Solow (1969) whose model was

$$\left.\begin{array}{l} \dot{p}_t = w_t - \dot{r}_t + k\dot{p}_t^e \\ w_t = f(U)_t \\ \dot{p}_t^e - \dot{p}_{t-1}^e = \theta(\dot{p}_t - \dot{p}_{t-1}^e) \end{array}\right\} \tag{7.25}$$

Here the shift factor is no longer attached to the wage equation. In the previous model, equation (7.23), the idea is that price increases are anticipated when wage demands are formulated, so that the rate of increase of money wage rates is raised, at any given unemployment rate, by an amount proportional to the expected rate of inflation. However, the Solow model assumes that firms anticipate cost increases when setting prices so that for any given increase in unit labour costs, the rate of price increase is raised by an amount which may be approximated by some proportion of the expected rate of inflation. Clearly these two explanations are not mutually exclusive, because although Solow deals with the product market, the approaches should give the same information provided that the markets are symmetric.

Solow used quarterly data for the period 1957(3)–1964(4). His reported equations are

$$\dot{p}_t = -0.233 + 0.081ulc + 0.002C_{u_t} + 0.809\dot{p}_t^e$$
$$\quad\;\;(4.77)\quad(1.83)\quad\quad(4.84)\quad\quad(8.11)$$
$$\dot{p}_t^e = 0.7p_t + 0.3\dot{p}_{t-1}^e$$

where t statistics are given in parentheses and

ulc = the rate of change of unit labour costs
C_u = capacity utilization (a measure of demand pressure)

Solow was concerned that from these results he could not reject the hypothesis of a unit coefficient on price expectations. This led him to use annual data (1956–1966) and a slightly different equation, with price expectations defined as in equations (7.25). The new results gave

$$\dot{p}_t = 0.0038 + 0.5815ulc_t + 0.098\dot{m}_t - 0.0169DL + 0.1803\dot{p}_t^e$$
$$\quad(0.978)\;(10.217)\quad\;\;(2.739)\quad(3.357)\quad\quad(1.395)$$

Solow was unable to explain the apparent discrepancy between his quarterly and annual results, but concluded that '. . . the trade-off may not be permanent but it is long enough'.

However, this interpretation must be treated with caution. Examination should also be made of coefficients other than that on price expectations. An alternative argument, that of Parkin (1978), is that ulc is a good proxy for expected factor price change and $\dot{m}$ is a proxy for expected import price changes. Thus the *sum* of the coefficients on 'expectations variables' should be tested to see whether they are different from unity. As this chapter is mainly concerned with unemployment, the remainder of this section concentrates on model (7.23) outlined above, using the expectations augmented Phillips curve.

Estimation of the expectations-augmented Phillips curve

An early examination of this model, in the absence of direct data on expectations, was made by Parkin (1970). He used the following model.

$$\dot{w}_t = \alpha_0 + \alpha_1 U_t + \alpha_2 \dot{p}_t^e$$
$$\dot{p}_t^e = \dot{p}_{t-1}^e = \theta(\dot{p}_t - \dot{p}_{t-1}^e)$$

which gives the reduced form of

$$\dot{w}_t = \alpha_0\theta + \alpha_1 U_t + (1-\theta)\dot{w}_{t-1} - \alpha_1(1-\theta)U_{t-1} + \alpha_2\dot{p}_t \qquad (7.26)$$

Parkin presented six numerical versions of this equation, using two different specifications of the error term for the entire period, and for 'policy-on' and 'policy-off' periods. Examination of these results leads to general dissatisfaction. The predictions of the 'no long-run trade-off' model are largely refuted by United Kingdom data. The coefficient on $\dot{p}_t^e$ is significantly different from unity in two of the three cases and in the third case the null hypothesis (of unity) is not rejected because of the large estimated standard error[38]. However, doubt concerning the specification is cast by the fact that the sign on the intercept is correct in only two cases. While some of this supports Parkin's attempt to show that incomes policies cause the relationship to 'collapse', he concludes that there is indeed a long-run trade-off.

This conclusion is challenged by Saunders and Nobay (1972), who take the Parkin wage equation but specify the formation of expectations as the ratio of two distributed lag functions. Thus

$$\dot{p}_t^e = \frac{\mu(L)}{v(L)} \dot{p}_t \tag{7.27}$$

where

$$\mu(L) = \mu_0 + \mu_1 L^2 + \cdots + \mu_{n-1} L^{n-1}$$

and

$$v(L) = 1 + v_1 L + v_2 L^2 + \cdots + v_n L^n$$

and L is a lag operator. Faced with the problem of finding the appropriate distributed lag the following specific form was applied (Jorgensen and Stephenson, 1967)

$$\mu_i = v_i = \gamma(1 - \gamma)^L$$

which yields a reduced form identical to that of Parkin. Saunders and Nobay then demonstrate that the adaptive expectations model used by Parkin underestimates the structural parameter on price expectations. This means that although their overall results, like Parkin's, give satisfactory signs for only the policy-off periods, the coefficient on price expectations is never significantly different from unity. For a long-run interpretation, the 'policy-off' periods are really the most relevant.

The use of distributed lag functions to construct hypothetical series for expectational variables is rather unsatisfactory. The main reason for this is that there is no guarantee that expectations follow a distributed lag, no matter how general the formulation may be. This has led to the use of direct data derived from questionnaire studies. For the United Kingdom, Carlson and Parkin (1975) have constructed a series of the rate of change of price expectations for consumer prices. This series is based on the percentage of the sample who believed that prices will follow a particular pattern[39]. Using the series they found that the first order adaptive expectations hypothesis could not be rejected, but the most satisfactory explanation appeared to be a combination of the second order error-learning process proposed by Rose (1972) with a devaluation effect. The second order process is

$$\dot{p}^e - \dot{p}^e_{t-1} = (1 - \gamma_0)\{\dot{p}_{t-1} - \dot{p}^e_{t-1}\} + (1 - \gamma_1)\{\dot{p}_{t-2} - \dot{p}^e_{t-2}\} \qquad (7.28)$$

Similar results were obtained for firms' expectations of wholesale and export price changes[40].

With these new series, which appeared to suggest some error-learning process, it was possible to test directly an excess demand expectations model. A testable model is derived by Parkin, Sumner and Ward (1976) whose final estimating equation is

$$\dot{w}_t = \alpha_0 + \alpha_1 U_t + \alpha_2 \dot{p}^e_{w_t} + \alpha_3 \dot{p}^e_{f_t} + \alpha_4 \dot{p}^e_{c_t}$$
$$+ \alpha_5 \dot{t}_{I_t} + \alpha_6 \dot{t}_{p_t} + IP \qquad (7.29)$$

where $\dot{p}^e_w$, $\dot{p}^e_f$, $\dot{p}^e_c$ are the expected percentage per annum quarterly rate of change of wholesale, export and retail prices respectively, and $\dot{t}_I$, $\dot{t}_p$ are the expected percentage per annum quarterly rate of change of the ratio of take-home pay to gross pay, and employers' pay roll tax respectively. IP represents a set of incomes policy dummies and U is the average rate of unemployment over the previous year.

The model was first tested over the period 1956(2)–1971(4) to find out if the hypothesis of no long-run trade-off could be rejected. When it could not be rejected they imposed appropriate restrictions on the model to give the preferred result. The restrictions are that

$$\left.\begin{array}{l} \alpha_2 + \alpha_3 + \alpha_4 = 1 \\ \alpha_2 + \alpha_3 + \alpha_5 = 1 \\ \alpha_2 + \alpha_3 + \alpha_6 = 0 \end{array}\right\} \qquad (7.30)$$

Their results are noteworthy despite the apparent lack of explanatory power, which is probably due to the construction of the data series. Domestic wholesale and retail price expectations appear to be the forces which generated the wage explosion of the late 1960s. But this may be a little misleading due to the obvious collinearity between wholesale prices and export prices. From the viewpoint of the excess demand protagonists, the results are even more satisfying in that the greater effect on wage changes comes from the demand side of the labour market. Their other important results are that the natural rate of unemployment, assuming a long-run increase in output per head of $2\frac{1}{2}\%$ per annum is 1.7%[41] and that unemployment remains the best proxy for excess demand. Finally, the fiscal variables appeared to make little contribution to the explanation of wage inflation no matter how they were constructed.

Two further issues are worth considering in relation to this study. The first is the obvious problem that during the periods when wages were exploding, unemployment was above the calculated natural rate. This is inconsistent with the excess demand hypothesis. Parkin (1978) argues that this is still consistent with the excess demand–expectations model provided there is a fixed exchange rate, so that export and domestic prices are influenced by world demand even if the domestic economy has excess supply. The second issue results from comparison of these results with those of Johnston and Timbrell (1973), using their bargaining model. Despite their different emphases, both models suggest that taxes and expectations are important. Furthermore, they suggest that it is possible for real wages to be rising below the trend, with marginal productivity at the trend, so that the cumulative difference will reflect the cumulative excess demand gap. With reference to this point the expectations-augmented Phillips curve estimated by Johnston and Timbrell does not really provide a fair comparison, as their price expectations variable is not at all in line with the measured expectations used by Parkin, Sumner and Ward (1976)[42]. The discrepancy over the failure of the tax variable may be explained in terms of indirect effects reflected through excess demand, thereby causing a possible ambiguity in the results.

Taking all these factors from his earlier work, Sumner (1978) dealt with a restricted model

$$\dot{w}_t = \alpha_0 + \alpha_1 X_t + \alpha_2 \dot{p}_c^e + \alpha_3 \dot{p}_w^e + \alpha_4 \dot{r} \tag{7.31}$$

where X is the excess demand for labour.

The substitution of the excess demand variable in the initial formulation arose from the failure of the earlier study to stand up to a data extension, notably the failure of the unemployment rate as a proxy for excess demand[43]. Clearly the disappearance of the short-run trade-off renders the problem of testing for a long-run trade-off irrelevant. Sumner found that by incorporating one intercept dummy for 1969–1974 and another for unexplained residuals in 1972, the previously estimated relationship, with its implications for a long-run trade-off, was restored. Sumner suggested that there may have been a once-and-for-all movement rather than a continuous movement in the Phillips curve. Furthermore the natural rate was 3.2% compared with 1.9% up to 1968, using the same productivity assumptions as before.

This summarizes the first part of Sumner's work and concludes the consideration of the role of expectations in wage, price and unemployment models for the United Kingdom. The second part of Sumner's paper was concerned with the behaviour of unemployment, and this is considered in the next section .

7.8 Conclusions

This chapter has been restricted to those models where excess demand is represented by the unemployment rate or where the latter is subsumed by other variables. There have, however, been other measures relating unemployment to excess demand. The use of the registered unemployment rate has been challenged, and some of the main points may be noted here.

There have been two main approaches to producing alternative series, one involving direct manipulation of the data and the other using regression analysis. The first is embodied by the work of Taylor (1972), who suggested that excess labour supply is better proxied using labour hoarding in addition to unemployment[44]. Taylor achieved some success with this measure when explaining earnings but found an insignificant effect when attempting to explain wage rates, a result later verified by Parkin, Sumner and Ward (1976).

The second approach stems from the fact that in most models the unemployment rate has been assumed to depend solely on the growth of output. However, social policy may be an additional variable operating on labour supply, in which case there has been a shift in the level of unemployment for any given level of excess demand. Thus any adjusted series will be necessary to deal adequately with the Phillips relationship. This has been pursued by Sumner (1978), who created an adjusted series that he claimed had been purged of 'voluntary unemployment' and used it with some success in a wage equation for the period 1952–1965. Although there have been alternative suggestions as to the nature of the unemployment equation (Apps and Ashworth, 1979), Sumner's work provides a useful line of advance. Further direct measures of expectations may also perhaps provide an improvement over the use of intercept dummies and the registered unemployment rate.

The vision arising from the large amount of work considered in this chapter is inevitably blurred. Clearly the issues are not resolved but the way forward would appear to be through a more detailed examination of the measures which are used to obtain proxies of the vital expectations and excess demand variables. But of course it must be remembered that the move from explanation to policy implementation may be unacceptable to many people.

Notes

1. For a fuller story of this period see Bronfenbrenner and Holzman (1963).
2. The various wage–wage, wage–price theories are outlined by Burton (1972).
3. The actual construction of $\dot{w}$ as a discrete approximation to a continuous variable is $\dot{w}_t = (W_{t+1} - W_{t-1})/2W_t$. The advantage of this over $\dot{w}_t = (W_t - W_{t-1})/W_t$ is explained by Lipsey (1960, n. 4).
4. Gilbert (1976) explains this point more rigorously. Further details of Phillips' method are given in Desai (1975, 1976).
5. This can be seen from *Figure 7.1*. In addition if demand were kept at a value which would maintain stable wage rates the associated level of unemployment would be 5.47%.
6. It should be noted that there is something of a problem here because while the Phillips relationship is between changes in money wages and the unemployment rate, the Lipsey approach would appear to be dealing with real wages.
7. It will be seen that E_j is a smooth curve, not two linear segments. This result is derived directly from the relationship between unemployment and vacancies. This is examined in detail in Chapter 4 of this book, and for the purpose of this chapter it should be appreciated that unemployment is only an approximate measure of excess demand.
8. There are many basic problems associated with the form of aggregation outlined in the text. See, for example, Peston (1971). An alternative approach outlined by Trevithick and Mulvey (1975) suggests looking for a theoretical base in the income–expenditure models and then disaggregating; thus putting a macro interpretation directly on to the Phillips curve.
9. No account has been made here of the size of the relative markets. Peston (1971) has shown that the Lipsey result could be significantly affected by the relative sizes of the markets. The result also depends crucially on the assumption that the functions for each market are identical. Bowers, Cheshire and Webb (1970) have proved that the results will not hold if this assumption is relaxed. This result is reiterated by Sargan (1971) who has shown that it is not true for either regional or industrial submarkets.
10. For an exposition of this idea see Bowen and Berry (1963).
11. Archibald (1969) and Archibald, Kemmis and Perkins (1974) have attempted to use σ_u as an explanatory variable to explain $\dot{w}$ and using both annual and quarterly data, claim better

explanatory power than the original Phillips curve for the UK. However, the evidence for the US over the same period is ambiguous.

12. This is a simplified viewpoint because the Samuelson and Solow (1960) use of $\dot{p}$ instead of $\dot{w}$ infers much more about the analysis. It can no longer be claimed that the Phillips curve comes directly from workings of the labour market, but instead it arises from a system of equations affecting different markets.

13. The Lipsey rationale for the Phillips curve and hence the estimating equation provides support for either the demand-pull or cost-push school. Excess demand for labour can be produced either by shifts in the supply curve of labour or the demand curve.

14. The data were derived in Dow and Dicks-Mireaux (1958) and subsequently used in Dicks-Mireaux and Dow (1959) and Dicks-Mireaux (1961).

15. This assumes that the government continues to pursue policies aimed at maintaining the rate of change of money wages at $\dot{w}_1$.

16. A more expanded version can be found in Smith (1970), the only difference being that he rationalizes the expectations augmented Phillips curve in terms of $\dot{w}^e$.

17. Both Friedman and Phelps accept some version of the Phillips–Lipsey relation between excess demand and unemployment and the rate of change of unemployment but their analysis differs in that it implies that there exists a level of unemployment at which excess demand is zero and inflation will be constant and equal to its expected rate. A further generalization can be found in Mortensen (1970) and a model which adapts to estimation can be found in Parkin, Sumner and Ward (1976).

18. A survey of bargaining models is available in de Menil (1970).

19. The possibility had been suggested by Dicks-Mireaux and Dow (1959).

20. Hines tried incorporating unemployment into the unionization equation but found no evidence to support its inclusion. Further, there was no evidence that union aggressiveness was dependent on labour market 'tightness'. Instead the model becomes a wage–price spiral. Price increases generate union pressure which generates wage increases. Hines also asserted that there was no association between $\dot{T}$ and the level of economic activity, but there has been evidence to the contrary by Richardson (1977). If this is the case then $\dot{T}$ may just track market pressures.

21. For example,

$$w_t = -7.537 + 2.9224 T_t + 0.317 \dot{T}_t \qquad R^2 = 0.9069$$
$$\quad (16.9) \qquad (7.04) \qquad\qquad DW = 1.57$$

22. Burrows and Hitiris (1972) and Godfrey (1971) have argued that small changes would militate against union 'pushfulness'. This point is rather less than satisfactory, as there have been large changes in membership in some unions even if the overall change is very small.

23. It should also be noted that Purdy and Zis cannot reject the possibility that serial correlation exists in the specification of the model. This would bias the significance of the coefficient. Their data construction may however have forced this 'serial correlation' on the model, as was seen in Section 7.3.

24. It is by no means certain that Purdy and Zis do not encounter this problem when testing using $\dot{T}_m$ and $\dot{T}_e$.

25. Strikes can be measured as number of workers, number of strikes, number of man-days, and strikes for particular reasons.

26. For more on the ambiguity of the expected sign on strikes, see Johnston and Timbrell (1973). Alternatively a comparison could be made of the arguments of Holt (1970) against those of Ashenfelter and Johnson (1969) and Godfrey (1971).

27. This real claim is not the actual claim which is made but the firm's belief of what the union would actually settle for. It should be noted that all bargaining models share a common theme of maximizing gains from trade and sharing these gains in proportion to the potential inflictable costs of confrontation.

28. This model has been extended by Chapman (1979) to incorporate a union decision-making process.

29. There are three constructions of c which are used giving different weights to cases where the target is beaten. The weights are either zero, one half or unity. Chapman (1979) states that the test of the model can only be considered very weak as he shows that it uses union objectives which are inconsistent with his constrained maximization approach.

30. The catch-up variable is significant when $\dot{p}$ is used instead of $\dot{p}^e$ and this also increases the correlation but Johnston and Timbrell express doubt as to its validity. There is also autocorrelation, indicating overstatement of significance, when $\dot{p}$ is used.

31. Sargan (1964) used a different price index but the equation looked similar and he used real wages which are replaced by real earnings. In addition, Henry, Sawyer and Smith do not use a government 'dummy'. Further discussion of Sargan may be found in Desai (1975).

32. Most price equations are based on scanty theory following the principle expounded by Solow (1969), 'In general one expects the rate of change of the price level to depend on the current and

recent changes in unit costs and on the supply–demand balance in the current period and recent past.'

33. This deals with the single equation case originally used by Perry (1966). If the model consists of a series of simultaneous equations, it is necessary to use the reduced form.

34. Policy-on periods were 1948(3)–1950(3), 1956(1)–1956(4), 1961(3)–1967(2). The definition of the unemployment variable is also very important because better fits were obtained for the 'policy-on' period using U_s, a five quarter moving average.

35. Parkin, Sumner and Jones (1972) have pointed out that this test is inappropriate because of the presence of serial correlation and as a result can only be a rough indication.

36. Hines' results exhibit the disturbing feature that for the policy-on period the coefficient on price change in the wage equation has a negative coefficient suggesting some mis-specification and so casting doubt on his interpretation. There are further studies using the separate equations approach but these tend to find no support for shifts of any kind. For examples of the work, see Taylor (1972) and Thomas and Stoney (1972).

37. They use U_t instead of $U'_t = (U_t + U_{t-1} + U_{t-2})/3$, claiming that U'_t increased the collinearity with $\dot{p}_t$.

38. This is at the 5% significance level, at 1% it is possible.

39. How the qualitative information is turned into quantitative data is described in Carlson and Parkin (1975).

40. See Parkin, Sumner and Ward (1976) and Smith (1978) for descriptions.

41. As noted this is not unlike the Phillips prediction but there is an obvious theoretical difference in that a trade-off was implied by the earlier work.

42. Henry, Sawyer and Smith's (1976) expectations-augmented Phillips curve can be treated in a similar manner.

43. The unemployment rate appeared with a positive sign in a study by Coutts, Tarling and Wilkinson (1976).

44. This is the case for empirical models although a case has been made for employing hidden unemployment. But this has been found to be insignificant in explaining w for the United States and so is not used. See Taylor (1970) and Perry (1970).

References

Apps, R. and Ashworth, J. S. (1979). *The production of an adjusted unemployment series*. University of Manchester Discussion Paper, No. 11

Archibald, G. C. (1969). The Phillips curve and the distribution of unemployment. *American Economic Review Papers and Proceedings* **59**, 124–134

Archibald, G. C., Kemmis, A. and Perkins, J. W. (1974). Excess demand for labour, unemployment and the Phillips curve: a theoretical and empirical study. In *Inflation and Labour Markets* (ed. by D. E. W. Laidler and D. L. Purdy), pp. 109–163. Manchester; Manchester University Press

Ashenfelter, O. C. and Johnson, G. E. (1969). Bargaining theory, trade unions and industrial strike activity. *American Economic Review* **59**, 35–49

Bowen, W. G. and Berry, A. A. (1963). Unemployment conditions and movements of the money wage level. *Review of Economics and Statistics* **45**, 163–192

Bowers, J. K., Cheshire, P. C. and Webb, A. E. (1970). The change in the relationship between unemployment and earnings increases: a review of some explanations. *National Institute Economic Review* **54**, 44–63

Brechling, F. (1963). Some empirical evidence on the effectiveness of prices and incomes policies. In *Incomes Policies and Inflation* (ed. by J. M. Parkin and A. R. Nobay), pp. 30–47. Manchester; Manchester University Press

Bronfenbrenner, M. and Holzman, F. D. (1963). A survey of inflation. *American Economic Review* **53**, 593–661

Burrows, P. and Hitiris, T. (1972). Estimating the impact of incomes policy. In *Incomes Policies and Inflation* (ed. by J. M. Parkin and A. R. Nobay), pp. 151–162. Manchester; Manchester University Press

Burton, J. (1972). *Wage Inflation*. London; Macmillan

Carlson, J. A. and Parkin, J. M. (1975). Inflation expectations. *Economica* **42**, 123–138. Reprinted in *Inflation in the United Kingdom* (ed. by J. M. Parkin and M. T. Sumner), pp. 112–140. Manchester; Manchester University Press

Chapman, P. G. (1979). Trade union objectives in the Johnston wage bargaining model. University of Dundee Occasional Paper, No. 14

Corry, B. and Laidler, D. E. W. (1967). The Phillips relation. A theoretical explanation. *Economica* **34**, 189–197

Coutts, K., Tarling, R. and Wilkinson, F. (1976). Wage bargaining and the inflation process. *Economic Policy Review* **2**, 20–27

de Menil, G. (1970). *Bargaining: Monopoly Power versus Union Power*. Cambridge, Mass.; M.I.T. Press

Desai, M. (1975). The Phillips curve: a revisionist interpretation. *Economica* **42**, 1–19

Desai, M. (1976). *Applied Econometrics.* Oxford; Phillip Allan

Dicks-Mireaux, L. A. (1961). The inter-relationship between cost and price changes, 1945–59: a study of inflation in post-war Britain. *Oxford Economic Papers* **13**, 267–292

Dicks-Mireaux, L. A. and Dow, J. C. R. (1959). The determinants of wage inflation in the United Kingdom, 1945–56. *Journal of the Royal Statistical Society Series A* **122**, 145–184

Dow, J. C. R. and Dicks-Mireaux, L. A. (1958). The excess demand for labour. *Oxford Economic Papers* **10**, 1–33

Friedman, M. (1968). The role of monetary policy. *American Economic Review* **58**, 1–17

Gilbert, C. L. (1976). The original Phillips curve estimates. *Economica* **43**, 51–58

Godfrey, L. G. (1971). The Phillips curve: incomes policy and trade union effects. In *The Current Inflation* (ed. by H. G. Johnson and A. R. Nobay), pp. 99–124. London; Macmillan; and amended in *Incomes Policies and Inflation* (ed. by J. M. Parkin and M. T. Sumner), pp. 138–150. Manchester; Manchester University Press

Godfrey, L. G. and Taylor, J. (1973). Earnings changes in the U.K., 1954–70: excess labour supply, expected inflation and union influence. *Bulletin of the Oxford University Institute of Economics and Statistics* **35**, 197–216

Henry, S. G. B., Sawyer, M. C. and Smith, P. (1976). Models of inflation in the United Kingdom: an evaluation. *National Institute Economic Review* **77**, 60–71

Hines, A. G. (1964). Trade unions and wage inflation in the United Kingdom, 1893–1961. *Review of Economic Studies* **31**, 221–252

Hines, A. G. (1968). Unemployment and the rate of change of money wage rates in the United Kingdom, 1862–1963: a reappraisal. *Review of Economics and Statistics* **50**, 60–67

Hines, A. G. (1969). Wage Inflation in the United Kingdom, 1948–62: a disaggregated study. *Economic Journal* **79**, 66–89

Hines, A. G. (1971). The determinants of the rate of change of money wage rates and the effectiveness of incomes policy. In *The Current Inflation* (ed. by H. G. Johnson and A. R. Nobay), pp. 143–175. London; Macmillan

Holt, C. C. (1970). Job search, Phillips' wage relation and union influence: theory and evidence. In *Microeconomic Foundation of Employment and Inflation* (ed. by E. S. Phelps), pp. 53–123. New York; Norton

Johnston, J. (1972). A model of wage determination under bilateral monopoly. *Economic Journal* **82**, 837–852. Reprinted in *Inflation and Labour Markets* (ed. by D. E. W. Laidler and D. L. Purdy), pp. 61–78. Manchester; Manchester University Press

Johnston, J. and Timbrell, M. (1973). Empirical tests of a bargaining theory of wage rate determination. *Manchester School* **41**, 141–167. Reprinted in *Inflation and Labour Markets* (ed. by D. E. W. Laidler and D. L. Purdy), pp. 99–108. Manchester; Manchester University Press

Jorgenson, D. W. (1966). Rational distributed lag functions. *Econometrica* **34**, 135–149

Jorgenson, D. W. and Stephenson, J. A. (1967). Investment behaviour in U.S. manufacturing 1947–60. *Econometrica* **35**, 169–220

Klein, L. A. and Ball, R. J. (1959). Some econometrics of the determination of the absolute level of wages and prices. *Economic Journal* **69**, 465–482

Knowles, K. G. J. C. and Winston, C. B. (1959). Can the levels of unemployment explain changes in wages. *Bulletin of the Oxford University Institute of Statistics* **21**, 113–120

Lipsey, R. G. (1960). The relationship between unemployment and the rate of change of money wages in the United Kingdom, 1862–1957: A further analysis. *Economica* **27**, 1–31

Lipsey, R. G. (1979). *Introduction to Positive Economics*, 5th edition. London; Weidenfeld and Nicholson

Lipsey, R. G. and Parkin, J. M. (1970). Incomes policy: a re-appraisal. *Economica* **37**, 115–138. Reprinted in *Incomes Policies and Inflation* (ed. by J. M. Parkin and M. T. Sumner), pp. 85–111. Manchester; Manchester University Press

Maki, D. and Spindler, Z. A. (1975). The effect of unemployment compensation on the rate of unemployment in Great Britain. *Oxford Economic Papers* **27**, 440–455

Mortensen, D. T. (1970). A theory of wage and employment dynamics. In *Microeconomic Foundations of Employment and Inflation Theory* (ed. by E. S. Phelps), pp. 167–211. New York; Norton

National Board on Prices and Incomes (1968). *Third General Report*, Cmnd. 3715. London; HMSO

Parkin, J. M. (1970). Incomes policy: some further results on the rate of change of money wages. *Economica* **37**, 386–401

Parkin, J. M. (ed.) (1973). *Essays in Modern Economics*. London; Longmans

Parkin, J. M. (1978). Alternative explanations of United Kingdom inflation. In *Inflation in the United Kingdom* (ed. by J. M. Parkin and M. T. Sumner), pp. 112–129. Manchester; Manchester University Press

Parkin, J. M. and Nobay, A. R. (eds.) (1975). *Contemporary Issues in Economics*. Manchester; Manchester University Press

Parkin, J. M., Sumner, M. T. and Jones, R. A. (1972). A survey of the econometric evidence of the effects of incomes policy in the rate of inflation. In *Incomes Policies and Inflation* (ed. by J. M. Parkin and M. T. Sumner), pp. 1–29. Manchester; Manchester University Press

Parkin, J. M., Sumner, M. T. and Ward, R. A. (1976). The effects of excess demand, generalised expectations and wage–price controls on wage inflation in the U.K.: 1956–71. In *The Economics of Wage and Price Controls* (ed. by K. Brunner and A. M. Metzler), pp. 193–222. Carnegie–Rochester Conference Series on Public Policy No. 2. Amsterdam; North Holland

Perry, G. L. (1966). *Unemployment, Money Wage Rates and Inflation.* Cambridge, Mass.; M.I.T. Press

Perry, G. L. (1970). Changing labour markets and inflation. *Brookings Papers on Economic Activity* 1, 411–441

Peston, M. (1971). The micro-economics of the Phillips curve. In *The Current Inflation* (ed. by H. G. Johnson and A. R. Norbay), pp. 125–142. London; Macmillan

Phelps, E. S. (1967). Phillips curves, expectations of inflation and optimal unemployment over time. *Economica* 34, 254–281

Phelps, E. S. (1968). Money wage dynamics and labor market equilibrium. *Journal of Political Economy* 76, 678–711

Phillips, A. W. (1958). The relationship between unemployment and the rate of change of money wage rates in the United Kingdom, 1861–1957. *Economica* 25, 283–299

Purdy, D. L. and Zis, G. (1973). Trade unions and wage inflation in the U.K.: a re-appraisal. In *Essays in Modern Economics* (ed. by J. M. Parkin). London; Longmans and reprinted in *Inflation and Labour Markets* (ed. by D. E. W. Laidler and D. L. Purdy), pp. 1–37. Manchester; Manchester University Press

Purdy, D. L. and Zis, G. (1974). On the concept and measurement of union militancy. In *Inflation and Labour Markets* (ed. by D. E. W. Laidler and D. L. Purdy), pp. 38–60. Manchester; Manchester University Press

Purdy, D. L. and Zis, G. (1976). Trade unions and wage inflation in the U.K.: a reply to Dogas and Hines. *Applied Economics* 8, 249–265

Richardson, R. (1977). Trade union growth. *British Journal of Industrial Relations* 15, 157–175

Rose, D. E. (1972). A general error-learning model of expectations formation. University of Manchester SSRC Inflation Workshop Discussion Paper 7210

Routh, G. (1959). The relation between unemployment and the rate of change of money wages: a comment. *Economica* 26, 299–315

Samuelson, P. A. and Solow, R. M. (1960). Analytical aspects of anti-inflation policy. *American Economic Review, Papers and Proceedings* **50**, 117–194

Sargan, J. D. (1964). Wages and prices in the United Kingdom: a study in econometric methodology. In *Econometric Analysis for National Economic Planning* (ed. by P. E. Hart, G. Mills and J. K. Whitaker), pp. 25–54. London; Butterworths

Sargan, J. D. (1971). A study of wages and prices in the U.K. 1949–68. In *The Current Inflation* (ed. by H. G. Johnson and A. R. Nobay), pp. 52–74. London; Macmillan

Saunders, P. G. and Nobay, A. R. (1972). Price expectations, the Phillips curve and incomes policy. In *Incomes Policies and Inflation* (ed. by J. M. Parkin and M. T. Sumner), pp. 237–249. Manchester; Manchester University Press

Smith, D. C. (1968). Incomes policy. In *Incomes Policies and Inflation* (ed. by J. M. Parkin and M. T. Sumner), pp. 48–84. Manchester; Manchester University Press

Smith, G. (1978). Producers' price and cost expectations. In *Inflation in the United Kingdom* (ed. by J. M. Parkin and M. T. Sumner), pp. 141–145. Manchester; Manchester University Press

Smith, W. L. (1970). On some current issues in monetary economics: an interpretation. *Journal of Economic Literature* **8**, 767–782

Sheriff, T. D. (1977). Some empirical evidence on the effectiveness of incomes policy in the U.K. *Applied Economics* **9**, 253–264

Solow, R. M. (1969). *Price Expectations and the Behaviour of the Price Level*. Manchester; Manchester University Press

Sumner, M. T. (1972). Aggregate demand, price expectations and the Phillips curve. In *Incomes Policies and Inflation* (ed. by J. M. Parkin and M. T. Sumner), pp. 163–181. Manchester; Manchester University Press

Sumner, M. T. (1978). Wage determination. In *Inflation in the United Kingdom* (ed. by J. M. Parkin and M. T. Sumner), pp. 75–92. Manchester; Manchester University Press

Taylor, J. (1970). Hidden unemployment, hoarded labour and the Phillips curve. *Southern Economic Journal* **37**, 1–16

Taylor, J. (1972). Incomes policy, the structure of unemployment and the Phillips curve: the United Kingdom experience, 1953–70. In *Incomes Policies and Inflation* (ed. by J. M. Parkin and M. T. Sumner), pp. 182–200. Manchester; Manchester University Press

Taylor, J. (1975). Wage inflation, unemployment and the organised pressure for higher wages in the U.K., 1961–71. In *Contemporary Issues in Economics* (ed. by J. M. Parkin and A. R. Nobay), pp. 120–138. Manchester; Manchester University Press

Thomas, R. L. (1977). Unionisation and the Phillips curve—time series evidence for seven industrial countries. *Applied Economics* **9**, 33–50

Thomas, R. L. and Stoney, P. J. M. (1972). Unemployment dispersion as a determinant of wage inflation in the United Kingdom, 1925–66. In *Incomes Policies and Inflation* (ed. by J. M. Parkin and M. T. Sumner), pp. 201–236. Manchester; Manchester University Press

Trevithick, J. and Mulvey, C. A. (1975). *The Economics of Inflation*. Bath; Martin Robinson

Wallis, K. F. (1971). Wages, prices and incomes policies: some comments. *Economica* **38**, 304–310. Reprinted in *Incomes Policies and Inflation* (ed. by J. M. Parkin and M. T. Sumner), pp. 130–137. Manchester; Manchester University Press

Ward, A. and Zis, G. (1974). Trade union militancy as an explanation of inflation: an international comparison. *Manchester School* **42**, 46–65

Zis, G. (1977). On the role of strikes variables in U.K. wage equations. *Scottish Journal of Political Economy* **24**, 43–55

Appendix

Table 7.1 Selected empirical results
See notes to Table for definitions of variables

[handwritten annotation: standard error in bracket]

Study	Data used / Estimation technique / Construction of rate of change variable	Regression
Archibald (1969)	Annual 1950–1966 / OLS / 3	$\dot{w}_w = -4.636 + 8.475U^{-1} + 0.348\dot{p} - 0.008\dot{U} + 1.729\sigma_R^2$ $\quad\quad\;(1.93)\;(2.29)\quad\quad(0.13)\quad(0.007)\quad(0.54)$ $\bar{R}^2 = 0.79 \quad\quad DW = 1.28$ A model using σ_I^2 instead of σ_R^2 gives similar results
Burrows and Hitiris (1972)	Quarterly 1955(1)–1967(4) / OLS / 2	$\dot{w}_w = 5.692 + 0.547D - 1.522U + 0.463US + 0.248\dot{p} - 0.318PS - 0.312\dot{N} + 1.386NS$ $\quad\quad\;(6.07)\quad\quad(0.76)\quad(0.77)\quad\quad(0.77)\quad(0.30)\quad\quad(0.32)\quad\quad(0.66)\quad(0.74)$ $R^2 = 0.498 \quad\quad DW = 0.766$ Similar results are found with slope dummies moving from policy-on to policy-off
Coutts, Tarling and Wilkinson (1976)	Annual 1960–1974 / OLS / 1	$\dot{w}_h = -2.15 + 2.09\dot{p}^e - 2.09U^{-1}$ $\quad\quad(6.32)\;(0.54)\quad\;(7.74)$ $\bar{R}^2 = 0.66$
Dicks-Mireaux (1961)	Annual 1946–1959 / 2SLS / 1	$\dot{e}_h = 3.90 + 0.3\dot{p} + 0.16\dot{p}_{-1} + 2.78LD_{-1/4}$ $\quad\quad(0.63)\;(0.13)\;(0.10)\quad\quad(0.82)\quad\quad R^2 = 0.99$ $\dot{p} = 2.47 + 0.27\dot{e}_h + 0.21\dot{m}_{-1/4} - 0.54\dot{r}$ $\quad\quad(1.39)\;(0.04)\quad\;(0.04)\quad\quad(0.16)$

Gilbert (1976)	$\dot{w}_h = 1.0892 + 10.524U^{-1.4496} - 0.0623\,(U^{-1.9503}.DU)$
Annual 1861–1913	$\qquad\quad\;\;(0.61)\quad\;\;(1.00)\qquad\quad\;(0.38)$
NL	Estimated standard errors on powers of U are 0.32 and 0.38 respectively
5	$R^2 = 0.748 \qquad DW = 1.984$
Godfrey (1971)	$\dot{w}_w = 0.6762 + 0.1589\dot{p} - 0.3536U^{-1.5} + 0.1055(S/100) - 0.0736\Delta(S/100)$
Quarterly 1957(3)–1969(3)	$\qquad\quad(0.24)\quad\;(0.19)\quad\;\;(0.56)\qquad\quad(0.05)\qquad\qquad(0.18)$
AIV	$s^2 = 0.258$
1	
Godfrey and Taylor (1973)	$\dot{e}_h = 1.957 - 0.234U_d - 0.233U + 0.349U_D + 1.4965 + 0.342\dot{e}_h^e$
Bi-annual 1955(1)–1970(1)	$\quad\;\;(1.27)\quad\;(0.08)\quad\;(0.39)\quad\;\;(0.18)\quad\;\;(0.57)\quad\;(0.20)$
CLS	$\dot{e}_h^e = 1.109\dot{e}_{h-1}^e - 0.109\dot{e}_{-1}^e$
3	$R^2 = 0.71 \qquad G = 0.82$
Hines (1964)	$\dot{w}_h = -1.9740 + 1.5947\Delta N + 0.1282N + 0.6804\dot{p} + 0.812\dot{p}_{-1} - 0.0441U$
Annual 1893–1961	$\qquad\qquad\qquad\;\;(0.24)\qquad\;(0.04)\quad\;\;(0.11)\quad\;\;(0.03)\qquad(0.11)$
2SLS	$R^2 = 0.9953 \qquad DW = 1.32$
1 for wages	$\dot{p} = -0.0779 + 0.6924\dot{w}_h + 0.0396\dot{m}_{-1/2} + 0.1346\dot{r}$
3 for prices	$\qquad\qquad\;\;(0.03)\qquad\;\;(0.02)\qquad\quad(0.07)$
	$R^2 = 0.9834 \qquad DW = 0.98$
	$N = 1.4014 - 0.1145N_{-1} + 0.4664\dot{p} - 0.0978\dot{p}_{-1} + 0.0149\Pi_{-1/2}$
	$\qquad\qquad\quad(0.01)\qquad\;\;\;(0.01)\quad\;\;(0.01)\qquad\;\;(0.005)$
	$R^2 = 0.98 \qquad DW = 1.31$

Study	Data used *Estimation technique* *Construction of rate of change variable*	Regression
Johnston and Timbrell (1973)	Annual 1959–1971 OLS 1	$\dot{w}_w = 0.074 + 2.72n + 0.758\dot{p} + 0.430C$ $\quad\quad\quad\quad\quad (3.48)\ (0.19)\quad (0.18)$ $\quad R^2 = 0.731 \quad\quad DW = 1.04$ $\dot{w}_w = -0.038 + 2.43n + 1.04\dot{p}^e + 0.271C$ $\quad\quad\quad\quad\quad\ (4.26)\ (0.37)\quad (0.24)$ $\quad R^2 = 0.606 \quad\quad DW = 1.97$ $\dot{w}_w = -3.19 + 1.71n + 0.60\dot{p}^e + 2.679U$ $\quad\quad\quad\quad\quad (3.63)\ (0.43)\quad (1.37)$ $\quad R^2 = 0.684 \quad\quad DW = 2.09$
Lipsey and Parkin (1970)	Quarterly 1948(3)–1967(2) OLS 2 Wage equations only	$\dot{w}_w = 4.147 - 0.891U + 0.482\dot{p} + 3.315\dot{N}$ $\quad\quad (0.97)\ (0.50)\quad (0.08)\quad (1.59)$ $\quad R^2 = 0.616 \quad\quad DW = 0.742$ *Policy-off* $\dot{w}_w = 6.672 - 2.372U + 0.457\dot{p} + 0.136\dot{N}$ $\quad\quad (1.15)\ (0.65)\quad (0.07)\quad (1.94)$ $\quad R^2 = 0.856 \quad\quad DW = 1.231$ *Policy-on* $\dot{w} = -3.919 - 0.404U + 0.227\dot{p} + 3.764\dot{N}$ $\quad\quad (1.72)\ (0.72)\quad (0.24)\quad (2.33)$ $\quad R^2 = 0.138 \quad\quad DW = 0.724$

Parkin (1970)	Quarterly 1948(3)–1969(1)	$\dot{w}_w = 3.034 + 0.021LD + 0.436\dot{p}^e$
	NLCLS	$\quad\;\;(0.88)\;\;(0.38)\quad\;\;(0.20)$
	2	$\lambda = 0.440 \qquad \rho = 0.483 \qquad s^2 = 0.701$
		$\quad\;(0.204)\qquad\;\;(0.229)$
Parkin, Sumner and Ward (1976)	Quarterly 1956(2)–1971(4)	$\dot{w}_w = 3.9838 - 0.6436U + 0.4010\dot{p}^e_w + 0.1265\dot{p}^e_f + 0.3263\dot{p}^e - 0.31077T_2$
	OLS	$\quad\;\;(1.99)\quad\;(0.92)\quad\;\;\;(0.19)\quad\;\;(0.23)\qquad(0.31)\qquad(0.53)$
	4	$\qquad\qquad\qquad\qquad\qquad\qquad\qquad\qquad\quad\; + 0.111T_1 + 0.1523I_1 - 1.0504I_2$
		$\qquad\qquad\qquad\qquad\qquad\qquad\qquad\qquad\quad\;\;(0.25)\quad\;\;(1.52)\qquad(1.50)$
		$\bar{R}^2 = 0.675 \qquad DW = 1.642$
Purdy and Zis (1973)	Annual 1925–1938, 1950–1961	$\dot{w}_h = 0.558 + 0.081N^m + 0.434\Delta N^m + 0.055\dot{p} + 0.222\dot{p}_{-1/2} + 6.368U^{-1}$
		$\quad\;\;(0.36)\;\;(0.05)\qquad(0.13)\qquad(0.13)\quad\;(0.12)\qquad(0.79)$
	2SLS	$R^2 = 0.963 \qquad DW = 1.670$
	3	$\dot{p} = -0.232 + 0.063\dot{r} + 0.239\dot{M}_{-1/2} + 0.682\dot{w}_h$
		$\quad\;\;\;(0.32)\quad(0.15)\quad\;(0.36)\qquad\;\;(0.08)$
		$R^2 = 0.930 \qquad DW = 1.668$
		$\Delta N^m = 10.054 - 0.40N^m_{-1} + 0.355\dot{p}_{-1/2} - 0.004\pi_{-1}$
		$\qquad\quad(2.07)\;\;(0.05)\qquad(0.08)\qquad(0.0005)$
		$R^2 = 0.6108 \qquad DW = 1.2312$
Solow (1969)	Annual 1948–1966	$\dot{p} = 0.0618 + 0.575u\dot{l}c + 0.093\dot{m} - 0.0453DC - 0.1147DL + 0.2109\dot{p}^e$
	OLS	$\quad\;\;(0.08)\quad\;(0.05)\qquad(0.006)\quad(0.005)\qquad(0.06)\qquad(0.06)$
	1	$R^2 = 0.9808$
		Assumed that adaptive expectations coefficient is $\quad \theta = 0.7\dot{p}^e_{+1} = 0.3\dot{p}^e + 0.7\dot{p}$
	Quarterly 1952(3)–1966(4)	$\dot{p} = -0.2325 + 0.0812u\dot{l}c + 0.00243CU + 0.8085\dot{p}^e$
	OLS	$\quad\;\;\;(0.49)\quad\;(0.05)\qquad(0.0005)\qquad(0.10)$
		θ assumed to be 0.7 $\qquad R^2 = 0.8443$

Study	Data used Estimation technique Construction of rate of change variable	Regression
Summer (1978)	Annual 1952–1974 OLS 4	$\dot{w}_w = 4.9054 - 1.4157U + 0.5183\dot{p}_w + 0.2436\dot{p}^e + 0.4627\dot{r} + 2.7478D_1 + 3.0240D_2$ $\quad\quad(0.77)\quad(0.59)\quad\quad(0.62)\quad\quad\quad(0.20)\quad\quad(0.17)\quad\quad(0.78)\quad\quad(1.15)$ $\quad\quad R^2 = 0.9558 \quad\quad DW = 2.0915$
	Annual 1952–1965	$\dot{w}_w = 6.4882 - 1.0323AU + 0.3352\dot{p}_w^e + 0.1152\dot{r} + 0.2260\dot{p}^e - 1.4006D_3$ $\quad\quad(1.46)\quad\quad(0.39)\quad\quad\quad(0.25)\quad\quad\quad(0.22)\quad\quad(0.34)\quad\quad(0.85)$ $\quad\quad R^2 = 0.8020 \quad\quad DW = 1.4850$
Zis (1977)	Quarterly 1956(2)–1975(4) OLS 4	$\dot{w}_w = 0.515 + 0.651\dot{p} - 0.935U^{-1.5} + 0.204S_{-1}$ $\quad\quad(0.53)\quad(0.09)\quad\quad(0.72)\quad\quad\quad(0.07)$ $\quad\quad \bar{R}^2 = 0.595 \quad\quad DW = 1.625$

Notes to table

A dot above a variable indicates a rate of change.
A superscript 'e' indicates an expectation.
For example if p is an index of prices, $\dot{p}$ is the rate of change of prices and $\dot{p}^e$ is the expected rate of change of prices.

AU	Adjusted unemployment	ρ	First order autoregression coefficient
C	Catch-up variable		
CU	Capacity utilization	S	Number of stoppages
D	Intercept dummy	s	Standard error of regression
DC	Cripps dummy		
DL	Lloyd dummy	σ_R^2	Variance of regional unemployment
D_1, D_2, D_3	Intercept dummies 1969–1972, 1972, 1962	σ_I^2	Variance of industrial unemployment
e_h	Hourly earnings	t	Time trend
I_2, I_2	Incomes policy dummies 1961–1962, 1966–1967	T_1	Expected ratio of take home to gross pay
L	Index of excess labour demand	T_2	Expected rate of change of employers' payroll taxes
λ	Adjustment coefficient		
m	Import prices	ulc	Unit labour costs
n	Proportion of workforce receiving pay increase	U	Registered unemployment (%)
N	Percentage of workforce unionized	U_d	Index of labour hoarding
NE	Net earnings	U'	$(U + U_{-1} + U_{-2})/3$
N^m	Same as N, but allowing for structural changes	U_D	Unemployment after 1966(2) zero otherwise
p	Prices	US, PS, NS	Slope dummies
Π	Profits	w_w	Weekly wage rates
r	Labour productivity	w_h	Hourly wage rates

Construction of rate of change variable

1. $\dot{w} = 100(W - W_{-1})/W_{-1}$

2. $\dot{w} = 200(W_{+2} - W_{-2})/(W_{+2} - W_{-2})$

3. $\dot{w} = 100(W_{+1} - W_{-1})/2W$

4. $\dot{w} = 400 \ln (W/W_{-1})$

5. $\dot{w} = 100 \ln (W/W_{-1})$

6. $\dot{w} = 100(W - W_{-4})/W_{-4}$

Estimation technique

AIV: autoregressive instrumental variables
CLS: constrained least squares
NL: non-linear estimates
NLCLS: non-linear constrained least squares
OLS: ordinary least squares
2SLS: two stage least squares

Unemployment statistics in Britain

8.1 Administrative sources

When a person becomes unemployed, he or she will normally wish to register for work at an Employment Office so that he is informed of suitable vacancies that occur. He will also normally wish to claim social security benefits and, if he does, he will be required to register for work. Until 1973 these two activities took place in the same office, illustrating the close association of registration for work with entitlement to benefits. Furthermore, the statistics of the registered unemployed are based on those registered as 'seeking employment' and accepted, on the basis of case law developed by National Insurance decisions, as being 'capable of and available for work'. Changes in regulations affecting entitlement to benefits can significantly affect the propensity of the unemployed to register for work, as has recently been reflected in statistics relating to married women. It is clear then that whereas registration-based counts of the unemployed quite specifically include a minority who are not making benefit claims, their coverage is heavily influenced by the social security system.

In total the administrative processes concerned with the unemployed represent a rich source of data, although their fragmentation at present prevents the formation of as comprehensive a picture as is theoretically possible. Despite inadequacies these sources yield most of the information quoted by political and academic commentators on unemployment. Within government the range of uses of data from these sources is vast: at one end of the spectrum the national monthly unemployment count is regarded as a principal economic and social indicator while at the other end counts relating to work at individual offices can be used to adjust their staffing levels.

There are five sets of administrative records which are, to varying degrees, used to provide statistical information on the unemployed— Employment and Careers Offices, Unemployment Benefit Offices, National Insurance contribution records, Department of Health and

Social Security (DHSS) local offices, and the National Unemployment Benefit System computers.

Employment and Careers Offices

The Employment Offices, including their Professional and Executive Recruitment offices and Jobcentres, are administered by the Manpower Services Commission with the purpose of matching job-seekers with vacancies. They deal in the main with the adult unemployed while most of the unemployed under the age of 18 are dealt with by Careers Offices which are administered by local education authorities. In turn, the significance of these offices from the statistical viewpoint is increased by the requirement that unemployed social security claimants register for work at one of these offices. And the vast majority of the registered unemployed are claimants.

Unemployment Benefit Offices

Unemployment Benefit Offices (UBOs) are administered by the Department of Employment acting as an agent of the DHSS. Although claimants have to be registered for work, it is at the UBO that they initially claim unemployment benefit or credits and attend there regularly to declare continuing satisfaction of the conditions for benefit for unemployment. The UBO checks the claimant's contribution record to establish whether he is entitled to unemployment benefit (which is a National Insurance benefit dependent on previous earnings-related contributions), checks that he is registered for work and then submits the claims to the insurance officer (the first of the independent adjudicating authorities who decide claims to benefit) for determination. If the insurance officer allows the claim, the UBO arranges payment of benefit (including any amount of supplementary allowance notified to the UBO) and, if necessary, arranges the notification of National Insurance credits.

National Insurance records

There are two ways in which the National Insurance contribution records held at the DHSS Central Office in Newcastle are involved in the course of a claim. First a check of the record has to be made to establish the claimant's contribution position and whether any other enquiry—reflecting another claim—has been made in a recent period which could affect entitlement during the current claim; in turn of course, the current enquiry with its date and type ('unemployment') will be recorded on the file. Secondly it may at a later stage be necessary to award, and record on this file, 'unemployment credits' to make up the deficiency in contributions resulting from the period of unemployment.

DHSS local offices

DHSS local offices have a wide range of responsibilities but in the current context their only role relates to the unemployed who are eligible for supplementary allowance in the absence, or on top, of unemployment benefit. This is the third office which must be contacted by such a claimant. It is here that entitlement to supplementary allowance is assessed but the actual payments are normally made by the UBO.

Benefit computers

The final but increasingly important element in this complex picture is the role of the National Unemployment Benefit Systems (NUBS) computers at Reading and Livingston. These hold information input direct from UBOs and their functions include establishing the claimant's contribution record via the Newcastle computer, calculating the amount of unemployment benefit due, issuing Girocheques (including any supplementary allowance) and recording entitlement to credits. When benefits for the unemployed become taxable it is likely that these computers will have a central role to play in that administrative process. The introduction of the system started in 1969 and is expected to serve the whole country by the end of 1981 though certain categories of claimant may continue to be excluded.

8.2 Department of Employment statistics

The main series

'The unemployment count' which is widely reported in the media each month is made public through a Press Notice prepared by the Statistics Division of the Department of Employment. The Press Notice is a wide-ranging summary of the latest figures in provisional form. It includes the numbers of unemployed by sex, region, and by broad duration category, the number of unemployed school leavers and seasonally adjusted figures on the numbers of unemployed and flows on and off the register at Employment Offices. It also gives the latest counts for the four categories of the registered unemployed who are excluded from the main unemployment figures, definitional notes and a range of vacancy statistics. Final versions of the figures appear later in the monthly Employment *Gazette* which also includes extra detail from the monthly counts, most notably the unemployment counts and corresponding unemployment rates for travel-to-work areas and for counties. Four main series of quarterly analyses are integrated with the monthly counts and summaries from each of these are also published in the *Gazette*. There is an industrial analysis (undertaken in February, May, August and November), an occupational analysis of those registered at Employment Offices (March, June, September and December) and analyses by age and duration (January, April, July and October) and by ethnic group (February, May, August and November). The February analysis by ethnic group also includes an age breakdown.

The statistics appearing in the *Gazette* are largely self-explanatory provided that attention is paid to the accompanying definitions and footnotes. The user is also greatly helped by the periodic inclusion of a range of articles in the *Gazette*. The June 1980 issue has an article on the flow statistics and the August 1979 issue explains the seasonal adjustment techniques. There is a wide ranging review of the unemployment and vacancy statistics in the May 1980 issue; this review includes a description of uses of the statistics, gives some emphasis to conceptual issues and provides details of what is included in, or excluded from, 'the count'. The key definitional point is that the principal statistics on the stock of unemployed relate to those who are unemployed and registered as seeking employment and who are accepted by the staff of the Employment Offices or Careers Office as being 'capable of and available for work, whether they are entitled to unemployment benefit or not'. But there are four categories of the unemployed who are excluded from the principal counts even if registered for work—adult students aged 18 or over seeking vacation employment, the temporarily stopped[1], the severely disabled[2] and those seeking part-time work and not claiming unemployment benefit or credits. The first three categories are included in the relevant DHSS statistics if they are claimants.

The information required for the counts of the stock of unemployed is available from the registration documents held by Employment Offices and Careers Offices. For those claiming neither benefit nor credits, the occupation recorded is that of their choice. Otherwise the recorded occupation reflects the instruction that '. . . in the light of registrants' general requirements and preferences and having regard to their qualifications, experience and personal qualities, the most suitable occupation for which they can be registered should be determined'. The industry recorded is generally that of the registrants' last employment provided that they have been in the employment field within the last 12 months. The figures for minority group unemployment relate to those who were born in, or whose

parent or parents were born in, certain countries of the Common-
wealth or in Pakistan.

The unemployment counts are always made on a Thursday,
usually the second Thursday in the month. The clerks at Employment
Offices and Careers Offices go through the registration documents
and add up the numbers in the required groups. Certain additional
figures (for example on the temporarily stopped) from UBOs are
incorporated and the numbers transferred on to a formal return to be
signed by the office manager (or Careers Officer). The returns are
sent to the appropriate Regional Manpower Intelligence Unit for
preliminary checking, incorporation of information on PER registrants from computer records held in Runcorn, extraction of material
for the Press Notice and forwarding to Runcorn for computer
processing. The Press Notice appears twelve days after the count
and at the same time regional and local statistics are released from
the Regional Manpower Intelligence Units and Employment
Offices. Statistics appear in the *Gazette* about five weeks later than
this and a range of unpublished information is available on request.

It will be apparent that counts undertaken in this manner and on
such a scale cannot be entirely accurate. However, there are controls
built into the system to ensure the quality of the figures. These
include comparisons with earlier returns and checks of totals but the
most important check is against an independent count of claimants
made at UBOs. There are detailed rules governing the level of
discrepancy which is acceptable at the local level and if any office
does not meet the specified tolerances careful checks have to be
made including, if necessary, a full matching of individual claims
against registrations. This check cannot of course cover the non-
claimant component of the count but this is a small part of the total.
Most difficulties arise from the interval between a change of
circumstances and its reporting to the registration and benefit
services. This can be systematically affected by changes in procedure;
the introduction of fortnightly signing for benefit in September 1979
is for example estimated to have increased the count by 20 000
(*Gazette*, November 1979) though the seasonally adjusted figures
allow for this.

These Department of Employment statistics represent key series
at the national level and supply detailed information at the local
level. The counts are frequent, rapidly and systematically released
and well-documented. It is because of the last two attributes that
they are here described much less fully than their pre-eminence
would otherwise warrant. There is however little flesh on the bones:
the counts are analysed by few variables and cross-analysed even
less. This is inevitable given the method of collection. To get further

information on who the unemployed are and their circumstances it is necessary to rely on future developments, the more detailed of the DHSS routine statistics, and surveys.

The periodic surveys of the characteristics of the unemployed

In 1961 and 1964 studies were carried out to assess the prospects of obtaining work, of a sample of the unemployed, and to shed light on certain characteristics which involve a degree of personal judgement by local office staff. Results from the surveys were published in the then Ministry of Labour *Gazette* in April and September 1962 and April 1966. In November 1972 the report of an inter-department working party on unemployment statistics was published as a White Paper (Cmnd 5157) and a working group, set up on its recommendation to consider detailed studies of the characteristics of the unemployed, conducted the 1973 'characteristics survey' which is reported in the *Gazette* of March, May and June 1974.

A similar survey was undertaken in 1976. The information is based on a 1 in 60 sample of the stock of registrants at Employment Offices on a day in June. Information for most of the questions was available in the registration records. The twenty questions cover each of the characteristics analysed in DE's regular unemployment statistics, and data on number of previous spells of unemployment, number of submissions to employers for jobs, whether a claimant, whether disabled, whether seeking long-term work and full-time work. Also covered were staff assessments on attitude towards full-time work and prospects of obtaining long-term work. Questions on training history covering apprenticeships and on the Training Opportunities Scheme (TOPS) and other sponsored courses were included. Two additional pieces of information—requiring offices to contact the registrants—were collected for those aged 55–64: these were the amount of any occupational pension being received and whether benefits or credits were being received. (The 1973 survey had readily been able to include information on the benefit position of the whole sample because Employment Offices also performed the functions now performed by UBOs.) For those leaving the register by January 1977, information is available on date and reason for leaving. The results are to be found in the June, September and October 1977 *Gazettes*. Another survey is planned to take place in late 1980 but this will not cover assessments of attitudes and prospects.

Future developments—JUVOS

The Department of Employment, together with the Manpower Services Commission, is proposing to introduce a computer-based

statistical system to provide national, regional and local unemployment and vacancy statistics, as well as management and other
statistics. The system is known as the Joint Unemployment, Vacancy
and Operating Statistics (JUVOS) system. It is hoped that the first
stage of the system will yield the unemployment statistics covering
the whole country from 1982/83. Central to the system are the NUBS
computers used for payment of unemployment and related benefits.
For claimants on NUBS, the data in the computer files will be used
for determining whether or not a person is unemployed on a given
day and will supply several characteristics of the unemployed (such
as age, sex and first day of unemployment). Other characteristics,
available only at Employment and Careers Offices (such as
occupation and industry) will be input to NUBS for transmission to
the JUVOS computer. Information on residual categories of the
unemployed will be collected by more traditional clerical means. It
is planned that statistics of vacancies notified to Employment Offices
will be collected and analysed through a computer network which
will be used to circulate details of vacancies between offices for
operational purposes.

Four significant advantages can be seen to accrue from JUVOS.
First, the greatly diminished clerical role in the actual counting
operations will, at less cost, give greater accuracy; accuracy at the
'final' figures stage will also be significantly improved by the ability
to reflect the retrospective notification of changes in status. Secondly
an immensely wider range of cross-analyses of the stock of the
unemployed will be possible, probably including statistics for local
authority areas based on postcodes. Thirdly, flow information will in
general be available in conjunction with a wider range of variables
than previously; this is not simply an ability to analyse the
characteristics of the inflow but also to analyse the duration of
completed spells, durations of non-unemployment and patterns of
spell repetition. Finally the resulting files will be suitable for
generating samples of the unemployed that may be required;
inclusion in such surveys would be subject to the individual's
agreement. A fuller outline of JUVOS can be found in *Statistical
News* (forthcoming).

8.3 Department of Health and Social Security statistics

Monthly inflow counts

The UBS1 return completed at UBOs simply shows the number of
claims to unemployment benefit or credits made during the four or
five weeks ending on the Saturday which precedes the first Monday

in each calendar month. The information on the form comprises just five figures: it shows the number of first claims in a benefit year (almost the same as a calendar year) and the number of other claims, giving males and females separately for each; and it shows the number of initial claims made under emergency benefit procedures[3]. The figures are obtained by adding together recorded daily totals, including cases dealt with by part-time offices under the control of the main UBO. The UBOs forward the returns to the appropriate 'regional statistical liaison officers' who check that all UBOs have submitted the returns before sending them on to the Statistics Division of DHSS at Newcastle Central Office. It will be apparent that the simple nature of the form prevents any checking of internal consistency; furthermore the volatility of inflows at the local level prevents checks based on comparison with earlier periods.

The forms are clerically processed to yield regional and national summaries each month and to cover a full calendar year. Figures are available about six weeks after the date of the return. The series started in July 1948 and figures are currently published in the Central Statistical Office's *Monthly Digest of Statistics* and in DHSS's annual *Social Security Statistics*.

The statistics are largely concerned with workflow. They are sometimes used as a base on which to express UBS4 figures (see below) as percentages. As with the Department of Employment's inflow figures, they can be related to the count of the stock to give a very crude indication of the mean duration of completed spells though the annual claimant statistics (see p. 246) now yield this information directly. Furthermore, because of the separate identification of first claims in the year they can also yield a crude overall estimate of the extent of spell repetition.

In the absence of possiblé checks on the data there must be some element of concern about the reliability. The variation between four- and five-week months and the need to include the sub-offices' elements must be sources of vulnerability. In the case of emergency benefit payments, the instructions specifically allow for approximate figures to be given when extreme conditions prevent exact figures being supplied.

Quarterly analysis of decisions of insurance officers

The UBS4 return provides for a quarterly analysis of insurance officers' decisions on doubtful claims for unemployment benefit or credit of contributions. The form is completed by the insurance officer, who usually serves a group of UBOs, on the basis of running records. The form specifies for each type of question that may require a decision, the number of such claims allowed, disallowed or referred direct to the local tribunal, and the results of decisions referred for review by insurance officers. There are some thirty categories into which decisions are classified, the most common being 'voluntary leaving', 'misconduct' and 'receipt of payment in lieu of notice or wages'. Decisions on applications for credit are separately listed and for decisions on seasonal workers males and females are distinguished. The returns are submitted to DHSS (Newcastle) via regional insurance officers who retain a copy for their own use. Processing is by computer though only a simple check on totals is possible; the results are also scrutinized for major variations.

Regional and national summaries are compiled each quarter and to cover a full calendar year. Figures are available about eight weeks after the date of the return. Their principal use is in the context of workloads and they are not routinely published. They have however formed the basis of recent publications by Layard (1979) and Fenn (1980). Such uses can be made of the figures provided that it is remembered that the firgures are no more than *decisions* on *doubtful* claims. There is no need for a decision on, say, seasonal working, if the claimants contribution record does not entitle him to unemployment benefit; and there is usually no need for a case to be referred to the insurance officer as doubtful before disallowing a day's benefit because a day's casual work has been reported. On the other hand one claimant, and one claim period, could give rise to several decisions on different questions or at different times.

Quarterly counts of the stock of unemployed claimants

The UBS2 return provides a broad analysis of the benefit position of unemployed claimants on a day in February, May, August and November; since February 1978 the day has been that on which the Department of Employment counts are made. The main figures comprise a simultaneous breakdown of claimants by sex (and marital status of women) and benefit position in eight categories.

(1) Unemployment benefit and supplementary allowance payable
(2) Unemployment benefit only payable
(3) Supplementary allowance payable—unemployment benefit not payable because exhausted
(4) Supplementary allowance payable—unemployment benefit not payable because title not yet determined
(5) Supplementary allowance payable—unemployment benefit not payable due to other reasons
(6) No benefit payable—unemployment benefit exhausted

(7) No benefit payable—unemployment benefit title not yet determined
(8) No benefit payable—unemployment benefit not payable due to other reasons

Emergency benefit cases are excluded from this breakdown and the totals given separately. UBOs submit the return, including any cases dealt with at sub-offices, to DHSS (Newcastle) through the regional statistical liaison officers. The returns are subject to computer processing though the only checks possible are on row and column totals which are included on the forms. However the procedures described here now apply to a minority of cases—about 15% in February 1980. In fact the NUBS computers now supply the information in respect of all live cases which have been input to the system: the clerical return now deals only with cases at the minority of UBOs not yet connected to the system, cases at other UBOs which are of types not input to the system (for example quarterly attenders[4] and emergency benefit cases) and other cases not input to the system because, for example, the claimants National Insurance number is not yet known.

Information on the individual UBOs is kept accessible for a limited time—principally to answer any Parliamentary Questions asked about particular localities—but only one table showing regional and national totals (and percentages within each) is produced about eight weeks after the date of the return. A series of similar information is available from 1947 but from May 1958 to August 1978 the figures included the registered unemployed not claiming benefit or credits. Results are published in the Central Statistical Office's *Annual Abstract of Statistics* in addition to the *Monthly Digest of Statistics* and *Social Security Statistics*.

These statistics form the basis for a broad monitoring of the benefit position of the unemployed and are a central component in forecasts of future benefit expenditure. But there are three weaknesses of which the user needs to be aware. The most serious—though fortunately visible—is that a significant proportion of claimants (11% in February 1980) did not have their entitlement to unemployment benefit determined at the time of the count but might subsequently receive the benefit in respect of that day (and this in turn might be substituted for the reported supplementary allowance). There was formerly some follow-up on these cases but a change in procedures brought the exercise to a halt; so far no acceptable method has been found but it is now being pursued in the context of wider changes. Secondly, the indication of whether the claimant is in receipt of supplementary allowance will not be completely reliable; the extent of the problem is relatively small and it arises mainly from the failure of DHSS local offices to notify UBOs of payments of supplementary allowance made direct to claimants early in their spell. Arrangements are in hand to overcome this problem. Thirdly, as with the Department of Employment counts, there is some inflation because of delays in UBOs getting to know of spell termination and this inflation has increased as a result of fortnightly signing. But on average the delay in notification to UBOs is less than the delay in notification to Employment Offices because of the involvement of money payments.

The UBS2 complements the UBS3—which is described next— and its particular value derives from its frequency and speed of processing relative to the UBS3, its role in providing grossing-up factors, the sub-national dimension which it adds and the limited information on emergency benefit cases.

Half-yearly sample of the stock of unemployed claimants

The UBS3 return supplies detailed information for a 5% sample (based on National Insurance number) of claimants counted in the May and November UBS2 returns. It is, like the UBS2, currently a hybrid of UBO and NUBS information. The variables presently comprise

(1) Sex
(2) Marital status
(3) Age
(4) Details of increases payable for dependants (unemployment benefit cases only)
(5) Current duration of spell
(6) Weekly rate of unemployment benefit or reason for non-receipt
(7) Days of unemployment benefit paid including days in linked spells
(8) Weekly rate of earnings-related supplement or reason for non-receipt
(9) Amount of reduction of earnings-related supplement or reason for non-receipt
(10) Tax year used for calculation of entitlement to earnings related supplement
(11) Days of earnings-related supplement paid including those in linked spells
(12) Whether supplementary allowance is in payment

The nature of these records is such that an exhaustive set of range and internal consistency checks to establish validity can be applied. The result is that about 30% of the clerical records are rejected and most have to be returned to the UBOs for correction before they can be re-input. When all the records are clean a count of the sample cases in each of the UBS2 categories is made to derive grossing-up factors to apply to the sample cases before tabling. These factors are important because the sample falls short of the nominal 5% to an extent which varies according to benefit position and sex. This is because there is a systematic—if unintended—shortfall arising from cases without a National Insurance number which cannot get into the sample. The rest of the shortfall is attributed to natural human frailty.

No sub-national tables are produced but this has not stopped the volume of output growing to a worrying 900 pages of computer print; this is in part an indication of the value of the data and hence the interest shown in it. Mainly because of the delays involved in dealing with the rejected clerical records, it takes about six months before the tables are produced. The return originated in 1949 but a number of the significant variables are recent additions. Routine publication is largely restricted to *Social Security Statistics* but with effect from the November 1978 return a set of summary tables has been placed in the libraries of both Houses of Parliament. Very heavy use of the data is made by DHSS for monitoring the effects of existing policy, exploring the cost and other consequences of changes of policy and for forecasting expenditure.

Problems in interpreting the data clearly include those which affect the UBS2. It is also apparent that the use of grossing-up factors to 'correct' for sample deficiencies is an imperfect solution. A further problem area is duration—an important variable. The problem is that for claimants whose present spell of unemployment was current when their UBO was taken on the NUBS system, the date of take-on is recorded as the date of spell commencement. A change in procedures has been agreed to prevent this happening in the future. In the interim—and it is a long interim—duration tables are excluding all cases at UBOs taken-on in the 18 months or so prior to the date of return and the resulting shortfall is being 'corrected' by a further set of grossing-up factors. Again there are dangers in this particularly as the take-on of UBOs shows a geographical bias, but the results do at least give a useable analysis of durations up to about a year and a quarter. The marital status of men is a new variable and one which may give rise to difficulties as it is not required for operational purposes; this may mean, for example, that changes in the course of a spell will not be reported.

The annual claimant statistics

This is a new series, starting with the 1978 calendar year, based entirely on information held on the NUBS computers. Forerunners to these analyses include exercises undertaken in the early 1950s and 1962–1964 (see Whitehead, 1974) and a pilot project undertaken in 1971/72, the results of which have not been fully published though Metcalf and Nickell (1978) quote a summary of the results on spell repetition. All of these earlier exercises were, of course, clerical enterprises which are costly and, as the 1971/72 pilot showed, give rise to serious problems of incomplete recording.

The objective of the exercise can be described as recording for analysis the complete claim history over the year for a standing 5% sample. In reality practical constraints, and an unwise decision to gear the records to yield the data required specifically for a limited number of pre-planned tables, causes the data to fall short of this objective. The items of information which are effectively available for every spell of every claimant included in the year's data are

(1) Sex
(2) Marital status of females
(3) Age
(4) Details of increases in benefit payment for dependants (unemployment benefit cases only)
(5) Total duration of spell
(6) Duration of spell within the statistics year
(7) Whether there has been unemployment or incapacity (shown separately) in the 13 weeks preceding the current spell
(8) Rate of unemployment benefit (if any) at spell termination or end of year
(9) Days of unemployment benefit paid
(10) Whether earnings-related supplement was in payment at end of spell or earlier in spell or not at all
(11) Rate of earnings-related supplement
(12) Days of earnings-related supplement paid
(13) Whether supplementary allowance was in payment at end of spell

For technical reasons the form of the records is more complex than this implies, which means that there is a small margin of uncertainty about some of the variables. The analyses are confined to those whose full-year history is reflected on the NUBS computers which gives rise to limited, but known, bias (the excluded cases were listed in the description of the UBS2 above).

Mainly because of the discretion that needs to be applied in using the data, no routine publication is yet planned. The data are, nevertheless, proving to be invaluable. They represent the only regular and systematic source of data on the duration of completed spells of unemployment and of the extent of spell repetition. (The definition of spell termination, relevant to these two quantities, is that a gap of one or more weekdays occurring between the days claimed represents a termination; this is a 'hard' definition but not necessarily inappropriate as such a gap most commonly results from the claimant taking casual work.) They also show distributions of the total durations of unemployment experienced in the course of a year. They have been used as the basis for estimates used in reply to Parliamentary Questions—for example, on the number of unemployed claimants receiving earnings-related supplement in the course of a year—and heavily used for a number of policy purposes. The data have been particularly helpful in illuminating two important issues concerned with plans to make taxable the benefits paid to the unemployed: they can be used to show claimants distributed by total duration of unemployment and total unemployment benefit received in a year—the basis for estimating tax yield; and the distribution of duration of claims is crucial to assessments of the workload resulting from making benefits taxable.

Statistics on unemployed recipients of supplementary allowance

The Annual Statistical Enquiry of supplementary allowance recipients yields exceptionally detailed information. On one day in the year, usually in November soon after the up-rating of benefits, forms detailing the circumstances of each individual in a 2% sample of supplementary allowance recipients are completed in DHSS local offices; the sample is based on every 50th case after a random start within each office and about 30 items of information—many of them with multiple entries—are recorded. In the case of unemployed recipients, some of this information has to be specially obtained from the UBO. The completed returns are forwarded to DHSS Newcastle where they are subject to extensive validity checking, resulting in the rejection of about 17% of cases, three-quarters of which are returned to local offices for correction before the records are tabled. The very extensive tables typically emerge about six months after the date of the return. The major vehicles for publication are *Social Security Statistics* and the Supplementary Benefit Commission's *Annual Report*, though the 1979 *Report* was the last from the Supplementary Benefit Commission.

The principal uses of the data are of course concerned with the monitoring and formulation of DHSS policy. Uses by those interested in aspects of unemployment other than benefit entitlement are limited as a result of the data relating to only those of the unemployed who are in receipt of the benefit—though at the time of writing they amount to a little under half of the total. However, significant uses do exist. First, they can be used in conjunction with the separate information on unemployment benefit recipients (from the UBS3) to shed light on the family characteristics of the unemployed: they can, for example, be used to estimate unemployment rates by family size and duration of unemployment. Secondly, they can be used directly for a detailed analysis of the long term unemployed because about four-fifths of those whose unemployment duration exceeds a year are in receipt of supplementary allowance; for these people the data available includes information such as the ages of wife and each child, tenure, housing costs, capital, and amounts and sources of other income.

The contribution records

Until April 1975 flat-rate National Insurance contributions were recorded by weekly stamps on contribution cards. Credits could be awarded in lieu of the contribution if the person was claiming unemployment or other benefits, subject to the satisfaction of a contribution test. Clerical records of contributions and credits were maintained at the DHSS Newcastle Central Office alongside a computerized system for recording earnings-related contributions from 1961 to meet the requirements of the Graduated Pension scheme. Samples of records from both recording systems have been used by Hart (1976), Disney (1979), Creedy and Hart (1979) and Creedy and Disney (1981), to examine individuals' experience of unemployment, incapacity and earnings over successive years.

Unfortunately—in the present context—Class 1 contributions are now wholly earnings-related and it is their annual (tax year) value, not the number of weeks to which they relate, which is recorded on the contribution records. Furthermore, credits when available are only used to supplement contributions to the extent that is needed to give entitlement to the flat-rate benefit. It follows from this that credits are not now needed in respect of many spells because contributions paid for much less than a full year can still give entitlement to the flat-rate benefit. Accordingly it is only in cases in which the credits might be 'needed' and spells dealt with by NUBS that procedures ensure that they are recorded in Newcastle. DHSS was however able to make some statistical use of these records in recent work which required an estimate of the extent to which the number of long-term unemployed would be increased if limited breaks in their registered unemployment, particularly those arising from incapacity, were treated as part of a spell of unemployment.

Future developments

The content of statistical series obtained as a by-product of administrative processes usually changes as a result of procedural and organizational changes, or of changes in policy or policy interests, or of changes in the availability of information 'within the system' which are usually related to one of the other types of changes. An example of the latter is the current intention of the government to make taxable the benefits paid to the unemployed; depending on what procedures are determined, this could render available at UBOs and NUBS information on pre-unemployment earnings. More straightforwardly, reducing or eliminating the unemployment benefit of those in receipt of sizeable occupational pensions in excess of a certain level, a provision being introduced in 1981, will simultaneously cause a need to collect, and provide a means of collecting, information on the receipt of such pensions. A major procedural change is the approach of full national coverage of the NUBS system. This gives rise to the consideration of whether the UBS2 and UBS3 returns, designed for an entirely clerical operation, continue to be appropriate. In fact it is intended that these returns be superseded by sampling records held by the proposed JUVOS system and supplemented by detailed benefit information relating to the same individuals. Important advantages of this approach are that DE and DHSS statistics should be rendered fully consistent and it should permit an improved understanding of the relationship between the characteristics of the unemployed and their benefit position.

8.4 Official surveys

Ad hoc surveys of the unemployed are common. They are highly variable in their quality, coverage of subject matter, geographical coverage, and sponsorship. However, the DHSS cohort survey warrants description, mainly because it is likely to be the unique source of information on a wide range of topics for at least several years.

The principal purpose of the DHSS *Cohort Study of the Unemployed* is to obtain information on the incomes, both in and out of work, of men experiencing unemployment, as measures of the financial incentives to work and of the level of income replacement when unemployed. Further, it is intended to relate this information to duration of unemployment, previous experience of unemployment, wives' economic activity and subsequent labour market participation. The sample is based on males 'flowing on' to the NUBS computers in the autumn of 1978 and was designed to be nationally representative but with a disproportionate number of family men. The information collected is based on two principal sources. First, detailed information, including amount and composition of benefits received and precise claim periods, is available from the NUBS computers in respect of the spell causing the men to be sampled and any subsequent spell within a year. Secondly, a series of three lengthy interviews—at the beginning of the spell and about 4 and 12 months later—yields very detailed information including total family incomes, household composition, the pattern of employment and unemployment, and details of employments obtained. Subsidiary sources of information on the sample members include records of incapacity available at DHSS local offices and, for those specifically agreeing, Inland Revenue records on tax refunds. The sample, comprising 2300 at the first interview, has suffered the usual attrition through non-response but the study is abnormally well-endowed with information to examine any resulting bias and any distortion arising from the respondents' knowledge that they are being studied: the full NUBS records are available both for non-responding sample members and for a control group.

There are a number of multipurpose Government interview surveys which shed additional light on the unemployed. A useful description of the potential of these sources is given by Hakim (1980). Their principal value lies in the additional information on the characteristics of unemployed individuals and their households particularly as they yield similar information on the non-unemployed thereby permitting direct comparisons on a consistent basis. They also yield data which include, and often specifically distinguish, those excluded from the administrative statistics because they have not registered as unemployed. They are therefore a useful corrective to the inclination to conceive of the unemployed solely in terms which reflect the nature of the principal counts. The annual *General Household Survey* (see for example Office of Population Censuses and Surveys, 1980), launched in 1971, is the most wide-ranging of these surveys. The achieved sample of about 12 000 households yields only a few hundred unemployed respondents but this has not prevented intensive analyses of the data (Nickell, 1977; Metcalf and Nickell, 1978). The annual *Family Expenditure Survey* (Department of Employment, 1980) is based on a rather smaller sample, is less wide-ranging but much stronger on financial aspects. Among its many other uses, it is the source of DHSS estimates of the take-up of supplementary allowance by the unemployed who appear entitled to it (Supplementary Benefits Commission, 1978). The DHSS' own *Family Finances Survey*—a one-off survey undertaken in 1978/79 with a subsequent follow-up of the respondents—has much the same content as the *Family Expenditure Survey* but is concerned solely with low income families with children, and has yielded a much larger sample of such cases. It will therefore shed clearer light on that category of the unemployed who fall within this group. The biennial *Labour Force Survey* (Office of Population Censuses and Surveys, forthcoming) sponsored by the European Community since 1973, has the advantage of a large sample covering nearly 90 000 households in the United Kingdom and yields data designed to permit comparisons with the other member countries. However the quality of the data tends not to be as high as for the other surveys mentioned because, for example, there is a greater acceptance of replies from those acting as 'proxies' for the relevant household member.

The main disadvantage of each of these sources lies in the quality of the data, particularly if a response is dependent on the level of the respondent's knowledge—for example on the composition of his social security benefits. The detailed wording of the questions is known to have a substantial effect on the nature of replies and consequently on the level of the figures. All of these surveys are vulnerable to bias resulting from non-response, all their results are subject to sampling error—often considerable, and all of them (except the *Family Finances Survey*) exclude those resident in hostels, hotels, and institutions. The decennial population Census is little affected by these latter problems but, because the form is for self-completion, quality of response will be imperfect. Its principal value in this context possibly lies in the detailed information on the unemployed that can be produced on virtually any geographical basis including very small areas. It can also be used as a check on the administrative sources. Its relative freedom from response bias and from the problems of small numbers associated with most surveys enables it to be used with confidence to explore complex relationships. An example is the relationship between the unemployment of economically active men and the number of dependent children in the family after standardizing for age and social class, with separate results for those with and without a working wife. For such reasons the decennial Census data represents an important supplement to the information supplied from surveys and from the administrative sources.

Acknowledgments

I am grateful to a number of colleagues in the DHSS and other Departments for assistance in the preparation of this chapter. In particular, the considerable efforts of Rosemary Butler in the Department of Employment brought about some improvement though not to the extent that she would have wished. The chapter describes procedures and plans as at the end of September 1980.

Notes

1. These are people who are suspended by their employers on the understanding that they will shortly resume work. They are available for work on the day of the count and are claiming benefit.
2. These are disabled people who are so severely handicapped that they are unlikely to obtain employment other than under special sheltered conditions.
3. These procedures are mainly designed to speed up or short-circuit normal procedures in UBOs when large numbers of workers in a particular locality are laid off or put on short-time working.
4. Certain claimants of benefit or credits are required to sign at the UBO, or by post, only quarterly. The main criteria determining qualification for quarterly attendance are that the claimant should be aged 50 or over and not have worked in the preceding two years.
5. The interval was 13 weeks until the linking rule was changed in September 1980. See also Chapter 6.

References

Central Statistical Office. *Annual Abstract of Statistics*. London; HMSO

Central Statistical Office. *Monthly Digest of Statistics*. London; HMSO

Creedy, J. and Disney, R. (1981). Changes in labour market states in Great Britain. *Scottish Journal of Political Economy* (forthcoming)

Creedy, J. and Hart, P. E. (1979). Age and the distribution of earnings. *Economic Journal* **89**, 280—293

Department of Employment (1980). *The General Household Survey 1978*. London; HMSO

Department of Health and Social Security. *Social Security Statistics*. London; HMSO

Disney, R. (1979). Recurrent spells and the concentration of unemployment in Great Britain. *Economic Journal* **89**, 109–119

Fenn, P. (1980). Sources of disqualification for unemployment benefit 1960–1976. *British Journal of Industrial Relations*, July issue

Employment Gazette, March 1974, **82**, no. 3, 211–221

Employment Gazette, May 1974, **82**, no. 5, 385–389

Employment Gazette, June 1974, **82**, no. 6, 495–502

Employment Gazette, June 1977, **85**, no. 6, 559–574

Employment Gazette, September 1977, **85**, no. 9, 965–975

Employment Gazette, October 1977, **85**, no. 10, 1122–1126

Employment Gazette, August 1979, **87**, no. 8, 780

Employment Gazette, November 1979, **88**, no. 5, 1151

Employment Gazette, May 1980, **88**, no. 5, 497–508

Employment Gazette, June 1980, **88**, no. 6, 627–635

Hakim, C. (1980). Social aspects of employment: data for policy research. *Journal of Social Policy* **9**, no. 1, 77–98

Hart, P. E. (1976). The dynamics of earnings 1963–1973. *Economic Journal* **86**, 551–565

Layard, R. (1979). *Guardian*, 5 November

Metcalf, D. and Nickell, S. (1978). The plain man's guide to the out-of-work: the nature and composition of male unemployment in Britain. In *Royal Commission on the Distribution of Income and Wealth, Selected Evidence Submitted to the Royal Commission for Report No. 6: Lower Incomes*, pp. 310–327. London; HMSO

Ministry of Labour Gazette, April 1962, **70**, no. 4, 131–137

Ministry of Labour Gazette, September 1962, **70**, no. 9, 347–349

Ministry of Labour Gazette, April 1966, **74**, no. 4, 156–157

Nickell, S. (1977). The effect of unemployment and related benefits on the duration of unemployment. Centre for Labour Economics, London School of Economics Discussion Paper No. 8

Office of Population Censuses and Surveys (1980). *The General Household Survey 1978*. London; HMSO

Office of Population Censuses and Surveys (forthcoming). *Report on the Labour Force Surveys*. London; HMSO

Social Security Statistics. Annual publication of the DHSS. London; HMSO

Statistical News (forthcoming) Central Statistical Office

Supplementary Benefits Commission. *Annual Report*. London; HMSO

Supplementary Benefits Commission (1978). Take-up of Supplementary Benefits. *Supplementary Benefits Administration Paper No. 7*. London; HMSO

Whitehead, F. (1974). Social security statistics. In *Review of United Kingdom Statistical Sources*, vol. II (ed. by W. F. Maunder). London; Heinemann

Index